Praise for *The Power of Nice, Revised and Updated*

"Shapiro eschews the academic 'win–win' style for the more practical 'WIN–win' approach which enables proficient negotiators to achieve beneficial results for themselves while simultaneously satisfying the basic interests of the persons on the other side. This is especially critical when on-going relationships are involved."

—CHARLES B. CRAVER, Author of
The Art of Negotiation in the Business World,
Freda H. Alverson Professor of Law,
George Washington Law School

"*The Power of Nice* offers essential tools that empower every negotiator. Shapiro's systematic approach to negotiations is easy-to-follow with classic and updated case studies throughout the book."

—MELANIE ALLISON, DNP, RN, ACNP-BC,
Vanderbilt University School of Nursing Faculty

"In *The Power of Nice*, the elusive elements of the 'art of negotiation' are broken down and explained to all in a concise, practical, and lively manner. Ron's sharing his career of negotiating makes us all better."

—RANDY LEVINE
President, New York Yankees
Of Counsel, Jackson Lewis P.C.

"This book, and the principles espoused within it, have helped me in innumerable 'difficult' conversations and discussions with faculty. The book has guided me towards being able to say either 'yes' or 'no' in a way that strengthens the professional relationship, underscores the person's value to the organization, and serves as a foundation for their career growth. Ron convincingly demonstrates how the essential elements of preparation, engagement, and personalization . . . . and truly listening . . . . are to getting to a mutual 'win.' His concepts move the negotiation from a one-time battle for supremacy, to a long-term conversation and a platform for collaboration and success."

—JUSTIN C. McARTHUR, MBBS, MPH, FAAN, Director,
Department of Neurology,
Johns Hopkins University School of Medicine;
Neurologist-in-chief, the Johns Hopkins Hospital;
Chair, School of Medicine Professorial Promotions Committee

"I have religiously used Ron's systematic approach for over two decades, and after reading this revised edition, I am not surprised to discover that even I can take my negotiation skills to a higher level."

—STEVE MOSKO, President,
Sony Pictures Television

"Ron goes beyond the practicalities of negotiating and shows how his philosophy of building strong relationships and paying attention to detail has an enormous impact on being successful—and not just in business."

—IRINA PAVLOVA, President,
Onexim Sports and Entertainment Holding USA, Inc.

"The new tools and stories in this updated edition of *The Power of Nice* demonstrate that Ron perfects his craft by practicing what he preaches. Anyone seeking to become a better negotiator should read this book!"

—EDUARDO DEJESUS RODRIGUEZ, MD, DDS,
Helen L. Kimmel Professor of Reconstructive Plastic Surgery,
Department of Plastic Surgery (Chair),
NYU Langone Medical Center

THE
POWER
OF *Nice*

HOW TO **NEGOTIATE** SO
EVERYONE WINS
—ESPECIALLY YOU!

REVISED AND UPDATED

RONALD M. SHAPIRO
with **JAMES DALE**

WILEY

For general information about our other products and services, please contact our Customer Care
Department within the United States at (800) 762-2974, outside the United States at (317)
572-3993, or fax (317) 572-4002.

Wiley publishes in a variety of print and electronic formats and by print-on-demand. Some
material included with standard print versions of this book may not be included in e-books or in
print-on-demand. If this book refers to media such as a CD or DVD that is not included in the
version you purchased, you may download this material at http://booksupport.wiley.com. For more
information about Wiley products, visit www.wiley.com.

ISBN 978-1-118-96962-5 (cloth); ISBN 978-1-118-96963-2 (ebk); ISBN 978-1-118-96966-3 (ebk)

Printed in the United States of America
10 9 8 7 6 5 4 3 2 1

To four generations of family:

My father, who was the exemplar in my life for the power of nice, and my mother, for always being there to support my endeavors with her love;

My darling wife, Cathi, for her guidance, wisdom, and love;

And my children and grandchildren, who never let a day pass without reminding me of the importance of living with the Power of Nice.

Contents

Foreword to the Revised Edition by Ambassador
   Charlene Barshefsky   xi
Foreword to the First Edition by Cal Ripken, Jr.   xiv
Acknowledgments   xvi

Introduction: Why Change What Works?   2

1   Negotiation   5
    "I'll Burn That Bridge When I Come to It"   5
    Your First Deal   7
    What Negotiation Isn't   11
    Filling the Negotiator's Toolbox   18
    What Negotiation Is   19
    What Negotiation Can Be   23
    Refresher   26

2   I Win–You Lose Negotiation—An Exercise in
     Flawed Logic   29
    Enemies and Entrenched Positions   29
    Hit and Run   32
    I'm Not One of Them, Am I?   35
    At Least One Dissatisfied Party   43
    Refresher   45

3   WIN–win Negotiation   47
    Myth and Reality   47
    Achieving WIN–win   49

Good Deals Echo, They Lead to More Deals   51

WIN–win Is Not Wimp–Wimp   52

Roadblocks, Minefields, and Wisdom   55

Putting It Together   57

Refresher   64

4   The Three Ps—A Systematic Approach   67

Prepare, Probe, and Propose   70

Refresher   79

5   Prepare… or Else   81

Preparation: The Aerobics of Negotiation   81

How Prepared Are You for Your Negotiations?   82

The Numbers and Letters Game   83

The Numbers and Letters Game Continued…   84

How to Prepare (and How Not To)   87

The Preparation Checklist   89

A Case Study: The Sur-Real Sales Challenge   97

Confidence Is the Secret Weapon (But the Real Secret Is

    That Preparation Is the Key to Confidence)   104

Sources of Information   105

Refresher   110

6   Probe, Probe, Probe   113

The Other Side Is Trying to Tell You How to Make

    the Deal   113

W.H.A.T.? The Probing Technique   120

The Don'ts—How Not to Probe   126

Listening   128

The Zoologist   133

Learning to Listen   135

Refresher   138

7   Propose–But Not Too Fast—Getting the Other

Side to Go First   141

Role Playing   141

Proposing for Real   146

The Three Rules Behind Propose   149

Making Counterproposals   153

Refresher   158

8   Difficult Negotiators   161

…And the Award for Most Difficult Negotiator Goes to …   162

Dealing with the Difficult Negotiator (without
*   Becoming One)*   166

Emotional Tactics—Nonemotional Responses   170

Challenging Personalities   173

Refresher   177

9   Negotiating from Weakness   179

Perceived Weakness versus Real Weakness   179

Expand the Goals   181

Locate Allies   182

Never Let Them See You Sweat   185

Brainstorming   187

Refresher   192

10 Unlocking Deadlocks   195

If Nothing Works, Change Something   195

Find Reasons to Agree   200

Get Creative   200

Objective Mechanisms   205

Sometimes No Deal Is the Best Deal   209

If Deal Fever Persists, Keep Saying "No"   209

Refresher   216

11 Building Relationships   219

Today versus Tomorrow: How Long Is the Long Run?   219

A Relationship Tool: Bonding   221

The Meet-and-Bond Style   222

Rebonding   225

No Faux Bonding   227

Practice Makes Bonding   228

The Value of Relationships   231

Refresher   234

12 Putting It All Together   237

The Major League Baseball Owners versus the Major
*   League Umpires (and the Major League Umpires versus*
*   Themselves)*   237

Refresher   244

Epilogue: Nelson Mandela—When the Power of Nice
     Changed a Nation   247
Reinforcement Tools Link   251
Post-Negotiation Assessment Questionnaire   253
Negotiator's Toolbox   255
Index   257

Foreword to the Revised Edition

You Can Be Nice, and Purposeful

By Ambassador Charlene Barshefsky

When I was Bill Clinton's chief trade negotiator, the United States Trade Representative, we negotiated over 300 market-opening trade and investment agreements across the globe. And as a private practitioner, I've negotiated countless agreements for both U.S. and foreign clients. Over the years, Ron Shapiro and I would always compare notes. His were more valuable.

I have been a Shapiro disciple for a very long time. *The Power of Nice* reminds us that negotiations are as much psychology and human interaction as substance and deal points. Understanding the other side's needs, concerns, and limitations, watching carefully, listening actively, and being agile enough to act as problem solver for both sides, is easily as critical as preparing your own substantive position and game plan. The goal is to bring home a great deal—a durable deal—for your clients or your business, not no deal because you couldn't get along with the other side. And it is not making a deal that looks good on paper but will never be implemented because you played "gotcha" once too often. Parents are often fond of reminding their kids that "what goes around comes around." Good advice. "Purposeful" and "nice" can and ought to coexist. Ron's very success is a testament to that.

The lessons contained in *The Power of Nice*, whether big or small, are invaluable. Take, for example, one of Ron's tactical tips on the pitfalls of restating your position. One of my earliest negotiations with the Japanese concerned telecommunications infrastructure. I explained the U.S. position, my Japanese counterparts listened intently, and were . . . silent. Thinking that they did not fully understand our concerns, I slowly repeated what I had said. They listened carefully, more time went by . . . and again, silence. I was just about to give it a third try, when a young staffer passed me a note of four words: "Ambassador Barshefsky—Stop talking." Why? Because Ron is right. Almost nothing is ever said precisely the same way twice, let alone three times. In fact, as *The Power of Nice* predicted, I had unintentionally altered my pitch, and telegraphed to the Japanese negotiators valuable clues as to my real position. The upshot? I never gave the third iteration, and waited, silently. After about 15 minutes of uncharacteristic American quiet, they began to talk—a lot. We got back on track, and I never made the same mistake again.

Or take Ron's points about forming relationships and not letting emotion overwhelm the talks. I was negotiating an intellectual property agreement with the Chinese, which went on for months on end, but during which my counterparts and I developed a very good relationship. The talks were sometimes tense or acrimonious, but never personal.

Late one night, the Chinese negotiator became highly agitated. I knew that he was under considerable pressure to conclude the talks without further movement on the Chinese side. In an uncharacteristic display, he lunged across the table (fortunately, it was a wide table and he was not particularly tall), and said, "That's it. No more. We are done." I could have yelled, "No we aren't," but I didn't. I knew that if I took the bait, we *would* be done, and I still had one final bit of ground to cover. So I weighed how best to defuse the situation, continue the negotiation for that last little bit, and not do anything that would result in the loss of face for my counterpart. I replied, calmly, "Mr. Minister. I am so sorry, but apparently, there has been a miscommunication. We are both tired. Let me suggest that we adjourn for the evening and resume early in the morning." With that, I stood, left the room, and returned the next day with essentially the same proposal. After a brief discussion, the deal was done.

Then there is the situation where your counterpart agrees to something that is too good to be true, and where Ron rightly counsels, no deal may be the best option. This almost happened in the case of a large trade agreement with Vietnam—principally because we did not fully appreciate their priorities (another Ron "must do").

By the early 2000s, the United States and Vietnam had yet to fully normalize relations, despite the decades earlier end to the Vietnam War.

Our proposed trade agreement had a twofold purpose: to slowly reform and open the Vietnamese market, and to serve as the last step in the normalization process—something both sides sought.

One day, after months of negotiation, my lead staffer called me from Hanoi so excited he could barely speak. "Today . . . well . . . . it's incredible. We are nearly done. What should I do?" This astonished me, because there is no way on earth the negotiation was nearly done. As we talked further, it became clear that the other side had simply decided to accept whatever we put forward. That would lead to an agreement that was never going to be fully implemented. I stopped the negotiation, called our team back, and invited the Minister from Vietnam to Washington. It was better to have no deal than to make a deal that wasn't good or wouldn't work.

Then I employed another Ron-ism: Preparation. Or, in this case, further preparation. We had prepared thoroughly for our negotiations in Vietnam. But as Ron teaches, preparation is not an end; it is an ongoing process, changing as the deal, the players, or the circumstances change. So we prepped again for the Minister's visit, analyzing his likely position, his needs and wants—empathizing, and determining our own true priorities, where we could give and where we could not.

When he arrived, we were ready for a heart-to-heart. As our preparation had indicated, for Vietnam, normalization was the overarching goal. For the United States, normalization was important, but so, too, was a strong, realistic agreement that could and would be implemented. So we simplified a number of our proposals, and revamped the agreement by phasing in various reforms over time. The United States and Vietnam normalized relations, and the agreement was fully implemented. No deal led to a better deal.

I could give countless additional examples of putting *The Power of Nice* to work—both as a systematic approach and an ethos. I was once told that as a negotiator I am tough, but reasonable, and funny— "purposeful" and "nice." This is, I am convinced, the best and most effective combination of winning, both in the short term and long. The proof is in *The Power of Nice*.

Foreword to the First Edition

Can You Say "Agent" and "Nice" in the Same Sentence?

By Cal Ripken, Jr.

Some people believe that successful professional athletes are prima donnas, and are only interested in how much money they can make. People may also think agents are aggressive, bloodthirsty sharks, who will promise anything to cut a deal. These stereotypes may be true in some cases but I hope my career proves there are exceptions. I know Ron Shapiro disproves this theory in his profession.

Just because you practice *The Power of Nice*, you listen to the other side, and everybody comes out a winner doesn't mean you're not a good negotiator. In fact, it shows that it is a more involved negotiation, and both sides end up getting what they want—a whole lot more. Ron Shapiro finds out how both parties can come out with a win. He is a real life example of a successful win–win negotiator.

When I first met Ron, I was about 18 or 19 years old. I was an up-and-coming baseball player and a lot of agents were interested in representing me. They wooed me pretty hard, trying to persuade me that they or their agency would represent me the best and the most aggressively, get me to the big leagues faster, get me a more lucrative contract, handle my money better, and get me more endorsements.

These agents had all kinds of not-too-subtle ways of convincing a player they were the best. Some of them would arrive in stretch limousines to take you out to dinner at the finest, fanciest restaurants: great big lobsters and New York strip steaks. They put the emphasis on glitz and glamour.

To tell the truth, I enjoyed it. After all, there were a lot of agents out there, there were a lot of good restaurants, and I like lobster and steak.

I would graciously accept the agents' invitations, go out, eat dinner, and listen. I referred to it as "the agent game."

One day, Mr. Shapiro called. Okay, I admit it, I'd heard of him and I called him. But he did call me right back. I now know his name is pronounced "Shap-eye-ro" but I called him Mr. "Shap-ear-o" and he called me "Carl." My parents and I made an appointment to hear his presentation so I could determine if I wanted him to represent me.

Right away, it was obvious that he was different from all the other agents. He said, "Let's meet at my office." So I thought, "This is okay. He'll show me his office and it's probably really posh, rich leather sofas, mahogany paneling, marble floors. Then he'll buzz for his driver and we'll go out to the fancy restaurant."

I arrived at his office and he introduced me to his staff. We talked baseball and what his approach would be for me. In some ways, it was similar to what others had said, but in a different atmosphere. The office wasn't posh. It was, what's the word— plain; no leather, no paneling, no marble. Eventually, it was lunchtime, and I was getting hungry, and I was anticipating that expensive restaurant. Ron had tuna sandwiches brought in and we ate at the conference table (which was oak, not mahogany).

In the end I chose Ron Shapiro. Why? Maybe it was everything he *didn't* do that told me how he'd act on my behalf. Maybe it was not living up to the myths of his profession but clearly being successful. Maybe it was that he asked me what I wanted and needed and actually listened to me instead of telling me what he was going to do. Maybe it was trust.

Or maybe I just guessed right. Now, after many seasons and All-Star games and contracts, and now a business career, I think I made the smartest decision any 18-year-old could make.

Over the years, I've seen every kind of dealmaker there is. I'll take Ron's kind every time. You can get what you want *and* you can live with yourself. Instead of making one-time deals, you make deals that lead to more deals. You build relationships. And, make no mistake, you'll outnegotiate the other side.

While I've enjoyed a record-setting streak of consecutive games played, Ron is on a streak of his own. I've seen him use his Power of Nice for over 30 years. My career, and those of many others in the worlds of sports and business, are testimony to its impact. The stories and lessons he tells in this book really work in real life, whether it be in everyday business deals or the hard-nosed negotiations of the big leagues.

Acknowledgments

I am grateful to Mark Jankowski for his significant contributions to the earlier editions of this book, and also for his work at the Shapiro Negotiations Institute during his years as my partner. I will always appreciate the opportunity I had to work with him in developing *The Power of Nice*. And thanks to Jim Dale for his valuable assistance in making this revised edition better than it would have been without him.

Thanks also go to the extraordinarily committed people who work at the Institute, including those who made special contributions to this revision: Todd Lenhart, Michael Blackstone, and Jeff Cochran. My friend and counsel, Michael Maas, our intern, Matt Legg, and my executive assistant, Kim Talbott, eased the burden of accomplishing the task through an array of contributions made by each of them. Andres Lares's and Samer Jassar's technology skills helped make the end product more contemporary.

I appreciate the efforts of my editor, Shannon Vargo, whose gentle guidance and belief in this revision inspired its publication. I also want to thank members of Shannon's team, Elizabeth Gildea and Deborah Schindlar, and my agent, Joe Spieler, for their support.

The editorial advice of Joann Davis and the legal guidance of Arthur Levine were given out of friendship and were crucial to bringing about the end product.

THE POWER OF NICE

Introduction

Why Change What Works?

> It's what you learn after you know it all that counts.
>
> —HARRY S. TRUMAN

After you write a book about negotiation, and it turns out that, yes, it works in the real world—enables people to get what they want more often, facilitates deals and partnerships, ends stalemates, heals wounds—why change it at all, why rewrite it, why update it? Because Harry Truman was right. Because in practicing what I preach, in teaching, in one after another real-life experiences, my approach evolved, was refined, got better, and became even more effective.

"Ron, can you help the new head of the Department of Psychiatry at Johns Hopkins negotiate the terms of his deal? He knows everything about the human mind but could use some help to change minds in this situation."

"Mr. Shapiro, you don't know me but I am a freelance web designer who feels I have been subjected to a fee–double standard compared to male counterparts. I'd like to raise my hourly rate . . . ."

"I've been named sales manager for the Network and I want to hone my skills at selling our sponsors and not discounting our rates."

"I'm a Deputy Fire Chief for Baltimore City and I have to make the case for the firehouse renovation program to a bunch of high-powered business leaders and I'm intimidated . . . . What do I do?"

"Ron, we have the opportunity to join the Big Ten. Can you help us negotiate our way in?"

"Pops, I have a problem with a friend and Mom said, 'talk to your grandfather.'"

In responding to these situations and countless others, I practiced and imparted the Power of Nice. But in each case the Power of Nice evolved, the tools were sharpened, the outcomes enhanced. Moreover, whether because of feelings of inferiority due to gender, age, culture, or experience, people who found themselves disadvantaged in negotiations, who felt they lacked power, utilized our systematic approach and became empowered. And, amazingly enough, there were successful negotiators who gained a whole new sense of empowerment by being systematic.

And in the course of those negotiations, and reflecting afterward, I continued to learn, and this book now reflects that learning. For example, the concept of WIN–win, or Big Win–Little win, is modified to "maximizing your win"—you get the *maximum* you can achieve at the time, but the other side doesn't leave the table in defeat.

What used to be the Preparation Planner is now the Preparation Checklist. It's a more streamlined, two-step system—Information Gathering Steps and Action Planning Steps—that facilitate the preparation process. Additionally within the Checklist, items such as the importance of knowing your bottom line, or, as described in the Checklist, your Walkaway, receive new emphasis. Also, the practice of Scripting has emerged to be so important to negotiation, with so much influence over outcomes, that it is now a step unto itself.

In this new version of the book, you will find some older stories updated, some older ideas modified, and some brand new stories and anecdotes that illustrate and teach today's Power of Nice. The systematic approach has evolved and, in total, is even more effective in more situations, more challenges, in more aspects of business and life. You will see the system at work. Most of all, you will find more than power; you will find empowerment. And nothing is nicer.

"We're going to try to negotiate first."

Negotiation

> Let us never fear to negotiate. But let us never negotiate out of fear.
>
> —John F. Kennedy

> Nothing in life is to be feared. It is only to be understood.
>
> —Madame Marie Curie

"I'LL BURN THAT BRIDGE WHEN I COME TO IT"

Early in my career, I had a law partner who loved his work. He was smart. He knew the law. He always had his clients' best interests at heart. And he liked nothing better than the challenge of negotiation. He had no fear of the other side. In fact, he relished confrontation. He paced outside a conference room like a blitzing linebacker. He had that same hungry look in his eyes, pacing and revving himself up for the kill. He couldn't wait to charge in and nail the quarterback (or the other lawyer) to the Astroturf (or the deal he was after). If a few bones were broken along the way, so be it . . . or so much the better.

He often got what he and his client wanted. But he only got it once. Nobody wanted or could afford to deal with him twice because he left nothing on the table. *Winner take all. Why take a share of the profit when you can take all of it? Why have investors when you can have sole control? Why pay commissions? Why give concessions to a union when you can break the union? Why not squeeze all suppliers to rock bottom? Why not drive all offers up to the last dollar? Why negotiate when you can dictate?* My partner literally destroyed the other side, and he reveled in it.

One day he strutted out of yet another of his "eat-the-opposition-for-lunch" meetings, fresh blood dripping from his teeth, having dismembered yet another adversary in the name of dealmaking. Instead of congratulating him, I asked him a question that took him by surprise. "What did the other side want?"

He looked at me with a combination of curiosity at my naiveté and astonishment at the irrelevance of the question. "I don't know, but they didn't get it," he answered.

I persisted, "Maybe they could have gotten what they wanted *and* you could have gotten what you wanted. What would have been wrong with that?"

Then he sighed like a wise old tobacco-chewing veteran and laid it out for the rookie who just didn't understand how to play the game. "Don't you get it? We won."

"Yeah," I protested, "but what if, some time in the future, the tables turn and the other side gains the upper hand and then they're in a position to change the deal?"

That's when my wise old veteran partner put his arm around me, took a long, dramatic pause, and said, "I'll burn that bridge when I come to it." That wasn't just his snappy comeback. He meant it. It was the embodiment of his negotiation philosophy.

That's the way a lot of people look at negotiation. Two S.O.B.s locked in a room trying to beat the daylights out of each other and may the biggest S.O.B. win. Even way back then, I thought there was a better way to make deals.

Over the years I practiced and perfected what made sense and worked for me: You can be "a nice guy" and still get what you're after. In fact, *embracing the systematic approach* of this book gives *you* the power and allows *you* to get better results, achieve more of your goals, and build longer-term relationships with even greater returns.

The Power of Nice Philosophy

The way to get what you want is to help the other side get what they want.

YOUR FIRST DEAL

What matters in negotiation is results. Everything else is decoration. To get results you must have parties who *want* to make a deal, each of whom has something to *gain*. Never forget, everyone who sits down at a negotiating table is there for one simple reason: They want something the other side has.

You picked up this book, so you must feel you have something to gain. As authors, we have already gained by making the book sale. So, have we won and you lost? Hardly. As you'll learn, we don't want a one-time deal; we want an ongoing relationship (your recommendation of our book to others, visiting our website, attending our programs, and buying our next print or digital book). You don't want a one-time deal, either. You want to learn to negotiate every deal well. Therefore, reader and authors have a common interest (another point I'll be making later) and that is *to make you a better negotiator*.

To achieve that end, we each have to make a commitment. Yours is to answer *two questions* with complete candor (even if it hurts). Ours is to deliver on four objectives that will make you an effective negotiator.

1. What negotiation have you handled recently that has not gone or is not going well? [Remember what I said about candor. Write out your answer and then show it to someone you can't fool (husband, wife, partner, friend, boss, client, mother)]

   _____

   _____

   _____

   _____

2. What would you like to be able to do differently after reading this book? *(Be realistic, but aim high.)*

   _____

   _____

   _____

   _____

Write down your answers and save them. You're going to want to look
back at them at the end of the book.

Four Objectives You Can Expect

1. **Displaying Confidence.** The most effective negotiators tend to
   be the most confident negotiators. Conversely, negotiators who are
   less confident are less effective. So, how do you get confidence and
   become a better negotiator? Get smart.

   Lack of confidence is mostly lack of knowledge. Knowledge is
   power. You will be armed with the knowledge it takes to deal from
   strength. You won't be cocky; you'll be confident. The former is imitating someone who knows what he's doing; the latter is the person
   who the cocky person is imitating.

2. **Achieving WIN–win.** Today, everybody talks about win–win negotiation. Both sides win. Both get what they want. Both are equally
   happy. How delightful. How unrealistic.

   If we negotiators were seeking truly equal terms and deals, like
   King Solomon, we'd simply divide everything in half. In reality, we're

out to achieve *all* (or most) of *our* goals, to make *our most desirable deal*. But the best way to do so is to let the other side achieve *some* of their goals, to make their acceptable deal. That's **WIN–win:** maximize your win, but don't forget theirs.

The most common approach to dealmaking is I Win–You Lose, the pound-of-flesh school—the only good deal for me is a bad deal for you. The unfortunate fate of too many negotiations is:

We both lose

or

If I can't win, nobody can.

We'll show you how to avoid both of these negative categories.

3. **Using the 3 Ps.** There's an old saying, "If all you have in your toolbox is a hammer, then every problem looks like a nail." The same holds true for negotiation. More tools enable you to solve more problems. Better tools enable you to find longer lasting, more enriching solutions. *Prepare, Probe,* and *Propose* are the first of the tools that we'll put in your negotiator's toolbox.

There is no secret formula that will enable you to get what you want every time you negotiate. But we have created a *systematic approach*—a step-by-step program—that, if repeated and mastered, will maximize your results. Like all good systems, this one is simple:

Prepare, Probe, and Propose.

That's it. Close the book, you've learned it. Well, it's not quite that simple. We'll show you how to *prepare* better than the other side; how to *probe* so you know what they want and why; and how to *propose* without going first and revealing too much, to avoid impasses or getting backed into a corner, but still achieving what you want. *As you'll see, negotiation is a process, not an event.*

4. **Handling Tough Negotiations.** Welcome to the real world of dealmaking. Unfortunately, it's full of tough negotiators and tough negotiations. Some people think you have to be a bad guy to be a good negotiator. So, they act the part. Some aren't really so awful but have to answer to an awful boss who demands that they act the part.

Sometimes, the negotiation itself may be brutal. The time, terms, or goals may be so difficult to meet that the *process* turns loathsome, even if the person opposite you isn't.

The tools in your negotiator's toolbox will enable you to deal with the toughest people and situations, from neutralizing animosity, to breaking deadlocks, to knowing when the best deal is no deal. You'll learn how to out-negotiate the bad guys without becoming one of them.

One more thing: If you've been around sports long enough, you know the value of a good pep talk—whether it's Herb Brooks talking to the 1980 U.S. Olympic Hockey Team—the "miracle on ice," Gene Hackman as the coach in *Hoosiers*, Babe Ruth talking to a sick kid in the hospital, or Pat O'Brien invoking the memory of the Gipper (Ronald Reagan in his second-most-famous role) in *Knute Rockne, All American*. It can make players play harder, forget their shortcomings, and literally change the fate of the game. This pep talk isn't just about getting your adrenaline going; it's about putting **PEP** into learning the lessons of negotiation.

PEP

Participate Be open to change. Read. Reread. Question.

Engage Throw yourself into this endeavor. Challenge yourself.

Personalize Relate what you learn to your career and your life.

If you read this book passively, you'll be cheating yourself. If you *Participate, Engage,* and *Personalize* you'll become a better negotiator, faster. Do the exercises in the book; ask others to help you practice; role play. Don't skip over parts you find difficult or unpleasant.

> What I hear, I forget. What I read, I remember. What I do, I understand.
>
> —CONFUCIUS

No, this isn't a normal textbook approach. But that's the point. To be more effective in negotiation, you have to stop using the same old "normal" approach. To harness the Power of Nice, you have to want change, accept change, and throw yourself into that change. The results will be worth it.

WHAT NEGOTIATION ISN'T

> People who fight fire with fire usually end up with ashes.
>
> —ABIGAIL VAN BUREN

Think of the word "negotiation." Quick, what images come to mind? Conflict? Confrontation? Battle? War? Or maybe: Debate? Logic? Science?

These are common interpretations that have fueled the negative approach to negotiation and are dead wrong.

Contrary to the fictionalized, Hollywood-ized, and ripped-from-the-headlines versions of larger-than-life moguls and the big-bucks business world that, up to a point, never seem to lose, from the investment bankers in *Barbarians at the Gate*, to Gordon Gekko in *Wall Street*, to Lehman Brothers in *Too Big to Fail*, to Jordan Belfort in *The Wolf of Wall Street*—dealmaking shouldn't be a stare-down in a stud poker game, a shoot-out at the O.K. Corral, hand-to-hand combat, a high-tech military maneuver, or an all-out atomic war. Despite the macho, swaggering, in-your-face lingo—winner take all, out for blood, call their bluff, raise the stakes, battle-scarred, make 'em beg for mercy, first one to blink, an offer they can't refuse, nuke 'em, meltdown, go for the kill, last man standing—negotiation isn't about getting the other side to wave a flag and surrender. *Negotiation is not war*.

Despite all the clinical, logical, rational, psychological, data-sifting analysis, graphs, pie charts, methods, and techniques from MBAs, CPAs, CEOs, shrinks, mediators, mediums, gurus, and astrologers, *negotiation is not a science*.

The problem is that war stories tell well. Wars have heroes and enemies and simplistic lessons: *Take no prisoners. To the victor belong the spoils.* (But war, you may have noticed, can lead to more war.) And science sounds like a formula. *If you do A, he'll do B, and you'll arrive at C.* Maybe. Unless he does D and then what do you do?

Negotiation as war and negotiation as science have each contributed to the popularity of the negative image of dealmaking, one by perpetuating the myth that the biggest, toughest thug wins and the other by way of the equally erroneous proposition that the coldest, least human calculator prevails.

Cultural conditioning (magazines, TV, movies, best-selling books, infomercials) has reduced dealmaking to images of brutal combat— often making great entertainment on film but lousy negotiation in reality. Gordon Gekko, the classic tough-guy negotiator from the movie *Wall Street*, played business hardball and never seemed to lose. (This is the movies, not life.) You may recall one scene where Gekko showed an adversary how the game is played (or Hollywood's version, anyway). In the scene, the well-dressed and self-impressed Sir Larry Wildman tries to bully Gekko into selling his shares of stock cheap so Wildman can pull off a takeover deal. Gekko, of course, is too shrewd to succumb to Wildman's intimidation. Gekko's protègè, Bud Fox, watches and learns. It went something like this:

Wall Street*

INT. GEKKO DEN—NIGHT

WILDMAN   I'm announcing a tender offer at 65 tomorrow. I'm expecting your commitment.

GEKKO   Showdowns bore me, Larry. Nobody wins. You can have the company. In fact, it's gonna be fun watching you and your giant ego try to make a horserace of it . . . (turns to Bud) Buddy, what's a fair price for that stock?

BUD   The breakup value is higher. It's worth 80.

GEKKO	Well, we don't want to be greedy, so what do you say to 72?
WILDMAN	You're a two-bit pirate and green-mailer, nothing more, Gekko. Not only would you sell your mother to make a deal, you'd send her COD.
GEKKO	My mail is the same color as yours is, pal. Or at least it was until the Queen started calling you "Sir." Now, you'll excuse me, all right, before I just lose my temper.
WILDMAN	. . . 71.
GEKKO	Well now, considering you brought my mother into it, 71.50.
WILDMAN	Done. You'll hear from my lawyers tomorrow. Eight A.M. Good night.
GEKKO	Well, he's right. I had to sell. The key to the game is your capital reserves. You don't have enough, you can't piss in the tall weeds with the big dogs.
BUD	"All warfare is based on deception . . . " Sun Tzu. "If your enemy is superior, evade him. If angry, irritate him. If equally matched, fight. And if not, split . . . reevaluate."
GEKKO	Hey, hey, hey, he's learnin', huh? Buddy's learnin'.

The Hollywood version of dealmaking makes good entertainment; it just doesn't make for good deals. The person on the other side of the table doesn't have to stick to the script.

Now, think of the word "negotiation" again. In order to practice the Power of Nice, start by wiping out everything you knew, thought, or felt about negotiation. Forget about winners and losers. Forget about verdicts. Forget about survivors and victims. Forget about keeping score. Forget about statistics. Forget about science. Forget about war.

Going into negotiation and counting on scientific results is like betting on the weather. If the forecast calls for a 20 percent chance of rain and you leave your umbrella home and it rains, you won't get 20 percent wet; you'll get soaked.

If you go into negotiation expecting war, bring a flak jacket. If you're armed for combat, the other side will be, too. If you have to win at all costs, so do they. Both sides attack, both sustain casualties. Neither side gives in, neither side gets what they want.

Negotiating a Phone Call

Imagine your car has broken down. You need to make a phone call for help and you have no cell phone. In the distance, you see a phone booth. You run to the booth but see there's a gentleman talking on the phone. How do you negotiate the man out of the booth? Do you wait patiently? Do you tap on the glass? How long is long enough to wait? Do you reach in and drag the man out?

Okay, change the facts. You had a car accident and your friend is near death in the passenger seat. You have to call 911. Now how do you negotiate? Do you wait patiently? Bang on the door? Throw the man out?

Change the facts again. You still have to call 911, but the man in the booth is Hannibal the Cannibal Lecter from *Silence of the Lambs*. Do you ask politely? Do you try to throw him out? Do you invite him to have dinner with your friend? Do you run for your life? As situations change, negotiation strategies must change. Negotiation isn't a science—there's no laboratory-proven answer. And negotiation isn't war—you don't attack Hannibal the Cannibal. Negotiation is a human interaction; it must be adapted and modified to fit the situation.

I Win–You Lose Becomes We Lose

Remember, if one party destroys the other, there's no one left to carry out the agreement. (Exacting exorbitant rents, punitive penalty clauses, or unrealistic noncompete terms often defeat their own purposes by creating disincentives; in other words, deals that are so good, they're bad.) The negotiation doesn't end when the contract is signed. If the other side is crippled by the deal, they will have every incentive to break the terms, literally having nothing to lose. You just made your first and last deal, instead of the first of many in a long-lasting relationship.

Nothing proves the point like history.

The Last Day of World War I was the First Day of World War II

It was 1919 and the Allies had defeated Germany. The story goes that the Allied representatives sat the vanquished German leaders down in a railroad car outside of Compiegne, France, to dictate the settlement that would eventually become the Treaty of Versailles. "Dictate" was the appropriate word. President Wilson had warned the Germans that the terms of armistice would be harsh—and they were.

German troops had to withdraw to a line six miles east of the Rhine River. Allied troops would occupy the evacuated territory. The German naval fleet was surrendered. Virtually all military supplies were given up to the Allies, including 5,000 cannon, 25,000 machine guns, 5,000 locomotives, and 150,000 railroad cars.

But the toughest demands were political and economic. Germany was ordered to pay huge reparations to the Allies in the form of cash and the removal of German assets and capital goods. France, which had been devastated by the German forces, regained Alsace-Lorraine and took over several German colonies. France was also given a 15-year lease on the Saar coal mines which, along with Lorraine, provided coal, iron, and potash to the development of heavy industry.

With a crippled postwar economy, it was soon clear that Germany could not sustain the burden of the payments. In 1923, the Dawes Plan was conceived to create a payment plan that Germany could meet. As a result of German reparation defaults, Belgium and France occupied the Ruhr district. By 1928, with Germany further behind, the Young Plan was a second effort to collect payments. Again, Germany was unable to pay. President Hoover called for a moratorium on reparations (and the United States forgave all debts from other Allied countries that were going to be repaid with monies they were to have received from Germany).

The Allies had won, Germany had lost. It was a classic I Win–You Lose negotiation. The Allies got to set all the terms. But the terms were unrealistic. *They made a deal that could not be carried out.* Instead of creating peace, they created further resentment. The loss of the Ruhr, the devastation of the German economy, the sacrifice of natural resources, all contributed to a latent, seething desire for revenge. Many historians feel that it was the ideal atmosphere for the rise of Adolph Hitler.

The deal that ended World War I, in effect, helped start World War II. In fact, when the Nazis invaded France, Hitler ordered that same railroad car, then housed in a museum, be the site where he would "dictate" the terms of the German occupation of France. I Win–You Lose became We Lose.

I Win—You Lose and its negative consequences seem obvious when the stakes are high and you have the historical benefit of hindsight. But the principle applies to even the simplest deal. In our seminars, we often begin with this game. You can try it yourself.

The $10 Game

Take 10 one-dollar bills. Find two people—two partners, husband and wife, people in your office, your kids. Tell them, "If you two can negotiate a deal in 30 seconds on how to divide the $10 between you, you can have the money. But there are three rules:

1. You can't split it, $5 and $5.
2. You can't say $7 and $3 or $6 and $4 and make a side deal to adjust the division later.
3. If you don't make a deal in 30 seconds, I take all $10 back."

Chances are, both parties will have a hard time resisting the urge to "win" and not "lose."
You'll hear the hard sell:

It's better for one of us to get it than neither of us so let's make it me.
I agree: As long as the one is me.

The soft sell:

Oh, gosh, whatever you think is fair.
Golly, how about $7 for me and, say, $3 for you?
No way!

The sympathy ploy:

I need the $10. I just ran out of gas.
At least you have a car.

The so-called logic ploy:

We've only got 30 seconds so you take $4, I'll take $6, and we'll both come out ahead.
Yeah, but you're more ahead.

The trust-me ploy:

> Give me all $10 and I'll make it up to you later. Trust me.
>
> **I've got a better idea. Give it all to me, and you trust me.**
> **BZZZZ! Time's up!**

Not only is it likely you'll keep your $10 with this game, but you can learn a lot about why negotiations *don't* work:

- When you have no preparation time, you don't think; you react.
- When you have time pressure *and* no preparation time, you revert to habits—usually bad ones. (When someone else is watching and judging your negotiations, it just adds to the pressure.)
- Most people revert to the habit of *I Win–You Lose*. Each one wants to win so much, is so convinced one can win *only* if the other loses, that they both lose.
- Sometimes *I Win You Lose* turns to *I Lose–You Win*. "I'll take $4, you take $6." In the quest to make a deal, any deal, people sometimes give away too much. Never forget, the goal should still be *WIN–win*—at least maximize and ideally, the big win is yours."

How Can You Achieve WIN–Win in the $10 Game?
Start with this premise:

> *Maximize your interests*. Determine what is the most you can come away with. Don't give away more than you have to. Get the most of a good deal, not the least of a bad deal. (That's another way of expressing WIN–win.)

Here are some interesting solutions we've seen in the seminars:

- **Look for points of agreement.** Rather than leaping into battle over who gets the most money, look for an idea upon which you both can agree. For example, "If we don't make a deal in 30 seconds, we both get nothing. So, let's start by splitting $8 of the money, $4 for me and $4 for you. Now let's just negotiate over the last $2." Once you've found one basis for agreement, you may well find more.
- **Remove ego.** Take subjectivity out and replace it with objectivity. Use a coin flip. "Heads, I get $6 and you get $4. Tails, you get $6 and I get $4." Both sides now have an equal chance to "WIN" or "win." And, regardless, it happened "fair and square."

- **Listen** carefully to the rules. They're limiting but not totally restricting if you're really creative. No one said you can't make change. Split the money $4.99 and $5.01. That's only a 2-cent windfall for the supposed winner.
- **Be creative—look for new approaches.** Increase the pie. Again, the rules allow for imaginative solutions. No one said you can't add to the total. Let's say, you put in an extra dollar. Now you're dividing $11. You take $6 and the other side takes $5. Both sides "WIN" by increasing the pie before dividing it.

Unfortunately, most people don't reach these solutions. They fall into the conventional traps of win–lose negotiation.

The Real or the Apparent Adversary?

What most people lose sight of in dividing the money is who they're up against. Each of the two negotiators generally sees the other as the opponent. They're wrong. In reality, they're up against the person holding the money. If the two negotiators don't succeed in making a deal, the one holding the money keeps the money. Before negotiators can find solutions, they have to identify their real obstacles, not just the apparent ones.

FILLING THE NEGOTIATOR'S TOOLBOX

How do you avoid the pitfalls of negotiation? Don't revert to the same old methods to solve your problems. If your only tool is a hammer, all problems look like nails; if the only tool in your negotiator's toolbox is **I Win–You Lose**, then everything turns into an I Win–You Lose situation. Negotiating becomes a battle of wills and/or egos. It isn't a good deal unless you defeat the other side in the process.

Conversely, if the only tool you have is **I Lose–You Win,** every negotiation will look like you have to give in, sacrifice, or settle for less in order to appease the other side's appetite.

Turn a mirror on yourself and ask, "What tools am I using in my negotiations?" The goal here is to put more tools in your negotiator's toolbox. By giving you the appropriate tools *and* an understanding of how and when to use them, you can become a more confident, and ultimately more successful, negotiator. Instead of dreading negotiation, you may even look forward to it.

WHAT NEGOTIATION IS

> Knowledge is power.
>
> —Francis Bacon

If negotiation isn't laboratory science or a bloody war, if it isn't the macho drama portrayed in the movies, what is it?

> Negotiation Is the Commerce of Information for Ultimate Gain

Let's take that definition apart. First, *the commerce of information*: Commerce is the business of trading. It's the stock market in New York, the commodities floor in Chicago, the street vendors in Tangiers. The difference here is that you're not exchanging corn futures for sowbellies or Moroccan francs for Persian rugs. *You're trading what you know for what you need to know.* In the negotiation market, information is the commodity. And in a negotiation, nothing is more valuable than information, whether it's two countries trying to make peace, two companies merging, two workers trading office gossip, or two kids swapping baseball cards. Is one veteran's card worth three up-and-comers? It all depends on information: What one kid wants and how bad. What the other kid has and is willing to give up.

Buzz I'll give you a Ichiro Suzuki. What'll you give me?
Bob I'll give you a Joe Mauer. But I won't give you my Derek Jeter.
Buzz That's okay, my cousin's got a Derek Jeter—he'll trade me.
Bob This one's in mint condition.
Buzz Well, all I got is a whole mess of rookie cards.
Bob Really? I got a rookie collection. Which ones you got?
Buzz Let's see. I've got an Adam Jones and a Matt Wieters.
Bob Not bad, but not enough for a mint Jeter.
Buzz Okay, see ya.
Bob You sure you don't have any others?
Buzz Well, my little brother has this Mike Trout.
Bob Too bad it's your brother's.

Buzz   He's only five and he says I can do whatever I want.
Bob   Really? Well, I have to think about it.
Buzz   I gotta go in for dinner.
Bob   Deal.

Kids swapping cards are no different from grown-up dealmakers. The commerce of information determines whether there can be a deal at all. Does one side have something of possible or real value to the other side, and vice versa? Do the sides want to make a deal or are they fishing? Is there competition? How deep are the buyer's pockets/resources? What are the terms of the deal? Who has decision-making power? Does either side have a deadline?

After feeling each other out with two players' cards either side would give up (*fishing*), Bob revealed he had the Derek Jeter card (*possible value*). Buzz wisely explained that he already could get a Jeter from his cousin (*competition*), which led to getting the information that Bob's Jeter card is in excellent condition (*real value*). Then, Buzz gave up information again, this time admitting he only had rookie cards (*limited resources*). Very smart move by Buzz. Either way, he learns. If Bob doesn't want rookies, there's nothing to talk about. But if he does, then there's plenty to talk about. It turns out Bob collects rookies (*value for both sides*). Buzz offers two rookies but Bob wants a third (*terms of the deal*). The third belongs to Buzz's brother, but Buzz can speak for his brother (*decisionmaker*). So now it's up to Bob to ponder whether it's a good deal. But Buzz has to go in for dinner (*deadline*).

Each side obtained information. Each side gave information. But one side got more than it gave. Each piece of information given out garnered key feedback, which better equipped that side for negotiation.

And that leads to the second half of the definition of negotiation, *for ultimate gain*. You enter a negotiation with a goal or goals—to get what you came for—to gain: a piece of land, a client, a lease, an option, a contract. You want to win but it *doesn't* mean the other side has to lose. In fact, it may not matter what the other side gains, as long as you achieve your goal. (You should even be willing to *help* the other side get what they want, *if* it enables you to realize your goal.) That's WIN–win or GAIN–gain or maximize your win.

But you're not just after gain; you want ultimate gain. That means two things. One, it may take a while. Be patient. Be ready to exchange as much information as possible. Let it sink in. Wait. Each deal has its own pace. (They can be sped up or slowed down, but not without affecting the results.) Allow each side to absorb the information, modify positions, evolve goals, adjust expectations, even save face. Ultimate gain means "ultimate" as in later, down the road, well past today's deal. It means the next deal that comes out of the first one, or a renewal of a contract, or forgiveness for late shipping, or offering a reference to your next prospect, or even making you a partner in their next deal. You never know when ultimate is coming but you can be sure it will arrive. That's when you find out just how good that deal was in the first place.

Now put the definition back together:

Negotiation is the commerce of information for ultimate gain.

Or in shorthand, *negotiation is using knowledge to get what you want.*

Everything Worthwhile in Life Happens after 10:00 P.M.

Some deals seem to come up over and over again. You face the same guy on the other side, who uses the same techniques to get the same results. He knows what he wants and you know what he wants. So you have lots of opportunities to do the deal until you get it right. But you never get it right.

You know the kind of guy I mean. He trades in the commerce of information better than you do. He attains ultimate gain better than you do. He's one of those shrewd but patient types, armed with dogged determination and relentless pursuit. Everybody has a negotiating nemesis like that. Mine is, or was, my stepson, William, now an adult but then only 11 and already a skilled dealmaker as I take you back to this scene:

It's dinnertime and William is perfect. "Mm, these lima beans are delicious." By 7:30 P.M. he's doing homework. He's quiet, he's studious, he's a model child at 8:00 ... 8:30 ... 9:00 ... 9:30 ..., right up until the minute hand creeps across the hour mark of 10:00. That's when William the Cooperative becomes William the Conqueror: because 10:00 is his bedtime. Theoretically. (Call our house at 10:25 any night and see who answers the phone.)

On weekdays, 10:00 is prime time, the start of *NYPD Blue, ER,* or *Law and Order.* Sometimes 10:00 is the bottom of the sixth inning with the score tied, Orioles 3–Yankees 3. But 10:00 is always when William engages in "the commerce of information for ultimate gain."

WILLIAM	My science teacher says kids my age only need six hours of sleep.
ME	I thought it was more like eight hours, William.
WILLIAM	Well, if you think I shouldn't believe my science teacher . . .
ME	Of course, I think you should believe your science teacher.
WILLIAM	Me, too. So, then I guess I should get to stay up later.

WILLIAM	If this was a playoff game, would you let me stay up?
ME	I guess if it was a playoff, maybe.
WILLIAM	This game could turn out to be the key game that decides if the Orioles make it to the playoffs. So it's really a playoff game for the playoff game.

WILLIAM	Have you ever seen *Law and Order*?
ME	No, I haven't.
WILLIAM	It's about lawyers, so it might help you do your job better. I'll stay up and watch it with you.

William knows that if he can get me interested in what he's interested in, I'll forget what time it is. Pretty soon, I'm caught up in Law and Order *and I'm asking William why the cop is lying to the DA. Or it's the eighth inning, the Orioles are up by two runs, and New York has the bases loaded.*

(William fishes with information until he hooks me.)

WILLIAM	The judge is in love with the woman who's accused of the murder.
	(He waits for the information to penetrate.)
ME	But the cop said the woman just moved from Boston.
	(William builds on it.)
WILLIAM	The cop is a bad guy, too. He and the woman are partners.
	(William works me slowly, patiently. Meanwhile, the clock is ticking. He's already getting what he wants, even in the process of negotiating.)
ME	How do you know?
WILLIAM	You'll see when the trial starts.
	(I modify my position.)
ME	Okay, just until the next commercial.
	(He trades more info.)
WILLIAM	The DA has a secret witness.
ME	Really? Who?
WILLIAM	They won't tell you until the very end.
	(He's got me!)

By now, it's close to 11:00 and I'm yawning. William, whose bedtime is absolutely, positively, without exception 10:00 P.M., is up, wide awake.

So, at my house, it was clear who was best at using "the commerce of information for ultimate gain": William, age 11, skilled negotiator.

WHAT NEGOTIATION CAN BE

Success is finding the right customers and keeping them.

—MBNA CORPORATE MOTTO

It's not the sale, it's the relationship that counts.

—MBNA'S JOE GATTI

Negotiation seems like a finite activity, with a beginning and an end: You're selling and I'm buying. You set a price, I offer, you counteroffer, I counter your counter, you modify, I accept, we sign, deal's done. Not necessarily.

Negotiation can be the initial step toward lasting business arrangements. It can yield clients, not just buyers. It can lead to repeat business, added business, referrals, even loyalty. Negotiation can result in partnership instead of one-upmanship. But it rarely does.

Most people act as if the deal they're making is the last one they'll ever make with the other side. In fact, the opposite is generally the case. Banks want to lend money to people who pay it back. People like to borrow from banks that give terms they can live with. Shopping centers try to retain good tenants. Tenants wish to remain where business is good. Sports teams want to hold on to their stars. Stars like to keep playing for good teams. Husbands who hate cleaning the bathtub hope their wives will trade for sweeping the garage. Most deals are just daily or monthly or yearly pieces of an overall deal . . . or they should be.

Name five of your negotiations that were truly one-time deals, with no ramifications, no chance for future deals, no openings for repeat business or for an ongoing relationship. Those five represent lost opportunities for long-term deals. The point is, you have nothing to lose by assuming you might do business again.

MBNA: The Credit Card Company That Started in an Abandoned A&P Supermarket . . . and Eventually Became One of Bank of America's Largest Acquisitions

MBNA was a company that didn't even exist before 1982. That's when a gentleman named Charles Cawley opened a fledgling credit card company in an old A&P store that A&P didn't want anymore.

MBNA had a simple philosophy: "*Success is finding the right customers and keeping them.*" It wasn't brilliant as much as it was sensible. The company didn't have many customers—and customers were hard to get. So, management figured when they found a good customer, they should hang on. Once they had one customer, they went after two and kept two, and then three, and ten, and a hundred.

In an industry that had become too complacent about the word "churn" (constant customer turnover), MBNA went on a crusade for retention. Throughout the office was posted one of the company's mantras, "*Think of yourself as the customer.*" When a cardholder called with a billing question or complaint, the goal was no more than two rings until a customer service representative answered. The staff was educated to be fanatically polite and knowledgeable. Good customers were automatically rewarded with higher credit limits without having to request the increase. Management often personally responded to customer inquiries.

Further, MBNA found new ways to bond with customers. The company pioneered affinity cards, credit cards tied to professional groups, universities, or other organizations to which the customer had loyalty. A University of North Carolina graduate could feel good that every time he made a purchase with his Tarheel MasterCard, he was supporting his alma mater. And he'd be far less prone to cancel his Tarheel card than he might be to cancel a card from an impersonal credit card company. MBNA soon became the industry leader in affinity marketing, with endorsements ranging from the American College of Surgeons to the Chicago Bulls. Needless to say, the company outgrew that original A&P store.

Headquartered in Wilmington, Delaware, MBNA became one of the top three credit card issuers in the world, with annual profits in excess of $500 million, and more than 14 million customers it served loyally and tenaciously (and, not surprisingly, had a very low churn rate).

The business philosophy at MBNA was: *There are no short-term, one-time deals.* Every customer was a potential customer for life, whether an affinity group, a partner bank, or the ultimate consumer/cardholder. In every town where MBNA did business, the company was determined to be the best corporate citizen, to stay and to have the communities want them to stay. Employees were taken care of the same way. MBNA recognized effort and dedication. The company didn't just give raises; it gave awards. It promoted from within. The result was a very low churn rate of employees as well.

In fact, MBNA's business philosophy ingrained itself so deeply that the employees became walking ads for the corporate culture. One of the top MBNA performers, Joe Gatti, came up to me in the parking lot before our first MBNA seminar even began, and, like the scene in *The Graduate* where the family friend offers Benjamin Braddock that memorable career-counseling wisdom ("I have one word for you, Ben. Plastics."), this executive looked at me and said, "It's not the sale, it's the relationship that counts."

At MBNA, it never was about the bottom line of any one deal. It was always about the cumulative reward over the life of the relationship. No wonder the company became so successful so fast. No wonder it became the model and envy of the credit card business, including much larger competitors.

And no wonder in 2006, the company was sold to Bank of America for $35 billion. Not bad for a company started in an empty supermarket.

As you'll read in Chapter 4, negotiation can and should be a *process*, not an *event*. But one aspect of that idea is, when you live from sale to sale, each sale becomes a measure of success or failure. If a competitor undercuts your price, you lose. If you overpromise and can't make good, you lose. Even if you make the sale, it pays a one-time profit and you have to start over with the same customer tomorrow. When you have a relationship with a customer, prices, promises, and results are measured in total return.

Sales pay one-time profits. Relationships pay dividends. It's a simple matter of economics. Which do you prefer?

REFRESHER

Chapter 1: Negotiation

What it isn't, is, and can be

Four Objectives

1. Display confidence. Confident negotiators negotiate better.
2. Achieve WIN–win. Both parties win, but you maximize your win.
3. Use the 3 Ps: Prepare, Probe, Propose.
4. Handle tough negotiations.

PEP

Participate: Be open to change, read, reread, question.

Engage: Throw yourself into the process of learning negotiation.

Personalize: Relate what you learn to your career and your life.

Lessons from the $10 Game

- Find ways to agree—create momentum.
- Remove ego—break deadlocks.
- Listen carefully to the rules.
- Be creative—look for new approaches. Increase the pie—before splitting it.

Negotiation is *not* war.
Negotiation is *not* a science.
Negotiation is the commerce of information for ultimate gain.

I Win–You Lose Becomes We Both Lose

With the Power of Nice you can:

1. Make deals.
2. Build relationships.
3. Make more deals.

P.S. Don't negotiate with kids. Chances are, you'll lose.

Kevin KAL Kallaugher, Kaltoons.com.

CHAPTER **2**

I Win–You Lose Negotiation—An Exercise in Flawed Logic

> The winning team, like the conquering army, claims everything in its path and seems to say that only winning is important. Yet, like getting into the college of your choice or winning an election or marrying a beautiful mate, victory is fraught with as much danger as glory. Victory has very narrow meanings and, if exaggerated or misused, can become a destructive force.
>
> —BILL BRADLEY, *LIFE ON THE RUN*

ENEMIES AND ENTRENCHED POSITIONS

I Win–You Lose is probably the most common (and least productive) approach to negotiation. Victory, not the achievement of goals, is the only acceptable outcome. And the counterpart of victory is defeat. In order for one side to gain what it wants, the other side must *give up* what it wants. There is no winner unless there's a loser. This is negotiation as war. The other side is the enemy. The success rate is about as good as that of war—seldom and rarely long-lasting—the opposite of the Power of Nice.

> I love the smell of napalm in the morning—it smells like victory.
>
> —Lt. Col. Kilgore, *Apocalypse Now*

Enemies

In I Win–You Lose negotiation, one side assumes the other is an adversary. Sometimes both sides assume so. They couldn't possibly each be business people or neighbors or siblings or even fellow human beings. They couldn't share wants or needs or fears or hopes. They have nothing in common. They're enemies.

And as enemies, there's no goodwill, no open-mindedness, no willingness to learn about each other's pressures, priorities, and goals in the negotiation. There is no trust.

> Whoever said "It's not whether you win or lose that counts" probably lost.
>
> —Martina Navratilova

If you subscribe to that outlook, there is no opportunity for mutual interests, creative solutions, and, least of all, building a relationship:

- The two parties may never learn that one party could have a delayed payout for tax purposes and the other party can meet a high price only if allowed to pay over time. Or that both sides must get the deal done by the end of the calendar year. Or that a third player has been talking to both.
- They may never experiment with shared profits instead of fixed payments. Or open books on both sides. Or lending each other talented employees. Or forming an alliance instead of trying to drive each other into oblivion.
- And they will certainly never explore how this deal might lead to others. Or joining forces instead of one buying out the other. Or one giving the other a "first look" or "second chance" on the next opportunity.

> The point is that you can't be too greedy.
>
> —Donald Trump

They are not at the table to reach their goals; they're at the table to defeat the enemy. And the assumption (usually erroneous) is that they will never encounter this same "enemy" again. They conveniently forget the cliché, "It's a small world," which got to be a cliché because it's true.

Entrenched Positions

If you believe there's no victory unless there's defeat, if you assume the other side is your enemy, then the negotiation process itself is nothing but taking a position, stating it, and restating it (sometimes louder for emphasis):

"My price is $1,000,000."

"*Is there any room for negotiating . . . ?*"

"My price is $1,000,000."

"*We don't have that much but . . .*"

"Too bad. We'll have to go to your competitor."

"*If we could have some time . . .*"

"The offer ends at midnight."

"*Maybe we could . . .*"

"My price is $1,000,000."

I Win–You Lose negotiators don't determine the individual circumstances, needs, or particular interests of the other party. They simply arrive at their offer or their price or their terms or all of the above. They often take it or leave it. (Their idea of an offer.) And, by the way, there's a deadline. (Their idea of an incentive.)

The one thing they don't do is listen. There's a cynical expression that describes the entrenched approach of the win–lose negotiator perfectly: *Don't confuse me with the facts.* Why learn when I've already made up my mind? Why compromise? Why meet halfway? Why try give-and-take?

Why look for common ground? Why find an innovative answer, creative terms, or a new route? You're the enemy. You're only trying to get the better of me. (After all, that's what I'm trying to do to you.)

Entrenched negotiators have a great deal of trouble completing deals. It's no wonder. They have so fixed their position, they have nowhere to move. Only a perfect coincidental match will work. You must need *exactly* what they have to offer, at the price they're offering, on the terms they're offering.

Meanwhile, deals are being made all around them and they wonder why.

HIT AND RUN

Don't Win–Lose negotiators ever make deals? Sure, it happens. In fact, there isn't a seminar we do where someone doesn't come up and say, "Hey, I know somebody who fits that win–lose description and I've seen them make great deals." Okay, it's true. How and why? When the quick-hit, I Win–You Lose negotiator is in an advantageous dealmaking position (i.e., desirable property, best talent, available space, an attractive client list, ready cash, an anxious buyer), he or she tends to opt for *Instant Deal Gratification*—get it all and get it now. Take cash, not an earn-out. If you get a higher offer, take it. Promises are nice, cash is better. How can they do it? They're *Hit-and-Run negotiators*. They get in, score, and get out, scoring one-time deals that make a fast buck and have a short life. No long-term relationships and very little repeat business.

But when their transactions are examined closely and over time, their apparent grand successes are often matched with equally grand failures. The sports agency business seems to have more than its share of Hit-and-Run negotiators. They're the agents who make headlines by bad-mouthing ball clubs, constantly making their players holdouts, and shamelessly shopping their players to get one-time, record-breaking contracts rather than life-fulfilling, career-making deals. They love to "leak" their big-dollar deals and their own prowess to the press.

What the Hit-and-Run negotiators don't like to mention, though, are the numerous times their strategies cost their clients money over the long term, waste years of a player's potential professional development or, worse, threaten or end a client's career.

I've Never Been on the Cover of *Sports Illustrated*

A case in point is the fame, or infamy to some, of NFL agent Drew Rosenhaus. He has represented prominent football players, from wide receiver Terrell Owens to tight end Rob Gronkowski to cornerback Jimmy Smith. There's probably no football agent (with the possible exception of the fictional Jerry McGuire) better known than Rosenhaus. There is no question that Rosenhaus is an adept promoter. The question frequently is: who is he promoting most, his players or himself? Rosenhaus is a nonstop Tweeter, a ubiquitous sports–talk show guest, and, in the ultimate irony (or professional courtesy?) he once actually wrestled a real shark in the water. In 2011, *60 Minutes* featured Rosenhaus. During the piece, CBS's Scott Pelley described Rosenhaus as "an agent who is at the same time revered, feared, and hated."

Rosenhaus is no stranger to headlines. The classic 1996 *Sports Illustrated* cover headline shouted, "The most hated man in pro football" next to a color shot of Drew Rosenhaus and his own words, "*I am a ruthless warrior. I am a hit man. I will move in for the kill and use everything within my power to succeed for my clients.*"

Inside, the article described Rosenhaus's negotiation style. "Deceit is part of his job. He will not only lie, he will also scream, cajole, threaten, and whine to defend his clients' interests ... He has been described as slithering and blindly ambitious." The story quotes other agents on Rosenhaus, "When you look up sleazeball agent in the dictionary, there's a picture of Drew," are the words of Craig Fenech and, according to Peter Schaffer, "Drew is the biggest scumbag in the business."

Pretty strong words: He may even sound effective with all that hype. But bloody victories that leave a trail of carnage do not necessarily make a successful negotiator. The ability to make deals and build relationships that lead to more deals is the definition of an effective negotiator. Will the Drew Rosenhaus clones, who have one-shot, headline-making wins, continue to have them, one after another, in the long run? Maybe.

But after reading the *Sports Illustrated* article, I said to myself with respect to Rosenhaus, "Give it some time and there'll be stories about how the Win–Lose approach blew up in his and his clients' faces."

Readers didn't have to wait long. The reports came fast and frequently. First there was *USA Today* columnist Bryan Burwell's piece on Errict Rhett, a well-known Rosenhaus client, headed, "Rhett's holdout turns out to be big bucks mistake." This is how Burwell described the situation:*

Say hello to Errict Rhett, poster child for the *really, really, really big, gigantic, jumbo, super-sized mistake*. As the Tampa Bay Bucs running back finally ended his 93-day-long holdout Wednesday, halfway through the NFL season, a few minor questions ran across my mind, such as: What was he thinking?

To review: The two-time, 1,000-yard rusher insisted he would not play for the $336,000 he was scheduled to earn this season. He rejected a six-year, $14.1 million offer from the Bucs during training camp, claiming the deal had most of the money back-loaded, then launched a lengthy holdout to force the Bucs to give him a better deal.

But when he finally showed up in camp on Wednesday, Rhett still had no new deal. Instead, this is what he did have: A bill for $5,000 a day in fines. Let me do the math for you—$5,000 a day at 93 days = $465,000. I'm no math whiz . . . . But, if you're only making $336,000 and you've already rung up $465,000 in fines, you might have what I might call a slight cash flow problem . . . . There are migrant farm workers who have a better deal than this, and the last time I checked, they didn't have . . . The Most Hated Man in Football representing them.

Player agent Drew Rosenhaus, a rather colorful, amusing, self-absorbed fellow who was given that title in a recent *Sports Illustrated* cover story, is the genius who navigated Rhett through this disastrous holdout. But let's be fair. In the history of ill-advised, bubble-headed plans, Rhett's three-month-long holdout was not the worst of all time. (Let's not forget these) 1. That little boat ride in *Deliverance*. 2. Christopher Darden saying, "Here, O.J., try on these gloves." 3. The CEO who said, "Hey, how about New Coke!"

Rosenhaus lost a client. Rhett lost millions of dollars, his starting position, and possibly damaged his career irreparably.

---

*Copyright 1996, *USA TODAY*. Reprinted with permission.

As for Rosenhaus himself, his style has kept his career in high profile. Whether that has always been what's best for his clients is a matter of opinion.

Hit-and-Run negotiators tend to leave victims in their wake, that is, customers, clients, investors, buyers, and sellers who've ended up on the lousy end (temporarily) of the Hit-and-Runner's abusive, shortsighted strategy. Rather than negotiators, they're opportunists. There's nothing wrong with opportunity. When it knocks, you should answer. But if that's all you do, you may miss out on the bigger rewards of deals that last years, renew, and lead to other deals (as well as the intangible benefits of long-term relationships).

I'M NOT ONE OF THEM, AM I?

Okay, readers, right now you're saying, "I don't have to worry about being a Win–Lose negotiator. I never beat up on the other side. I don't need to read this book. Everyone I negotiate with needs to read it."

None of us likes to think of ourselves as Win–Lose negotiators, but there are times when we give in to the temptation of the moment, when we hold the cards, or want to get (just a little bit) even with the other side, and we give in to the dark side and go for the kill.

We've all been there. Truth be told, we all speak from experience. There are four situations that arise when even the most dedicated WIN–win negotiators may be tempted to cross over to Win–Lose:

1. When you've been hit (hurt, damaged, taken advantage of) and have the urge to hit back.
2. When you allow principle (I'm going to teach them a lesson) to cloud vision or become a rationalization.
3. When you think you have the upper hand and underestimate the other side.
4. When you oversell, driven by the desire to make *a* deal rather than to make the *right* deal.

The stories that follow are each examples of giving in to the temptation of Win–Lose negotiation and the negative outcomes that inevitably result. The first illustrates that even though I've tried to take a WIN–win approach throughout my career, I, too, have fallen victim to the lure of Win–Lose.

Oprah Before She Was Oprah! (Or, I Was Hit and Wanted to Hit Back)

Okay, it's humility time. I'm the guy who represented Oprah Winfrey before she became so big she only needed a first name. I was her agent in Baltimore and I did my best to get her what she was worth as her talent began to manifest itself. I offered my counsel and advice. I urged her to move fast without moving too fast: the right mix of patience and ambition. As she embarked on her climb up the major market ladder toward Chicago, I helped navigate the journey.

Oprah was hot. You could sense it. And getting hotter. She really came into her own at the ABC affiliate in Chicago. She was magnetic. Audiences were drawn to her. Magic was happening. The magazines and tabloids picked it up. There was, as they say, a buzz.

Not surprisingly, as her star ascended, she reexamined many things, including her career management. It happens to Triple A ballplayers who are brought up to the majors and have a red-hot rookie season, it happens to repertory actors who toil anonymously and suddenly win the lead in a Broadway show, to state governors plucked by their party to be national candidates, to painters, authors, and rock musicians. Are they being managed as they reach for the top as well as they were managed on the way up? Certainly, it's a legitimate question, one over which I've gained a few clients, but rarely lost one. This proved to be the exception.

I could argue all I want about what a good job I was doing, but ultimately it wasn't my decision; it was hers. She had to do what she thought best. It wasn't long before I got a call from Oprah. She started with, "Ron, this is really hard to say, but...." She went on to tell me how much she appreciated everything I'd done for her, how much she respected me, and how she hoped we could stay friends and maybe even work together again someday. I was hurt, but I wished her well.

Some time later, I read that Oprah thought she no longer wanted a "nice-guy agent." If that's so, I can't argue with the label. Naturally, there are different styles of negotiation. Some clients are comfortable with one type, some with another, and some change from time to time. I believe you can be a nice guy and get what you and/or the client want at the negotiation table (hence this book).

I lost Oprah Winfrey. But that's not the humbling part of the story. I had a contract with Oprah. According to one of my partners, she still owed us commissions. Even though she was no longer a client, he said we were entitled to the revenue. On a strictly legal basis, he was probably right. My instinct told me, legal basis or not, drop it. But I didn't follow my instinct. *I had gotten hit and I wanted to hit back*. I said, "Okay, go after the money." Our firm explored legal action. Both sides retained attorneys. Eventually, we settled and got our money, the short-term gain. But we lost the possibility of future good will. Maybe we'd never have done business with Oprah again. But maybe we would have. After we sued, it wasn't even a question.

Postscript: Whenever I reflect on what might have been, I take some consolation from an observation later made by a key player. When Oprah retired in 2011, Dennis Swanson, at that time the president of station operations for Fox Broadcasting, retold the story of the negotiations that enabled her to move from Baltimore to Chicago and ultimately to the national stage. He said, "Well, you know, she had the best attorney in Baltimore, Ron Shapiro, who handled Brooks Robinson, and a lot of the Orioles who were a championship team at that time. The tricky part of it was, her contract didn't expire until the end of the year. But then, the people who had the contract had a 60-day option in there, and I said to Shapiro, I said, 'We'll wait till January 1, because she's worth waiting for, but I can't wait the 60 days beyond that.' He negotiated out of that. We put her on the air the first of January, and we were in last place when we put her on the air—and we won the February (ratings) less than a month later."

If It's a Circus, How Come No One Is Smiling? (Or, When Principle Clouds Vision)

For years, Ringling Brothers and Barnum & Bailey Circus performed in the Baltimore Arena. And every year was a sellout. But in the late 1980s, the arena, previously owned by the city, was privatized. The new operators and Ringling Brothers management had a history of bad relations. Neither side trusted the other. Both sides accused the other of bad faith dealings in the past and now stood their ground as a matter of "principle." As a result, each could only see their own side and could not yield. Each was convinced they had to make the other back down, and each was convinced the other couldn't live without them. So what had been a profitable endeavor for both performer and venue was now jeopardized.

Without going into the ugly details, the negotiations were not "entertainment for the whole family." The arena wouldn't budge. Ringling Brothers wouldn't budge. I was asked to intercede. I tried to mediate and actually made some headway. But the progress was only temporary. The talks broke down. Ringling threatened to pull out. The arena called Ringling's bluff, figuring that Ringling would come to its senses and call back in a few days. Or, the arena thought it could bring in another, equally appealing circus. But there were no calls from Ringling and no other circus matched Ringling's market appeal.

Ringling, for its part, was sure the arena management would think it over and make a better offer. No offers came. Both sides waited longer. Nothing.

Finally? No deal. Two principle-driven devotees became entrenched I Win–You Lose negotiators who set out to out-macho each other, each wanting a win that came out of the other's hide. What they got was nothing at all. "The Greatest Show on Earth" wasn't the greatest show in Baltimore. The circus didn't come to town.

P.S. It took a few years, but wisdom and mutual gain finally overcame overblown principles. With the specific goal of starting a fresh relationship, the CEO of Ringling went to his counterpart at the top of the company that manages the Baltimore Arena and other venues. In contrast to prior dealings between their companies, the two men put that I Win–You Lose history behind them; they made a deal on a handshake in all of 30 minutes and also agreed to work together at other venues. Some stories, even those with a rocky middle, have a happy ending.

The Baseball Strike, Score 0–0 (Or, When You Think You Have the Upper Hand and Underestimate the Other Side)

There is probably no better lesson in I Win–You Lose than the negotiations over the Major League Baseball strike of 1994 and 1995. The subtleties, nuances, and techniques of dealmaking are all here. And all wrong. The baseball strike is a "How-Not-To" case study for anyone negotiating anything.

During 1994, the Major League Baseball Players Association and the team owners had been talking—I wouldn't even call it negotiating—for months. Both sides were talking, but neither side was listening. And both were convinced they had the upper hand.

The owners said payrolls were getting out of control. They wanted a salary cap. Not surprisingly, the players, who were on the receiving end of those escalating salaries, wanted no such hard-and-fast limit on their earnings: maybe something more creative, but nothing that resembled a cap. The owners wanted a cap, nothing more creative, hard-and-fast, just the way the players didn't want it.

I talked with representatives of both sides throughout. I can only say that they were equally unrealistic. My contacts among the owners made it clear that there was one thing they were positive the players wouldn't have the guts to do: strike. I cautioned the owners not to be so sure.

In late summer of 1994, the players struck. The surprised, but unmoved, owners responded with their favorite refrain. They wanted a salary cap. By now, that was fairly clear.

There was another other thing the owners told me they were sure the players wouldn't do: stay on strike. The owners followed a strategy based on the premise that those "greedy" ballplayers would miss their inflated paychecks, break ranks, and return to the field. Again, I offered my doubts about the owners' outlook. Again, the players surprised the owners. The players stayed out for 10 games, 20, 50, and still didn't give in.

My contacts in the players' union were just as sure (and just as wrong) as the owners. The players were positive that those "greedy" owners would miss all that advertising and attendance money, the TV revenue, souvenir sales, the hot dogs, beer, and pretzel profits, the parking fees, the licensing deals, and that they would cave in on the salary cap. I offered a similar caution to the players as I had to the owners. "Don't be so sure." But they didn't want to hear it (at least not yet).

Game after game was missed. All told, 668 regular season games were canceled In 1994. (Eventually, another 261 games were wiped out in the spring of 1995 for a total of 929.)

Then the unthinkable happened. In September of 1994, Acting Commissioner Bud Selig announced that the World Series was canceled. Even the national despair of the Great Depression wasn't enough to stop the World Series. The Second World War couldn't interrupt the World Series. The San Francisco earthquake of 1989 didn't thwart the Series.

But the owners and players had stopped their own game. If they hadn't killed the golden goose, they certainly had their hands wrapped around its throat. It was classic I Win–You Lose negotiation. The only thing both sides agreed on was that the other side was dead wrong (and would have to back down).

Fay Vincent, the commissioner of Major League Baseball who had been forced by the owners to resign prior to the showdown, recalls, "I could not talk these people out of having that battle, didn't have the political skill or the ability not to have this war, and I regret that."

While the two parties were battling to a standstill, both were forgetting the third party, the one neither could live without—the fans, a.k.a. consumers. With every missed game, they became less attached, less devoted to their favorite pastime, a dangerous disaffection. Without consumers, there is no game—no fans in the stands, covered in logos, inhaling hot dogs and beer, nobody at home in front of the TV or glued to the radio, exposed to all those ads, buying all that stuff the ads hawk.

A good negotiation is about dividing the pie so that both sides get a satisfactory piece. A better negotiation is one that finds a way to grow the pie (increase revenues, add market share, strengthen resources) so both sides get a bigger piece. But baseball was playing out the worst scenario possible. What had been a 2.5-billion-dollar pie was actually shrinking. It had taken decades for it to reach that size and, in a matter of weeks, it was losing revenue by the millions.

If the battle kept up, the two sides might be fighting not over slices of the pie, but crumbs. The economic impact of the strike is hard to fully assess. It wasn't just the teams, the sponsors, and the media: every major league city lost revenue from people *not* stopping for dinner before the game, restaurants *not* ordering extra food and beverages from suppliers, *not* hiring extra help for game nights, the help *not* earning extra tips, fans *not* buying gas to drive to the games, *not* parking in lots by the stadium, *not* fueling the local economies from Boston to San Diego. Spring training cities held their breath for fear of suffering the same fate.

Finally recognizing that more than playing the game was at stake and that common sense had failed, as had government mediators, President Clinton stepped in. He suggested turning to a distinguished private mediator and asking both sides to enter into voluntary mediation.

If ever there was a well-intentioned effort, this was it. Maybe, just maybe, the intervention of the President of the United States could move both parties in the right direction. The President asked William Usery, a former Secretary of Labor, and a highly respected man, to mediate. Hope turned to whispered optimism. Mr. Usery and his staff met with both sides in early November 1994. Each party opened up to Mr. Usery. The meetings appeared to go well. But appearances were deceiving.

Mr. Usery telephoned me a few weeks later to ask my views of the parties and their positions. He was searching for clues to opportunities for compromise, where he could find common ground, what might open a closed mind. He had been asking the players and the owners these same questions since November and he was getting nowhere. He said, "In order to walk on water, you have to know where the rocks are, and I'll be damned if I can find them."

So, William Usery, distinguished former cabinet member and statesman, had run into the wall of distrust that had been building for years. It was a power battle and each side thought they had more clout and it was time to show it. From the perspective of the majority of the owners, it was a game of "break Don Fehr and his union." To say they were hard liners doesn't do justice to their resolve. On the other side, the union was built on a rock-solid ideology of a free market economy and a deep-seated mistrust of the owners dating back to their illegal collusion in the 1980s. In the past, with the game making record profits, commissioners of baseball had managed to persuade the owners to accede to the players on several controversial issues. By now the union had begun to feel that compromise wasn't necessary. But, unfortunately for both sides, times had changed.

More weeks passed. The winter wore on. The public relations game, which both sides always played, now seemed to be the World Series of the baseball strike. Who could score with the politicians? Who could come across better with the press? Who could play better to the public on a talk show? They went "off the record" and "on the record." They pitched and they spun. The union made a serious effort to persuade Congress to repeal baseball's long-standing antitrust exemption, a long shot at best. Ballplayers lobbying members of Congress did nothing but sap energy from the process of negotiation. The owners were no less guilty. They leaked their versions of each story, provided their named and unnamed sources, did their spinning, wooing, and pitching. And the fans were getting weary of it all. If we were getting nowhere slowly before, now we were getting nowhere fast. Spring wasn't far off.

In late 1994, a White House contact and I were lamenting the shrinking baseball revenue, the impending disaster of canceling spring training, and the immeasurable damage being done to a national icon. He asked me if I held out any hope for the mediation process.

I wanted to say "yes." But honestly, I was losing faith. As we talked, I recalled memories of another White House–orchestrated mediation: Jimmy Carter brokering the Israeli-Egyptian peace treaty of 1978. By no means am I comparing baseball to Middle East peace, but I am comparing the dynamics of two seemingly intractable parties. The Camp David peace process demonstrated how confidentiality—knowing that what was said would go no further—enabled discussions to take place that could never have occurred in a public forum. Why not offer a similar safety shield to the players and owners? Why not get away from the press, the klieg lights, the microphones, and the tape recorders?

An interesting thought, but it was never to be. In fact, the opposite atmosphere prevailed. On a Sunday evening in early 1995, I walked into Washington's Mayflower Hotel (the collective bargaining headquarters) and found the lobby had been turned into a media war room. Interviews and exclusives, hot lights, writers on laptops, reporters on cell phones, producers shouting to cameramen. You couldn't get to the elevators without tripping over cables. Hardly the setting for confidential talks.

Then I saw how bad it really had become. Across the room, I spotted Mr. Usery and his press assistant giving a press briefing. The man whom the President had asked to be mediator now apparently had a full-time press assistant. And, the two of them gave regular press briefings. He had fallen prey to the same media promiscuity as the players and the owners. Now the circus had three rings.

Instead of moving the parties out of the spotlight to where they might be able to let their respective guards down, Mr. Usery had done the opposite. This wouldn't lead to settlement. It would lead to a ratings war: Who was getting the best coverage?

As the mediation effort was heading to a close, things got downright embarrassing. The President had requested a meeting with Mr. Usery and representatives of each side. He also asked the mediator for a recommendation. I spoke to the representatives of each side that day and I realized that each side's perception of what was going to occur was diametrically opposed to the other's. Evidently, they had each been told different stories, led to believe different recommendations would be made in order to get them to come to the meeting. Perhaps, the thought was, if they both showed up in front of the President of the United States, they'd almost have to agree to some kind of settlement. It was a naive plan at best.

Word got out (because word always gets out) that the mediator was going to make a recommendation to the President that would ignore the union position (by supporting a luxury tax plan; in effect, a salary cap). The union wasted no time in making sure that the White House got the message that if the President supported this proposal, he would be publicly repudiated by the Players Association. In simple political terms, a Democratic President was about to be snubbed by a labor union. Not good politics.

On the flip side, when the owners heard that the President was leaning toward the notion of binding arbitration, they sent a clear message back: "Don't." The unstated part of the message concerned alienating potential big contributors. After all, there was an election coming up.

Baseball visited the White House that evening, but it was a night to forget. Oh, there was hand shaking and some photo ops, but behind every smile were gritted teeth. The players felt mistreated and so did the owners. No one trusted the mediators. The President was host to a No–Win situation. The mediation effort died right there in the White House.

What are the lessons of the strike? Everything that could be done wrong was done wrong.

1. Each side perceived it had the upper hand and underestimated the other side. Each side was determined to make the other side back down. All the other "wrongs" stemmed from that premise.

2. What should have and could have been handled with delicacy, privacy, and confidentiality, was allowed to deteriorate into the worst sins of *Win–Lose* negotiation. There's no victory without defeat. My gain is your pain.

3. It was a negotiation between enemies. Royalty and Peasants. Labor and Management. North and South.

4. It was a battle of entrenched positions. Over the course of the entire year, neither side materially modified nor compromised its stance. Every meeting was an echo of the last. Repetition replaced innovation.

5. Despite how long it took, it was a hit-and-run deal. Baseball finally resumed on a delayed basis in 1995. But it wasn't the result of negotiation; rather, it was by virtue of a judge's ruling (and it's worth noting for the historical records that the judge was future Supreme Court Justice Sonia Sotomayor). Unfortunately, it was a short-term solution; though the strike had ended, the issues remained.

6. The parties' differences were not resolved. Both parties walked away dissatisfied. The distrust did not abate, it festered.

7. *I Win–You Lose* turned to *We Lose*. The players and owners both dealt from *I Win–You Lose* postures. Who won? Nobody. Who lost? Everybody: including baseball's constituency—the media partners, the advertisers, and the fans. For a long time to come, they were all skeptical and they were vulnerable to other suitors—football, hockey, basketball, golf, or any form of entertainment that captured their fancy and didn't let them down. The great American pastime struck out.

Of course, eventually, Major League Baseball did learn its lesson, but far later than it should have.

AT LEAST ONE DISSATISFIED PARTY

In an I Win–You Lose negotiation, one thing you can count on is that somebody will walk away unhappy. The approach practically demands it.

If the winner really wins what he or she set out to win, then it was at the expense of the loser. The loser goes home with nothing, except maybe a long memory. If these two ever sit down again, you can bet the loser will be out for more than a deal. The loser will want revenge: *Wait until it's my turn to be the tough guy*.

Because of the nature of I Win–You Lose negotiation, its adversarial, non-accommodating approach, the impasses it creates, there's a good chance that *at least* one party will not only walk away without the deal they sought, but will come away with practically nothing.

REFRESHER

Chapter 2: I Win–You Lose Negotiation

I Win–You Lose Negotiators

- Treat each other as enemies.
- Stake out entrenched positions.
- Adopt hit-and-run philosophy.

Win–Lose Negotiators

1. Leave a trail of victims.
2. Miss out on deals that last, renew, and lead to more deals.
3. Lose the intangible benefits of long-term relationships.

Even if You Mean to Be WIN–win, You May Give in to the Temptation of Win–Lose When

- You've been hit and have the urge to hit back. (Oprah)
- You allow "principle" to cloud vision. (The Circus and the Arena)
- You think you have the upper hand and underestimate the other side. (The Baseball Strike)

Hit-and-run negotiators' successes are usually matched by equally or more devastating failures.

"They're offering a deal—you pay court costs and damages, they drop charges of breaking and entering."

CHAPTER 3

WIN–win Negotiation

> When you win, nothing hurts.
>
> —Joe Namath

MYTH AND REALITY

The Myth of Win–Win

Negotiation experts (and amateurs) have been preaching win–win for some time. The trouble is, it's unrealistic. The expression win–win has become more of a pop cliché than a negotiating philosophy. It's either a winner's rationalization for lopsided triumph, a loser's excuse for surrender, or both sides' phrase for when everybody is equally unhappy. There's rarely such thing as both parties winning identically, that is, both getting all of what they want. One party is bound to get more and one less, *even if both sides are content with the outcome*. The latter is possible. Both parties can be satisfied, but both do not usually win to the same degree.

The Reality of WIN–win

If someone is going to come out ahead, it would be great if it's you, but at the very least you maximize your interests.

For example, in the $10 bill game in Chapter 1, rather than quickly retreat to a division of $4 for you and $6 for them, one way to maximize your return is by making change, a split of $5.01 and $4.99. Even if you end up with the $4.99, you have substantially increased your return over the $4 split.

WIN–win is realistic. It isn't easy—it requires focus and discipline but it is achievable. And it doesn't turn negotiation into war. Because it's not WIN–lose, WIN–clobber, or WIN–ransack-pillage-and-obliterate, you don't have to destroy the other side. On the contrary, you want them to survive, even thrive, in order to make sure the deal lasts and leads to future, mutually beneficial deals. That's the Power of Nice and WIN–win is what that power delivers.

In the Super Bowl, There's Only One Winner . . . Or Is There?

When offered the opportunity to purchase the Baltimore Ravens NFL franchise in 1999, Steve Bisciotti structured a deal that is a model for the WIN–win books. At the time, it was common knowledge that then the Ravens' owner, Art Modell, was struggling financially and had set out to sell the team so that he could leave his family on solid financial footing. When given the chance to pursue the sale, Steve, in contrast to most buyers in such circumstances, set a twofold objective for the transaction: He offered to address the financial needs for the Modell family and he did so in a way that showed respect for Art's legacy in the NFL. And in doing so, he enabled a transition for both himself and Art Modell. Steve had decided early in his life that a key to success in any endeavor was to eliminate distractions and focus on a single area of expertise. He would now be leaving his earlier business ventures and ultimately giving his total focus to the team business. So he proposed to stage the purchase of the team—not taking over on day one but rather in a way that allowed Art Modell to transition *out* of the majority ownership and allowed Steve to transition *into* this new field of business.

With the help of some talented attorneys and accountants, Steve and Art staged a four-year transition in ownership in which Steve would first become a minority owner and then over time, the majority owner. The structure was innovative in the business of professional sports. The new owner of a team franchise typically can't wait to take control and revel in the acclaim and excitement of professional sports.

Steve said, "It was important to honor Art in this way and at the same time, I had the objective of learning the business and slowly making a positive impression on the community. So the transition phase was self-serving in a way, but also the best combination for both Art and me."

In 2001, Art's life-long dream came true; he hoisted his, and the Ravens', first Super Bowl trophy with Steve in the background.

But Steve learned well in the ownership transition, and in 2012, Steve and the Ravens hoisted another Super Bowl trophy. A WIN–win indeed.

ACHIEVING WIN–WIN

Know What You (Really) Want–Know What They (Really) Want

To achieve WIN–win, the first order of business is to identify your own interests and goals, what you really need to achieve from a potential deal. You may say, "Hey, I do that automatically." But that's the problem. What you automatically assume to be your goal may not be what you really require to make the deal worthwhile. For example, you may assume you must get a certain price for a piece of real estate. Do you make the assumption because you hear that's the current market value? Or because another seller supposedly got that price? Or because you promised your partners a given return? Is your price really engraved in stone? Will you take less if it's a cash offer but insist on more if paid out over time? How about the emotional aspects of the deal? Are you trying to get out from under a burdensome property? Are you saddled with nervous investors? Perhaps you need peace of mind more than money. Or vice versa.

You can't satisfy your interests until you know what they are. And they're rarely as obvious—or simplistic—as you might assume. But, if you force yourself to think through your priorities, your interests will clarify. You will learn the true parameters of your needs, what you can sacrifice, and what you can't.

Before you go into a negotiation, ask yourself what you want out of it. Then challenge your own answers. Take apart your demands. Make hypothetical offers to yourself, each with different terms. Rank your needs. Force yourself to give up goals from the bottom of the list up, until you're left with the one most important goal of the deal. Now you know what you want.

But you're only halfway there. You have to do the same for the other side. Try to determine their needs and interests. Just as you can make the mistake of assuming your goals, you could make the mistake of assuming theirs: *You want to get as high a price as possible so they must want to pay as low a price as possible.* What if you learned that they might pay substantially more if you let them push the deal into their next fiscal year? Or that while you have investors clamoring for a return, they have shareholders who are in an acquisitive mode? Or that while your constituents want land, they want security?

Determining someone else's needs isn't easy to do alone. Get some-one to play the Devil's Advocate, thinking on behalf of the other side. By role-playing, the advocate will look out for and reveal to you real interests of the other side, instead of your having to rely on your assumptions. Or, if you have the opportunity, directly probe the other side for its interests.

Chances are, their interests are as complex as yours. The earlier you know what their interests are, the greater your leverage will be. Some of their goals may become apparent as you negotiate. But that may be too late to react or counter.

The chapter that follows this one deals with the 3 Ps, one of which is *prepare*. It means, among other things, learn all you can about the people with whom you're negotiating, what motivates them, and, importantly, what they must achieve in a given deal. Find out as much of what they need as you can *before* you sit down at the bargaining table. You will discover even more once you're at the bargaining table, during the probe phase, which follows prepare.

Satisfy Your Interests Well–Satisfy the Other Side's Interests Acceptably

Once you know what the other side needs, you can determine how their interests conflict and/or mesh with yours. You can find areas of mutual benefit: your price and their terms; their divestiture and your expansion; their capital needs and your investment strategy.

You each have strengths and weaknesses. But, if you do your homework, (and if you probe effectively) you have an advantage. You know what you want *and* you know what they want. You may be tempted to fulfill all of your own needs and to disregard theirs. Believe it or not, that's not in your best interest. No matter now much stronger your position may be, make sure they achieve some of their goals. That's what enables a deal not just to be made, but carried out.

Let's say you're negotiating with three suppliers for a season's worth of embroidered NBA logos for hats—in round numbers say 24 million logos. Your goal is to lower the cost by .017 cents per logo, but to main-tain the quality of those little woven Bulls, Heat, Knicks, Spurs, Thunder, Cavaliers, and Magic. (Ideally, you'd like this season's 24 million hats in your warehouse by tip-off of the first game.) You've had multiple logo suppliers in the past but now you're willing to give the entire 24-million-logos order to one company if they can meet your specs.

The first supplier, Econo-Emblems, comes in with the lowest price, but only on the condition that they can sew logos with a slightly lower thread count per centimeter. The second supplier, Logo-Motion, can meet the thread-count quality standards but at a cost of .003 cents more per logo, which really adds up when you multiply it by 24 million. The third supplier, Sew-What Ltd., meets the lowest price and the thread count but they ask for staggered delivery dates. They'll deliver 8 million logos a month, feeding fan demand as the season goes on. You could reject their request for staggered delivery. And they might give in. After all, this is the biggest order in the industry.

But you know their needs, their real interests. By staggering the delivery dates to you, they'll fill factory capacity over several months, eliminating downtime, keeping the best workers employed throughout the year, thereby increasing profits on other, previously unprofitable jobs, all of which enables them to give you both the price and quality you want. If you force them to meet the original schedule, you run the risk of sacrificed quality to make the dates or missed dates to maintain quality. And even if they make the dates and maintain the quality, their overall operation will likely lose money and never be able to meet the same specs again.

Remember the one goal at the top of your list. Lower the price without sacrificing standards. You WIN, in capital letters. Now let them win on the delivery schedule. Their win assures your WIN. It enables them to carry out the agreement. Instead of what might be, at best, a one-time, one-sided win, or, at worst, a one-time disaster, you now have the makings of a long-term relationship. Remember, the essence of negotiation is not just making a good deal; it's building relationships.

GOOD DEALS ECHO, THEY LEAD TO MORE DEALS

Often, the best way to get what you want is to help the other side get what they want. There are very few deals in business or life, in general, that are truly one-time, never-again transactions. The world of negotiation is a small one. How often have you:

- Done business again with someone with whom you did business what seems like a lifetime ago?
- Awarded a job to a supplier who was the runner-up last time you bid them?

- Discovered a familiar name as a reference on a resume?
- Called on an old acquaintance for an opinion?
- Hired a competitor?
- Invested in a rival?
- Found yourself a seller to the same party to whom you were once a buyer?

Too many people negotiate as if they'll never again see or do business with the person across the table. That was the modus operandi of my ex–law partner, the bridge-burner. In fact, the opposite is true. Chances are, you will associate and do business with the same people again. More leases are renewed than written from scratch. More suppliers are retained than replaced. More contracts are extended than begun. More shipments go to old customers than new ones. There's an old business adage that says it takes five times the time/effort/money to win a new client as it does to keep an existing one. The same, with varied multiples, applies to anyone on the other side of a transaction.

If you treated your last deal as your final deal with that party and left them with a bad taste, or worse, bad business results, next time they'll either come to the table with revenge on their minds or not come at all. But, if you did your best to make sure they got some of what they wanted, if you made sure they achieved a win (lowercase), you have the potential of making mutually beneficial deals ad infinitum.

WIN–WIN IS NOT WIMP–WIMP

We've established that WIN–win is not win–win. It's clearly, unashamedly designed to maximize your return or even tilt the scale in your favor. It's not pretending that both sides go away with separate but equal smiles. But, importantly, it also stands in sharp contrast to win–win's mutated relative, Wimp–Wimp. That's where you want to make a deal so badly, you make a bad deal. You give in, give up, and give away; anything to get the deal done.

We've identified five notorious Wimp–Wimp negotiator types. Here's how each would negotiate the purchase of an automobile:

Wimp–Wimp Negotiators: Buying a Car

- **Addicted Wimp.** The addicted negotiator walks into the dealership, falls in love with the red sports utility vehicle, and decides he or she wants it and wants it now. Addicted negotiators don't really care about the terms of the deal, the financing, the extras, or even the undercoating. They will concede all of it and pay full list price, as long as they can drive it home today. These negotiators want to do a deal, any deal, so badly that they make unnecessary and harmful concessions just to get the deal done.

- **Anxious Wimp.** The anxious negotiator walks into the dealership and thinks, *"I hate doing this. All these salespeople know how to play the game, and I always lose. I don't want to look bad. I don't want to look stupid. I just want to get this thing over with as quickly as possible. Next time I'm going to CarMax so I can avoid this whole negotiation thing."* These negotiators will accept the first offer put onto the table just so they can get the process over with.

- **Apathetic Wimp.** Apathetic negotiators think that negotiating is not worth the hassle. They know they could get a better deal, but they also know it means shopping around to different dealerships, reading *Consumer Reports*, and even going back to the same dealer several times to work the price down. They know they could get a better price using this strategy, but they just don't want to put in the time or the energy to make it happen. This negotiator justifies that the time and energy *saved* in *not* negotiating makes up for the higher price they inevitably pay.

- **Aristocratic Wimp.** The aristocratic negotiator walks into the dealership, refuses to speak with any of the salespeople, and demands to see the manager. He or she tells the manager he or she is going to spend top dollar and does not want to get into a haggling scene over the price. *"Just give me a price and I will tell you whether or not I will buy the car."* Aristocratic negotiators rationalize that negotiation makes them feel "cheap" and, therefore, they claim to be "above petty haggling." They do not want to engage in the game of negotiation and often leave plenty of lost money on the table.

- **Amiable Wimp.** The amiable type walks in and immediately gets into a long conversation with the salesperson about their families. Before you know it, the amiable person knows everything about the life history of the salesperson, including the fact that he or she is one car away from getting that bonus that will help to pay for Junior's braces. In the end, the amiable person just takes the deal that is offered because he knows that it will help the salesperson out and really feels that he and the salesperson can become good friends—and he would not want to negotiate with a friend. In the end, it is more important to be liked than to get the best deal. And Amiable Wimpiness isn't just a buyer's trait. It can just as easily be the salesperson who gives in by reducing the price before any negotiation even begins, just to make the sale and to be nice to the customer who is now his or her friend.

Regardless of variety, the Wimp Negotiator becomes a Wimp in the quest for a deal. This isn't disastrous if the other side is also a Wimp. The real danger is when you become a Wimp and the other side doesn't. Then you become something worse than a Wimp; you become a Loser. The process turns to *Lose–Win*.

We had a participant in our seminar—a broker with a prominent national investment firm who specialized in retirement plans. He confessed that he knew he suffered from a Wimp–Wimp approach but found it almost impossible to unlearn. His story illustrates the old maxim, "Old habits are hard to break."

The Man Who Sold Retirement Plans so Cheaply, He Could Never Afford to Retire Himself

The broker stood up at the seminar and told his ironic story. He had all the business he could handle, in fact, maybe more than he could handle. But his problem was a lot of his business wasn't profitable. When asked why he took on unprofitable business, he explained that the industry had become ferociously, even blindly competitive. Winning clients at all costs had become the goal. Scorekeeping and body counts had replaced bottom-line results. He wasn't about to lose a client to another broker. So, he bid lower and lower, cutting his own commission to the point where there was virtually no profit left. He'd do anything to win the client. Even make a bad deal.

He was willing to lose and he did. He lost time and money on more and more clients. (He was living out the old auto dealer sales pitch. "We *lose money on every car but we make it up in volume.*")

Naturally, he didn't have time to service his low-commission clients as well as he should have. So, even though they were paying him very little, they weren't very happy. And he resented what service he did give them because he was losing more money with every extra minute he spent. Eventually, many of the client victories he had "bought" left him anyway, thereby turning into losses. Yet, he kept on underbidding, low-balling, and losing money in order to win clients.

Despite his own recognition of his pattern, the broker had difficulty breaking the Wimp–Wimp cycle. It took an ice-cold slap in the face to snap him out of it. He had an opportunity to bid on what could have been a very good piece of business. Out of habit, after he assessed the situation and arrived at a reasonable bid, he then preemptively lowered his bid to rock bottom to *assure* his winning it. Then he sat back and waited for the call from the client saying, "You win."

He never got the call. Two weeks later, he got a different call altogether. The potential client called to say, "Sorry, you didn't get my business."

The broker was stunned, *"Wasn't I the lowest bidder?"*

The client said, "Yes, by far."

"But, *but, but* . . . ."

The client explained, "My policy is to throw out the highest bid and the lowest bid because neither is likely to be the right bidder. One is overcharging, the other is underdelivering."

That stopped the broker cold. Imagine, it took a buyer's insight to show the seller how self-defeating a Wimp–Wimp or lose-in-order-to-win approach can be.

From that day on, the broker began to assess each prospect differently. He used his own experience and judgment, coupled with a projection of future potential, to arrive at a bid he could live with in the short run and which had promise of long-term return. His track record of client wins has since gone down, but his profits have soared. In fact, his entire definition of winning has changed. He's not counting clients anymore. He's counting results.

ROADBLOCKS, MINEFIELDS, AND WISDOM

Okay, it's simple, right?

1. Know what you want. Assess your needs and wants *before* negotiating.
2. Find out what they want—probe, dig, ask, learn.
3. Satisfy your interests well.
4. Satisfy their interests acceptably.

What could go wrong? Nothing: If the path to a WIN–win deal was a straight shot. But it isn't. It's almost always littered with barriers, hurdles, detours, potholes, hazards, and all manner of obstacles to keep you from getting to where you want to go. Here's what they look like.

Insufficient Planning

When we harp on the need to prepare, it applies to both sides, yours and the other party. Unfortunately, we can only influence your side. The more prepared you are—the more you know about your goals and their goals, your absolutes and theirs, flexibilities, time limits, creative alternatives, pressures—the greater the opportunity to make a good deal.

As for the other side, the less prepared they are, the more difficult it may be for you to make a deal. The process will surely go slower. They're likely to be skeptical of even the most reasonable offer. Unlike you, they have not thought through various scenarios in advance. They're worried about what they don't know, even paranoid, and therefore less willing to compromise. They may obsess on issues of contention (whether they're meaningful or not) instead of focusing on the bigger issues (on which you could be in agreement).

Why would people not prepare? It's natural. Planning is not fun. Doing is fun. Planning is tedious. (Even if it makes the doing better.) Vacations are fun. Packing isn't. Arriving without socks is not fun. Eating is fun. Flossing isn't fun. Root canals are as unfun as it gets. Spending is fun. Saving isn't. Bankruptcy is only fun if you're a bankruptcy lawyer.

Ineffective Communication

Many negotiators think they're outstanding communicators because they're good talkers. They have big vocabularies, are never at a loss for words, always have a snappy comeback. The problem is, most negotiators aren't good listeners.

When they talk, they're saying what they want to say, instead of answering the concerns and needs of the other party. They're not communicating their ideas clearly; they're uttering words they want to hear themselves say. Or worse yet, the communication takes place through legal representatives and documents, rather than face to face, human to human.

Often, if the other side doesn't communicate effectively, they don't listen well either. They may listen through a negative filter. They suspect what is being said; they're skeptical of motives. It can't be good; it's someone trying to get the better of them. In the end, both parties end up in disagreement, not necessarily over issues, but over the manner in which the issues and positions were expressed.

In the chapter on probing we'll talk about *Listening*. We'll show you that listening is more than waiting to speak. It's an art and a science. You can practice it and get better. Listening may be the single most powerful tool in achieving WIN–win because it can inform you what the other side really wants and needs to make the deal.

Inexperience

It seems like too many negotiators' jobs are filled by the following help wanted ad: "No experience necessary," because too many perfectly good deals go bad simply as a result of inexperienced negotiators.

Novice negotiators just haven't made enough deals to know what matters and what doesn't. In their quest to avoid a bad deal, they often avoid making a deal at all. They sometimes take a hard line when it isn't necessary. They offend the other party either accidentally or because someone told them that negotiators are supposed to be tough guys. They believe, out of naiveté, in win–lose negotiation. If they can't win, they'd rather walk away. They react emotionally instead of rationally: all of which can be the undoing of an otherwise promising deal.

The experienced negotiator should know how to handle an inexperienced counterpart. Don't take it personally (no matter how offensive). Don't get hung up on tactics (no matter how crude). Do exercise patience. Let the novices make mistakes, say the wrong thing, back themselves into corners, rant, rave, and demand. While they're ranting, you're thinking. When they're demanding; you're strategizing. They are actually giving you time to calmly assess (or reassess) your position, your method, and your priorities.

PUTTING IT TOGETHER

When you can put all the elements together, get past positions, when you can identify what you really want, what the other party really wants, when you can satisfy your interests well and the other side's interests acceptably, that's when you can make a WIN–win deal. Here's a case in point:

Cal Ripken's Five-Year Contract (That Took Almost a Year to Negotiate)

When we began to negotiate Cal Ripken, Jr.'s 1992 contract, we and the Orioles were a mere $30 million apart. The team wanted a four-year deal and they cited as their precedent the salaries of the top shortstops in the game. They proposed almost $20 million over the four years. We wanted a five-year contract and we cited, as our precedent and benchmark, the top players in the game, regardless of position. Our proposal approached $50 million (not so much by today's standards but very aggressive at the time).

Over the next 250 to 300 days, most of the negotiation was about the money/time ratio. The Orioles slowly edged toward five years (fully justified by the trends in the game) and the dollars worked their way north of $25 million over the life of the contract. Our position moved down to the $35 million range. The key to coming together was recognizing each other's interests.

Throughout the talks, the Orioles negotiator was Larry Lucchino, former tough trial lawyer turned baseball executive under then team owner, Edward Bennett Williams, and subsequent owner, Eli Jacobs. Larry was one of the prime movers behind the creation of Camden Yards, was later CEO of the San Diego Padres, and today is President/CEO and part owner of the Boston Red Sox. He's a good friend but (unfortunately) he never let that stand in the way of saying "no" to me and the ballplayers represented. Similarly, I didn't let our friendship get in the way of asking for an aggressive, market-value contract for my client.

We were in the position phase—that is, I said, "This is why it's right for Cal Ripken to get at least $35 million," and he said, "This is why it's right that the Orioles only pay $25 million"—wherein both parties repeat high-minded statements of belief and make very little practical movement. Our pronouncements were impassioned and sincere. Our verbal exchanges were heated and not always what you'd expect from friends. We each had clients and/or employers to represent.

How did we move from this phase to discovering each other's real interests? We changed locations from our offices, usually my conference room—jackets on, jackets off, sleeves rolled up, ties pulled down, crumpled yellow papers, cold coffee dregs in Styrofoam cups and a lineup of Diet Coke cans, and still little or no progress. We moved to my farm—outside, breeze blowing, overlooking a quiet pond, birds chirping in place of car horns. (Not everyone has a farm or a retreat, but a change of location can do wonders when you're stuck. From a cold, serious office to a hotel lobby, someone's den, or a comfortable restaurant.) On the day in early summer when we sat at the farm, I thought another change might help: A deadline, not a threat, just a date we could all aim for. It was Cal's birthday later in the summer, in August. It was far enough in the future that we both thought it was a good idea.

It was then that we started to hear each other, began to understand the other side's issues and interests. Cal wanted a contract that acknowledged the totality of his accomplishments to date and took into account his contributions to community projects, his outside business ventures, and his future security. The team wanted a figure that acknowledged his recent decline in offensive statistics (though it was short-lived) and met the team's interests—fiscal responsibility, setting future contract precedents, yet still retaining one of the game's all-time greats. Larry was finally beginning to hear us. We were finally beginning to hear Larry and the Orioles.

We started to talk about ways to recognize Cal's contribution to the team in ways other than standard salary. For example, the Orioles eventually agreed to give Cal post-career compensation guarantees, which added dollars to the overall contract but did not raise his pay for active years. (Interestingly, these very dollars were later traded for during-career compensation in his next contract.) They gave him merchandising rights in the stadium, another way to provide additional revenue for what Cal had come to represent, but not pay for performance, per se. This helped Cal provide funding for his recently created foundation. The team offered special hotel accommodations on the road, designated parking, seats and a skybox for his family (which he paid for), all in an effort to provide added security as his increased visibility brought increased vulnerability.

Each of these creative solutions answered Cal's "interests." They provided the compensation he felt he had earned for his unflagging performance for the team and the town. At the same time, this form of reward allowed the club to maintain what it wanted, fiscal responsibility. They could hold his annual pay to a level they could live with.

On his birthday, August 24, 1992, Cal signed the biggest contract of his career, 333 days after negotiations began. It was classic WIN—win. Both sides won. We felt Cal won a little more. The Orioles wanted only a four-year deal. Cal wanted five years. Cal got his five. The Orioles didn't want to pay the highest salary of the day. They didn't. Cal would have been eligible for free agency a month and a half after the contract was signed. The bidding would have easily passed the $35 million mark, heading for $40 million. Instead, Cal got $32.5 million; he netted a top contract (albeit briefly) by getting a combination of revenue streams; and he got something else he truly wanted—to stay in the city he called home.

It doesn't usually take 11 months to get past the impasses. In this case, it was definitely worth it. The dollars and the length of the deal made that clear. However, in most deals that's not necessarily the case. Determining how much time is warranted is important . . . but not easy to assess. Many people, particularly salespeople, don't look closely enough at the time they spend on a deal, sale, or challenge to see if they are spending it wisely.

WIN–win and maximizing your interests means not just the size of the deal, the profits, or other benefits, but also the time you invest to make the deal—literally the ROI on your efforts. You must ask yourself, "Does what I'm doing make sense?"

To help you answer that question objectively, we've created the Value/Pay Grid.

First, let's define Value. This is the regard your customers hold for your product or service compared to other options in the marketplace—average, good, better, best. And how they regard you as their representative. As for Pay, that's just what it says, how much your product or service is worth compared to other alternatives—the same, less, or even a premium. And "pay" is not only dollars; it can be in the form of other gain, need, or benefit.

Let me give you some examples for each of the boxes in the grid. In the upper right quadrant, Value/Pay, people or customers who fall in this quadrant might say, "I love what your product offers us. I'm confident it's the right product for us. I love you as our sales rep and that you make sure we are always taken care of. Keep doing what you're doing and we'll have a long and productive relationship."

Those in the lower left quadrant, No Value/No Pay are the exact opposite and will say so, "I don't care about your product or what it has to offer us. I don't particularly care for you as a sales rep and have no interest in working with you or your company."

Those two quadrants are easy to identify. The other two are where the challenges come.

In the lower right quadrant, No Value/Pay, customers may say, "I don't care about your product or what it offers us, nor do I particularly care for you as a sales rep. However, my boss says we need the product, or thinks highly of you, so I'm required to work with you. Just understand, the moment it's up to me, I will stop buying."

In the last quadrant, Value/No Pay, customers sound like this, "I love what your product offers us. And I love you as our sales rep and that you always make sure we're taken care of. But . . . I just don't have the budget to give you any business. So, keep doing what you're doing and one day I'm sure we'll do business together."

Now, before you decide how to deal with each customer or quadrant, first go back to that ROI question, "Does what I'm doing make sense?"

Value/Pay—They love you and/or your company. Keep doing what you're doing. The key is to not forget about them and their loyalty. Sometimes we take good customers for granted. As time goes by, these customers can start to resent the lack of attention. They value you. You must value them.

No Value/No Pay—Even though they don't value your product or your personal service, it's good to know where they stand. After some effort, if you can't accomplish the goal of demonstrating value of your product, you may decide to spend less time and resources on them.

No Value/Pay—Some people will look at this quadrant and think it's terrible, or certainly tenuous business. But while you prefer customers who appreciate your product and dedication, this is not entirely bad business to have . . . *if* it's priced and serviced correctly. You may wish to move them into the Value/Pay quadrant, but if you can't, and if you realize they may leave at the first opportunity, in the meantime, you can have a profitable, realistic relationship.

Value/No Pay—This is the worst quadrant of all. That may surprise some but when you think about it critically, these are the time- and resource-suckers. They tell us how much they value what we do, but they can't work with us right now, or can't pay enough. They ask for research, proposals, ideas, free consulting, and we keep giving it all to them in hopes that someday we might get some business. But in the meantime, they're chewing up valuable time. You have to either move them into the Value/Pay quadrant . . . or into the No Value/No Pay quadrant, and then move on to spend your time more wisely.

Many people won't fall unquestionably into the middle of a particular box. They may be a little bit of one, leaning toward another, or straddling a line. But eventually it should become clear where they fall. Your job is to analyze each of those relationships as objectively as possible. Ask yourself, "Does what I'm doing with them make sense?"

Sometimes *Maximizing Your Win* even means walking away. It may be the best use of your time, the highest ROI on your time investment. (See Chapter 10: No Deal.) You and your company's time, resources, information, and people have value. If you don't believe that, no one else will either.

Here's a real-life story of how the Value/Pay grid can work.

Finding a New Cure for the Common Pharma Rep

My partner, Todd Lenhart, and the SNI team worked with a global pharmaceutical company on introducing a new commercial sales model that would redefine the way the sales force operated. Our client decided to move away from a traditional "reach and frequency" sales model—sending as many reps to see as many doctors as often as possible—to a more focused sales mode, concentrating on more sales per rep and per doctor. This meant a reduction in the client's sales force from 2,000 to 1,200 reps and simultaneously giving the existing sales team more autonomy over the allocation of their time and resources. Physicians that used to have three or more representatives calling on them would now have one. But the sales reps were given more freedom to call on those physicians that helped them achieve their sales goals, and could call less often or not at all on those doctors that did not account for substantial prescriptions.

SNI utilized the Value/Pay Grid to help the sales team face the challenge. The first objective was to shift the traditional mindset from the old model and help them prioritize limited time and resources. The client's analytics team provided us with the previous 12 months of sales activity and helped the sales team plot every physician in their territory on the grid. This analysis was based on time and resources invested positioning the product (VALUE) and the actual prescriptions written by physicians (PAY).

The result of this exercise was that a larger portion of the physicians landed in the "Value/No Pay" category than most wanted to initially believe. Sales reps had been spending a large portion of their time pitching products to physicians who claimed to believe in the efficacy of a drug, but did not actually write prescriptions for patients. We invested the next six months in working with the sales team on their habits and strategies to move physicians in their territory toward the Value/Pay quadrant or off the grid all together. The result was that the sales team no longer spent precious time and money just hoping physicians would write prescriptions at some unknown point in the future (Pay). The new, more focused sales model resulted in increased sales growth over the next 18 months. Not surprisingly, the Value/Pay Grid is an important component of every sales representative's quarterly business review as they analyze how to allocate time and resources effectively.

REFRESHER

Chapter 3: WIN–win Negotiation

Myth of win–win: Both parties may benefit, but there's rarely such a thing as truly equal deals or wins.

Reality of WIN–win: If someone is going to come out ahead, it would be great if it's you, but at the very least, you maximize your interests.

Achieving WIN–win

- Know what you want. Assess your needs and wants *before* negotiating.
- Know what they want. Find out—probe, dig, ask, learn.
- Satisfy your interests well.
- Satisfy theirs acceptably.

The best way to get most of what you want is to help the other side get some of what they want.

Good deals echo—they lead to more deals.

WIN–win Is Not Wimp–Wimp

- Don't turn into a negotiating wimp.
- Don't lose in order to win.
- Don't give in just to get the order.

Five Wimp–Wimp Types

- Addicted—anything to make the deal.
- Anxious—accepts the deal to get it over with.
- Apathetic—time saved is worth overpaying.
- Aristocratic—negotiating is beneath them.
- Amiable—more important to be liked than to get a good deal.

Roadblocks to WIN–win

- *Insufficient planning*: Someone isn't ready or prepared to negotiate.
- *Ineffective communication*: Someone isn't listening.
- *Inexperience*: The novice is negotiating the way they do it in war or in the movies. That makes the process hard for both sides.

Maximize your Time and Resources Using the Value/Pay Grid

- Don't waste your time in the Value/No Pay quadrant.
- Analyze your relationships as objectively as possible. Ask yourself, "Does what I'm doing with them make sense?"
- Sometimes maximizing your Win requires you to "walk away" or reallocate your time.

"*I do have a fallback position, but it involves firearms.*"

The Three Ps

A Systematic Approach

> I wish I could tell all the young women I work with, all these fabulous women, "Believe in yourself and negotiate for yourself. Own your own success." I wish I could tell that to my daughter, but it's not that simple.
>
> —SHERYL SANDBERG

> The more I see people overcome their fear of negotiation by embracing the systematic approach, the more I am convinced people can have their "power" and "nice," too.
>
> —RON SHAPIRO

You need to use a systematic approach in order to become a better negotiator. Why is a systematic approach better? My former partner Mark Jankowski's story about skydiving makes the point.

Why a Systematic Approach Is Particularly Helpful When You're Hurtling through Space toward the Earth . . . or Negotiating

I have five friends and once a year we do an "adrenaline rush" thing. We've done bungee jumping, white-water rafting, swimming with sharks. One year, we decided, "Here's something we haven't done. We've never jumped out of an airplane." So, it was time to go skydiving.

The five of us went to an airfield in Delaware. Once you get there, the skydiving company trains you for six straight hours. From 6:00 A.M. until noon, they train you and then, after noon, you finally start jumping. We had declined the tandem jump and the static line jump and chosen the most advanced jump they'd let us learn, the freefall from 10,000 feet. (We wanted to get our money's worth.)

From 6:00 A.M. until noon, there were only five things they taught us.

1. How to step out on the wing of the plane and let go.
2. How to arch your back so you maintain your aerodynamics.
3. How to pull your ripcord so you remain in your aerodynamics.
4. How to get your lines untangled if they get tangled.
5. And, very important, how to land.

There were only those five things they told us. The good news was, they were pretty simple. The bad news was, we had to practice each one for over an hour.

We did every single step, over and over. They had me suspended from a hanger, with white cords leading down to blue straps, simulating a parachute. They spun me around and purposely tangled up all the white cords. Then they'd say, "If your white cords get tangled, grab hold of your blue straps and kick like a bicycle." So, I'm up there, doing this exercise for 30 minutes, then 45 minutes, and I say, "I get it, I get it." The instructor says, "Nope. We're going to do this for an hour. We're going to spin you around and tangle up the cords. You grab the straps and kick like a bicycle. Just kick like a bicycle." Finally, it's 12:00. That's enough. We got it. It must be time to jump.

The skydiving company owned one small prop plane, which could only take one skydiver up at a time. My friend, Brad, had arranged the whole trip, so he got to go up first. The rest of us were on the ground, watching.

It took about 20 minutes for that little prop plane to climb to 10,000 feet. Finally, we see a little dot in the sky. It's Brad. He jumps. We're watching him and thinking, this is going to be great. We can't wait to get up there. Meanwhile, Brad is coming down 10,000 feet . . . 8,000 feet . . . 6,000 . . . 4,000 . . . . Then his chute opens up. We're watching and feeling like this is going to be the best of all our adrenaline rush things. This is going to be great!

As Brad is floating through the atmosphere, he's receiving ground instructions through a walkie-talkie strapped to his harness. We were told, in advance, to do whatever your walkie-talkie guide tells you to do—steer left, steer right, and, most important, put on the brakes. The walkie-talkie guide that day was Gus, who was about 89 years old and looked like he flew with the Wright Brothers. The very veteran Gus was talking Brad down. "You're looking good, Brad. Yep, a little left, now a little right. Looking good. Looking good. You're coming in, you're coming in, you're coming in...." BOOM! Brad hits the ground at about 40 miles per hour. Gus forgot to tell him to put on the brakes. Brad stands up. Brad falls down. He had a spiral fracture from his ankle all the way up to his knee. Fortunately, the paramedics were nearby. They stabilized Brad's leg, gave him something for the pain, and loaded him into the ambulance.

As the ambulance pulled away, Gus turns to us and says, "Okay, which one of you guys is next?" Pointing to each other, we all said, "Him!"

I was the last one to go up. Everybody else before me had some kind of problem. One guy blacked out up there. One missed the landing area. Another person jammed his ankle. Literally, every single person had a problem. As I was putting on my parachute, I heard two young instructors talking. One says to the other, "Get Gus off the walkie-talkie. He's killing these guys." I immediately started thinking of graceful but still semi-macho ways to back out. "Gee guys, I just remembered, ever since the Gulf War, I've had recurrent mortophobia—fear of death." Just then, another instructor puts his arm around me and said, "Mark, I'll be talking you in today." I think, "Thank God, no Gus!"

I confidently strode over to the plane, got on, and who do I see is flying the plane? Gus! Oh boy. I rationalize, maybe he's a better pilot than walkie-talkie guide. We go up; I have my parachute on; I feel good. We get to 10,000 feet and it's time to jump. I wave goodbye to Gus and jump out of the plane.

Wow! This is great. I'm thinking, "I knew I'd be the one who would not screw any of this up." 10,000 feet . . . 6,000 feet . . . 4,000 . . . . It's so easy. Time to pull my rip-cord. I pull my ripcord. One problem. They told us to pull it straight out to maintain aerodynamics. But I made the mistake of reaching *across* my body to grab it. I started to spin in the air like a top. My chute opened, thankfully, but when I looked up, all my white lines were tangled *and* all my blue straps were tangled, too. They never told us what to do on the ground if your blue straps got tangled. But one thought popped into my mind: Kick like a bicycle! And I did. I was riding the stationary bike from hell up there! I kicked like a bicycle and kicked and kicked. Slowly, finally, my straps untangled. I grabbed them and then got my cords untangled. I put on the brakes and landed.

What was the lesson I learned from this experience (besides never going sky-diving with Gus again)? The key to learning how to skydive was not memorizing 45 different ways to get on the wing of the plane or 75 ways to get your lines untangled. I learned only five basic things—it was simple. They taught us a sequence—it was systematic. They made us simulate each step in the sequence over and over. It was practiced until it was mastered.

We do not teach people the 45 best opening lines or the 75 greatest closing tactics. Instead, we opt for a simple, systematic approach to negotiation. If you learn it—that is, practice and master what we preach—when the pressure hits, you'll revert to your new, learned habit and you'll be a more effective negotiator.

And perhaps equally important, the systematic approach will empower your negotiation prowess. You will overcome a lack of confidence or feelings of inferiority—be they cultural, experiential, or gender-based—that would otherwise impede your effectiveness in the negotiation. And you won't be tempted to use aggressiveness to camouflage your inferior feelings.

> When people are under pressure, they revert to habits. In order to create new habits, you need a simple, systematic approach that you can practice and master.

PREPARE, PROBE, AND PROPOSE

The 3 Ps comprise our *systematic approach* to negotiation. There's no magic here; just a simple set of disciplines. That's what a system is or should be. Follow the disciplines and you'll make better deals. Ignore them and every deal will be left to chance. And without them to empower you, you may revert to the habits of insecure negotiators, ranging from being overly aggressive to dangerously submissive.

Many people view negotiation as an event—haggling or trading offers at the bargaining table. To be an effective negotiator, that view must change:

> Negotiation is a process—not an event.

That is the essence of the 3 Ps. Prepare, Probe, and Propose. You prepare for the negotiation *before* it occurs. You probe for information *before* and *during* the negotiation. You propose *after* preparing and probing. You *continue* preparing and probing as you respond to an offer . . . and so on, until a deal is struck. Even then, the negotiation isn't over because the deal made may well lead to future deals.

As with all disciplines, these demand diligence. The 3 Ps, each explained and demonstrated in detail in Chapters 5, 6, and 7, are like exercise, homework, vitamins, a good night's sleep, and flossing your teeth. You may not get a big kick out of them, but the results are undeniable.

Prepare

If negotiation is the commerce of information for ultimate gain, then you need information. Obtain all the information you can about the other side while controlling the flow of your own. The more you know *before* the dealing begins, the better your position.

Prepare. Research. Study. Stockpile knowledge. Don't go into a meeting until you know everything you can about your position, evidence for and against you, comparable situations in the past and present, what you're aiming for, what you're willing to settle for, and all you can about the other side, its position and views.

Probe

Doing your homework isn't enough. You have to go beyond research and background. You have to go to the source. An excellent source of information about the other side is the other side.

Probe. Ask questions, and listen, and an amazing thing happens: You get answers. Most people don't ask questions. (And even if they do, they tend to be poor listeners.) They seem to think asking questions is a sign of weakness, as if they should already know everything. And they're reluctant to go to a key source of information about the other side, *which is the other side itself.* Ask direct questions: What do they really want? Why have they taken that position? What are their short-term goals? What are their long-range plans? Ask indirect questions: Where the other person lives, where they went to school, what they do when they're not working. Listen for clues as to how the other side thinks, acts, and feels.

Everything you learn about the other side's needs and interests can affect the deal. For example, from the direct questions that you ask of the other side, you may find you can enable them to attain their long-range aims even if you can't meet their short-term price or goal. And when you're listening, what they don't say can have as much or more impact as what they do. If they won't reveal their bottom-line hope for the deal, maybe they haven't formulated it yet and your negotiations will shape their final desire. From the indirect questions, you'll learn what to talk about when you take a break from negotiating. You'll find things in common (hobbies, humor, religion, politics) and you'll learn what to avoid like the plague (hobbies, humor, religion, politics).

In Chapter 6, you will not only learn to hone your skills for asking questions, but also the practices that enable you to be a better listener.

Propose

When you finally propose a deal, your proposal will only be as good as your preparation and probing.

Propose. Try not to make the first offer. When you do make an offer, aim high—make it strong, solid, and reasonable. And be open to change it as the process unfolds.

As it is usually better not to make the first offer, there are a number of ways to draw a proposal from the other party (covered in Chapter 7). But even if the other side leads, you will have to respond to their proposal, which is a proposal in itself. So remember, a proposal is a starting point: Smart, revealing, but not final. Never forget, there's another side opposite you. Give them something to think about. Don't just give them something to accept or reject, to take it or leave it. (That would be a sure way to turn a potentially tough negotiator into a truly tough one.) A good proposal should lead to conversation: Exchange, swapping of needs and wants. The process allows both sides to formulate and prioritize. Where do you go from here? What is most important?

Don't start by asking for the moon, and don't start by asking for the least you can live with. Always know, *before you propose,* where you're willing to go next. *Plan* to make concessions. If you know in advance where and what you can concede, they won't be losses, they will be part of your plan. You gave and it didn't hurt. And the other side has gotten something.

Brooks Robinson's Final Contract or One "P" Out of Three May Be a .333 Batting Average, but It's Lousy if You're a Negotiator

One day in 1976, not long after I had left my job as Maryland's Securities Commissioner to go into private law practice, I got a call from Jerold "Chuck" Hoffberger, owner of the Baltimore Orioles. He asked if I could help one of his ballplayers straighten out some financial troubles. While I wasn't salivating at the prospect of sifting through shoe-boxes of old receipts, trying to balance hopelessly screwed-up checking accounts, and, with luck, undoing some fly-by-night deals, I had two problems with declining. First, I just like to help people. It's hard for me to say "no." Second, it was especially hard for me to say "no" to Chuck. My total hesitation got as far as, "Uh, Chu . . . " when he interrupted, "Ron, it's Brooks Robinson." I said, "When do I start?"

Brooks Robinson wasn't just a ballplayer; he was a legend with one foot already in Cooperstown. He *couldn't* be in financial trouble. He had to keep his mind on third base and the Orioles' pennant hopes. To skip to the happy ending, we managed to turn Brooks's ink from red to black.

So when Brooks called after the 1976 season and asked if I'd negotiate his final contract with the Orioles, I said the same thing: "When do I start?"

Brooks was paid $100,000 in 1976, but the Orioles were trying to impose the maximum allowable reduction of 20 percent and take him down to $80,000. (Imagine walking into work tomorrow and being told your salary is being cut 20 percent!) They said Brooks was a *former* superstar, with declining statistics in his declining years. Legend or not, they said, Brooks's best days were behind him.

I attacked my job with a fervor that would make some of today's agents seem comatose. I was a combination pit bull–grad student–evangelist, staying up day and night to formulate a thesis that would forever change the sports world. Straining at the leash, I was hungry and unstoppable—a man on a mission and a marathon. Brooks Robinson didn't deserve a 20 percent cut, or even 10 percent. He deserved a raise! He should get $105,000 at the very least. And I was going to get it for him!

I was a glutton for *information*. I read. I dug. I scoured. I researched. I refer-enced. I cross-referenced. My aim was to learn everything there was to know about the Orioles, their organization, and their financial condition. Did they make money? How much? Who called the shots? What did they pay other players? How did the Orioles compare with other clubs?

Fortunately, the Orioles were a public company so they filed their financial data with the Securities and Exchange Commission. Yes, they were profitable. Modestly. Though they were among the winningest teams in baseball, wins didn't equal dollars. They ran on a tight budget—really tight—and they had every intention of staying that way.

They made money but didn't part with it easily. How did they feel about the value of past glories?

I talked to everyone I could who was in any way connected directly or indirectly with the club or anyone in it. The Orioles did want to keep their ties with the past greats alive and well; they knew that name players brought fans and also helped the transition to the next stars. Frank Robinson, Boog Powell, Dave McNally, and Paul Blair had all recently retired. Management wanted these past greats to lead the way to the new generation of fans and players.

How much was that transition worth?

I kept digging, kept preparing. I studied the negotiating *personality* of the man I would face, Hank Peters, the Orioles' general manager. Was he a hardball player, out for an I Win–You Lose negotiation? Or was he a WIN–win type? Did he negotiate in confidence, behind closed doors, quietly and subtly? Or did he use the press as a tool to float offers and preempt counteroffers? Was he stubborn? Was his ego on the line? What effect would this negotiation have on his career? Did he and Brooks have a past and was it a plus or a minus? Did he have a sentimental bone in his body? Was he a soft touch for a legend getting ready to hang up his number, or was he a numbers cruncher who delivered budgets as if they were RBIs?

I went back to my *network*. I talked to reporters. I read sports stories. I read what the Orioles' media guide said about Peters, talked to employees and former employees in Baltimore and in other big league cities. I listened to what people who liked Hank said and what people who didn't said. I learned that he was a tough negotiator, but a fair one. He valued marquee players, but he never forgot that he was part of an organization that ran on and believed in really tight budgets. He hadn't kept his job by throwing money around.

Hank looked like a guy who couldn't be swayed by an emotional pitch. But what if emotional value could be translated into bottom-line numbers?

Next I went looking for *precedents*. How did Brooks' numbers compare with those of other ballplayers? More research, more digging. I pored over Major

League Baseball statistics. I put Brooks up against every third baseman; every player making $100,000; superstars in their prime; superstars in the twilight of their careers—Willie Mays, Joe DiMaggio, Ernie Banks, Yogi Berra, Ted Williams, Stan Musial, Mickey Mantle; other Orioles of the past and other Orioles last season. I was searching for anything and everything that would justify $100,000 (and negate a salary reduction) for a player of the caliber and stature of Brooks Robinson.

I didn't find it.

The hard fact was that before 1975 and the beginning of free agency, lots of Hall of Famers–to-be were *underpaid* and they took *pay cuts* as their careers faded. Even players with stats comparable to Brooks's weren't earning six figures. Existing precedents weren't supporting the $100,000 goal.

Was the research wasted? Hardly. It was all the more valuable. Now I knew what Hank Peters might know. I would have to be prepared for it and be prepared to counter it.

Now it was time to determine my client's *real goals*. What was it worth to Brooks, not just to the Orioles, for him to finish his career in Baltimore? If we got another $10,000 from New York, was it worth it to move? Did it take $20,000 or $30,000 more to live there as well as he lived in Baltimore? Even if he got more from one of the expansion clubs like Toronto or Seattle, was it worth it for probably only one more season? What about life after he left the field? Would he want to be back in Baltimore anyway?

The answer was pretty clear: Brooks was tied to Baltimore. After turning his finances around, he had good business prospects here and he was part of the community. He hoped to expand on his relationship with the Orioles—maybe in the front office, maybe behind a microphone. Going to another club to finish his career might dull the luster on Mr. Oriole as it had, for a short time, when Mr. Colt, Johnny Unitas, left Baltimore for San Diego. And that might lessen Brooks's future earnings.

It was time to explore *alternatives*. True, the precedents weren't in our favor. And Brooks *wanted* to stay in Baltimore. I knew it, and probably Hank Peters knew it. But Peters didn't know if Brooks was *willing* to leave. I evaluated the option of going to other clubs. Only the expansion clubs would meet or exceed the $100,000. Established clubs didn't care about his intangible value—Mr. Oriole didn't mean anything at Fenway Park or Tiger Stadium.

He wasn't a hometown hero. (They had their own Carl Yastrzemskis and Al Kalines.) To them, he was an aging third baseman who might not be able to spear a scorcher up the line anymore. Our option was new clubs where an "old star" might be a draw and have an impact on developing younger players.

Time to take *inventory*. Where did all this preparation leave me? The Orioles weren't going to overpay—Peters would be persuaded with numbers, not nostalgia.

The precedents of comparable players spelled a pay cut. Established teams wouldn't pay a premium for Brooks, though expansion teams might. Brooks wanted $100,000, but would take less to stay in town.

Would I have been better off not knowing all this? Absolutely not. What if Peters knew it all and I didn't? What if I pursued avenues that were blind alleys? It's as important to know your weaknesses going in as it is to know your strengths: Maybe more important.

It was going to be a tough battle, but we had one route open, the intangible called "economic impact": the money Brooks generated by *being there*. Economic impact is a commonly used term today in financing major civic projects like stadiums and convention centers. Back then it wasn't. Even now, it is never an exact calculation—more the art of fiscal conjecture. So I created my own guesstimate of Brooks's impact. I looked up newspaper and magazine articles. I gleaned every fact, trend, and anecdote that indicated how his presence in an Orioles uniform, on the field, and in the line-up might boost attendance, sell souvenirs, and line people up for beer and hot dogs. I estimated the value of Brooks at every home game. I calculated the return, in dollars and cents, of a "Thanks Brooks Day." I looked at Brooks as a one-man public relations office for the Orioles and tried to assess the positive community impact of the Orioles keeping Brooks and the potential negative impact of not keeping him.

Tough battle or not, I was ready. I knew where the mines were planted. I knew every number, every fact, every stat for and against us. I could make the case for $100,000 without stepping into a trap. I could make the case, in dollars and cents, and I could back it up. And because of what I had learned, we weren't stuck on getting $100,000 in straight salary. We were willing to accept creative ways to get there.

Bring on Hank Peters. Let him ask me anything, let him challenge me, let him put me on the spot. I was prepared, prepared, prepared.

I went into Hank's office. I looked over at him and I didn't see a general manager. I saw the jury. My case would win them over. I spread notebooks out and laid newspaper articles across the tables. I propped pictures up. I circled figures and percentages. I unfurled my spreadsheets. It was impressive, to say the least, and it took almost an hour. From fact to fact, from figure to figure, and finally to the finale: I made my closing argument to the jury. "Hank, clearly, undeniably, absolutely you can see this evidence demonstrates beyond any doubt that Brooks Robinson is worth at least $100,000."

I rested. I looked at Hank Peters, my jury. I waited. Confidently. It was time for an impressed Hank to furrow his brow, scratch his head, stick out his hand, and agree with me.

There was one problem. Hank hadn't read the script. He just looked across the table and said, "Thanks Ron, I'll get back to you."

What? *"I'll get back to you?"* He didn't say "yes." He didn't even say "no." After my brilliant performance! *"I'll get back to you?"* Had I not made an ironclad case? Was he just not listening? Oh, he was listening, all right. He heard everything. Because I told him everything I knew, all at once.

I *was prepared, but I didn't probe*. I didn't ask one question. I didn't get one insight from Hank Peters. I didn't even ask how the traffic was that morning.

I *was prepared, but I didn't properly propose*. I said, this is what we'll take. I didn't try to get him to go first, or give me an idea of *where* or *how* or even if he'd make an offer.

I *didn't negotiate*. I orated, I speechified, I pontificated. But I didn't engage in "the commerce of information for ultimate gain." I revealed our entire position without getting one shred of information from him. He could take his time, mull over our position, respond to every argument, and defuse, disarm, and negate my points, one by one.

Most of all, I *didn't listen*. Listening is a critical link in probing and throughout the process. I wasn't open to input that might have changed the outcome. I wasn't attuned to the cues from the other side. I heard only what I already knew, not new information that might have changed the outcome of the negotiation.

Hank said, "I'll get back to you" because he knew how to negotiate. And he did get back to us with an offer of $80,000. And he gave us his reasons, which by now were honed to perfection. Brooks accepted.

There is a P.S., though. We never burned our bridges. And that paid off down the road. Late in the season, in anticipation of getting into the World Series, the Orioles wanted to make a roster move, that is, make room for a younger player by moving an older player off the roster. Hank Peters called and asked if Brooks would be willing to move off. I took the opportunity to remind Hank that Brooks had acted and played like a true professional throughout the season, despite never feeling quite comfortable with the outcome of our contract negotiations. Hank knew that was true and said he was going to make up the salary difference retroactively so Brooks would, in fact, make $100,000 for the year. The team even held their "Thanks Brooks Day" to recognize his career contributions to the Orioles. It was an early lesson in the value of building relationships. There's much more about that as you read on.

So, unlike me with Hank Peters, don't fail to put all 3 Ps in play. In the next three chapters, we go into detail on each of them—Prepare, Probe, and Propose. We'll provide you a systematic approach to insure that you understand them, refine them, practice them, and employ them and empower you to . . . yes, maximize your win.

REFRESHER

Chapter 4: The Three Ps—A Systematic Approach

Empower yourself with a systematic approach:

Prepare, Probe, Propose

1. *Prepare*: Research, study, stockpile knowledge.
2. *Probe*: Ask questions and listen; you'll get answers.
3. *Propose*: Try not to make the first offer. When you make an offer, aim high—make a strong, solid, reasonable offer, and be open to change it.

Remember the Brooks Robinson contract—one P is not enough

Preparation: gathered information, studied other side's personality, went to personal network, looked for precedents, determined client's real goals, explored alternatives, took inventory.

Other side's response: "I'll get back to you." Preparation alone is not enough.

Prepared, but—didn't probe—didn't learn other side's real goals/ interests, didn't properly propose, went first without creative options.

"This, of course, adds a new element to our negotiations."

CHAPTER 5

Prepare . . . or Else

> If I had eight hours to chop down a tree,
> I'd spend six sharpening my axe.
>
> —ABRAHAM LINCOLN

PREPARATION: THE AEROBICS OF NEGOTIATION

The first phase of any negotiation is the preparation phase. It is the most important phase and sometimes the most neglected. You can't control the other side, outside events, and often not even your own position—but the one thing you can control is your preparation. If you are not prepared for a negotiation, you might as well not show up. You have given the other side an undue, unearned advantage.

Preparation is the only aspect of negotiation over which you have control.

Preparation is like exercise. Sure, it's good for you, but while you're "stair-mastering," ab-crunching, and treadmilling, you feel tired, bored, and, afterward, sore. It's only months later when you're running through an airport for a plane and you *don't* get winded that you appreciate all that sweat.

Don't expect a thrill from preparation while you're gathering background information, checking sources, networking, referencing, fact checking, and strategizing. *Do* expect to be exhilarated when you sit down at the table and get few surprises from the other side. The more you know about them, their expectations, aspirations, limits (time, money, resources), their perceptions of you, the deal, and its ramifications, the better position you are in to make the deal you want. *Preparation is power.*

> By failing to prepare, you are preparing to fail.
>
> —BENJAMIN FRANKLIN

Successful negotiators are prepared negotiators. Preparation is an exercise in patience and persistence that pays off. Remember, most people see negotiation as a finite incident. The opposite is true. *Negotiation is a process, not an event.* The process begins with preparation. Use it or lose it.

HOW PREPARED ARE YOU FOR YOUR NEGOTIATIONS?

How Prepared Are You for Negotiations?

In my preparation, I . . .	Circle One		
• Try to learn real interests of the other side.	Always	Sometimes	Never
• Look for precedents for either side.	Always	Sometimes	Never
• Understand both sides' alternatives.	Always	Sometimes	Never
• Consider impact of deadlines.	Always	Sometimes	Never
• Determine my strengths.	Always	Sometimes	Never
• Consider strengths and weaknesses of the other side.	Always	Sometimes	Never
• Establish the highest goal I can achieve.	Always	Sometimes	Never
• Determine my walkaway point.	Always	Sometimes	Never
• Assemble a team to assist me.	Always	Sometimes	Never
• Assess the other side's negotiators.	Always	Sometimes	Never
• Commit my strategy to writing.	Always	Sometimes	Never

If six or more of your answers were "Always," you have good preparation habits, which this chapter will hone further. (If all of your answers were "Always," c'mon!)
If five or more of your answers were "Sometimes" or "Never," this chapter will immediately improve your next negotiation.
If three or more of your answers were "Never," read this chapter as fast as possible.

The following exercise demonstrates the impact of preparation.

THE NUMBERS AND LETTERS GAME

Part 1—Numbers

Don't look at the numbers below yet. When you do, you'll see a graphic of scattered numbers. Pick up a pencil. Ask someone to time you or time yourself. From the moment you look at the graphic, you have 30 seconds to connect as many numbers in order as you can. Okay, start now!

11   6

9

16

17   14 26

12

5

19   22

7

1   10 24

21

15   2

13

25   20

4 18

3   8

23

THE NUMBERS AND LETTERS GAME CONTINUED ...

Part 2—Letters

Don't look at the letters that follow yet. When you do, you'll see letters of the alphabet. Do not pick up your pencil. Ask your timer to give you 60 seconds to study the placement of the letters. Then, pick up the pencil. Have the timer give you another 30 seconds to connect as many letters, in order, as you can. Ready? Go!

L

C   E J

M   X

O

A

R   W

B Z   Y

S

D   U

F N

G Q

K   H

V

T   I

P

What impact did the 60 seconds of preparation time have on your results with the letters (versus your results without prep time with the numbers)? More importantly, what impact did that 60 seconds of preparation have on your level of confidence in doing the exercise?

Most people experience a much higher confidence level after they have prepared for the letter exercise. They are able to map out where they want to go, establish a system to use, and work through the exercise mentally before putting pen to paper. This preparation increases their confidence level, which, in turn, increases their performance level.

How Do the Numbers and Letters Exercises Relate to Daily Negotiation?

How do you feel when you're unprepared (or less prepared than you should be) for a negotiation? *Scared? Overpowered? Defensive? Anxious? Angry?* How do you feel when you're totally prepared? *Confident? Like a winner? Strong? Calm?* What are some possible negative results of being unprepared? *Embarrassment? Confusion? A bad deal?*

The way you *feel* about your preparation is an important factor. In the previous exercise, some people do reasonably well with no preparation time. But the vast majority do measurably better when they've had time to prepare. That means two things: (1) Preparation helps; and (2) *feeling prepared* helps. Yes, you *might* do fine without preparation, but why walk into a situation without giving yourself every possible advantage?

Remember, confidence is important. But it doesn't take the place of real preparation. In this next story, I had plenty of the former but not enough of the latter.

Selling My First Home (Learning the Hard Way)

This is what I called "my first grownup transaction." I had a good start on my career as a lawyer; we had begun a family; we bought and were ready to sell our first home. You never forget that first house. It was the late 1960s and we'd bought a detached, three-bedroom, brick home on a little piece of land in a nice family neighborhood. We paid $26,000 for the house (it seemed like a lot at the time!). With two children and one on the way, a dog, a station wagon, and a new swingset in the backyard, we were a living, breathing ad for American middle-class family life. And, after three years in the house, we were about to outgrow it.

The real estate market had not been great. It had been flat to moderate. But, we had made some improvements to the house—repairs, painting, decorating. I figured, the house had to be worth somewhat more simply because (1) it was three years later and (2) we had improved it.

We decided we'd sell it for $30,000. It seemed like a fair price—not greedy, not desperate. I remember we came to our decision on Thursday evening. We were ready to put the house on the market the following week.

Then, on Friday morning, I remembered this friend, another lawyer named Gene who had always said that he and his wife, Carol, liked our house and its location. In fact, they'd said, "If there's ever a home for sale in your neighborhood, let us know." When I got to the office, I found Gene and told him we would be selling the house the next week but we'd give them first crack at it. So if he bought it, we'd both save by not having brokers' fees.

He was excited and said he and Carol would come look at the house that evening. At 5:30 Gene and Carol walked through our house, tried every light switch, opened every cupboard, and flushed every toilet. And, thankfully, everything worked, closed, and flushed. I was getting pretty excited myself. Then, I overheard Carol in the third bedroom say, "I think we'll paint this room yellow." She didn't say, " . . . *if* we buy the house, we *would* paint this room yellow." She said, "we'll" as in "we will" *when* we buy the house, not *if* we buy it. We practically had the sale made.

Then we adjourned to the negotiation center of all homes—the kitchen. Before anyone could say anything, Carol looked out the window and saw the swingset. She said, "Would you throw the swingset in with the deal?" I thought to myself, "You mean the really heavy, cumbersome swingset that I desperately don't want to move?" I took a thoughtful pause and said, "Okay, we'll throw in the swingset." This deal was all but done. Gene asked how much we were selling the house for and I replied, "$30,000." Gene didn't flinch on the price. He said they'd go home, talk it over, and call on Monday. I was feeling great. We'd sold the house in one day.

The weekend passed; Monday came and Gene didn't call. Tuesday came and went; no call from Gene. Wednesday morning came and still no word. But, walking down the street that day, I saw Gene. He said the words you never want to hear in dealmaking, "Ron, I was going to call you." In other words, 'I have something to say to you that I don't want to say so I've been putting it off.' He said, "We bought a house."

I said, trying to be calm, gracious, and all kinds of things I wasn't feeling, "Really? Where?"

He said, "About seven houses down the street from yours."

I had to know. "Gene, do you mind if I ask how much you paid for it?"

"$27,500," he said, adding, "You know, we've been looking for a house in your neighborhood for a while and there have been six houses that have sold or are for sale with the highest asking price of $28,000."

"Oh," I said weakly, "congratulations."

What a lesson. In that simple transaction, or missed transaction, I learned the importance of preparation. If I had walked through my own neighbors' homes during their open houses, I'd have seen how much they were expecting and how their homes compared with mine. If I had examined the public records of selling prices in the area or if I had used a professional broker, I'd have better understood market value. If I had done research and utilized the available resources, I'd have been better prepared and a better negotiator.

In the end, of course, we sold the house. The sale price was $28,000. So it didn't cost us anything. Or did it? We had to make three more months of mortgage payments.

HOW TO PREPARE (AND HOW NOT TO)

Before anything else, preparation is the key to success.

—Alexander Graham Bell

I don't know that there are any shortcuts to doing a good job.

—Sandra Day O'Connor

How to Prepare: Why Don't People Do It?

We humans fall back on excuses (and they sound a lot like the ones we tried to get away with when we didn't do our homework in grade school).

- *"I know it already. I don't need to prepare."* Sure, it's your business or profession or investment so you ought to know it inside and out. You assume you're up to date, but you may not be. Give yourself a review. You're likely to find some surprises. Just because it is your business, you could be too close to it and take too much for granted. Step back and try to take an outsider's look. We guarantee you'll learn something.

- And no matter how much you know about your side, you don't know enough about their side.

It's what you learn after you know it all that counts.

—Harry Truman

- *"There's not enough time."* Preparation is actually a time saver. The more you know about your side and theirs, the more shortcuts you can take in negotiation. Concepts require less explanation. Jargon is already understood. Major issues separate themselves from minor ones. When people tell us there's not enough time to prepare, we say "baloney." If a deal starts to turn into a disaster, there always seems to be enough time to postpone the deadline and hope for an eleventh-hour miracle, so surely there was enough time up front to avoid that last-minute disaster. Simply put, if you invest in preparation now, you will make fewer mistakes later and save yourself the time of implementing corrections of those mistakes.

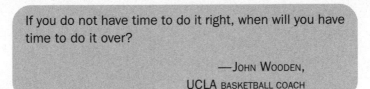

If you do not have time to do it right, when will you have time to do it over?

—John Wooden,
UCLA basketball coach

- *"I don't know what to prepare."* This one may appear to have merit. But it's not acceptable. Yes, there's a lot of background you could gather, perhaps limitless information. Yes, some information is more valuable and some less. No, you can't absorb all of it, nor do you want to. But what you can, and should, do is use a preparation plan to maximize your exposure to relevant data and minimize wasted effort and time.

How to Prepare: A System

We've learned that taking the time to prepare can build confidence and effectiveness. But the reality is we don't always have enough time to prepare as fully as we might like. In that case, having a plan or using a system for just that contingency can still be empowering. What do you do if you're faced with an almost immediate need for a response? Size up the situation quickly and say, what can I do to increase my preparation in a matter of seconds or minutes? Remember the numbers exercise on page 83?

If you didn't have time to review them in advance of having to connect them sequentially, your confidence and effectiveness might be lower. But your confidence and results improve if you were given, and could apply, the following system: *Draw a vertical line down the center of the page. Note that all of the odd numbers are to the left of the line, and all the even numbers are on the right.* Despite the apparent lack of time, understanding that system empowers you to go further in connecting the numbers in sequence than if you did not have it. Even when you are short on time, you will be more effective if you have a system in place.

That's what we're going to provide—a system for when you don't have time, and one that, of course, works very well when you do have time, that will maximize your results. In negotiation, that system is the Preparation Checklist.

THE PREPARATION CHECKLIST

The Preparation Checklist is a tool that gets you in the habit of preparation to make sure you're ready when you sit down to negotiate. It is broken down into six "Information Gathering Steps" and two "Action Planning Steps." At the end of this section, we provide you with a Preparation Checklist that you can use as a guide before every negotiation. Here are the components.

Six Information Gathering Steps

1. *Situation Summary*. Briefly describe what this negotiation is about. Identify your objectives and overall goals. Include who, what, when, and why as they apply to this deal. Though you may think you have the

facts firmly implanted in your mind and know your objectives, writing them down helps you both organize your thoughts and clarify your understanding of the challenges you face.

2. *Precedents*. Knowing precedents gives you the *power of the past*. You can quote or cite, as well as learn from those events that have already happened, thereby giving credence to your position. Knowing how similar transactions, particularly those involving the other side, unfolded in the past may guide you in structuring this one.

   Do not just focus on a single precedent, such as one that supports your position. Be familiar with precedent(s) the other side might use. Case in point: Cal Ripken's 1992 contract negotiation. Our precedent was the highest paid players in the game of baseball—$6 million per year. Their precedent was the highest paid shortstops in the game—$4 million per year. We knew our precedent and we knew theirs so we were ready.

3. *Interests*. You most likely know your own interests, but theirs are the keys to getting past what seem like rock-hard positions. Determining interests means getting beyond what they *say* they want to what they *really* want, things that may not be readily apparent but may well bear on the outcome of the transaction. Dollars may define positions (prices, salaries, and so on), but noncash value may often define interests (settling quickly, service, security, experience, recognition). Effective probing may uncover their real interests.

> First, you have to know what you want. That sounds self-evident, but you'd be surprised by how many people don't actually know what they want with the kind of precision that a negotiation demands. Then, you have to think of the 2,000 ways to get to where you want to go: what the trades might be, what the arguments might be, what the moves might be on the other side. And you watch carefully, and listen carefully, talk less, and remain persistent.
>
> —AMBASSADOR CHARLENE BARSHEFSKY

4. *Alternatives, including Highest Goal and Walkaway*. Alternatives make you less dependent on one kind of deal and more open to

variations. There's no take it or leave it when you have alternatives; therefore, there are far fewer impasses. Further, knowing their alternatives to doing the deal with you may guide you in accessing their leverage. Employing alternatives gives you the *Power of Options*. Going into a negotiation without options is like going into battle with one weapon. What if the battering ram won't knock the door down? Did you bring grappling hooks to fling over the walls? If not, you're not going to get inside.

> If you don't know your options, you don't have any.
> —DIANA KORTE, WOMEN'S HEALTH ADVOCATE

You also must know your *Highest Goal* and *Walkaway* positions. You will not achieve a lofty goal unless you aim for it. Where would you ideally like to come out? If you don't make that ask, you will not get it. At the same time, know where your bottom line is: How much would you give up to make the deal? If you don't face that hard question in advance, you may find yourself repeatedly lowering your expectations as the deal progresses.

Be willing to walk at a certain point. But decide where that point is *before* you start negotiating and write it down.

Developing a *Walkaway* is an important step of the Preparation Checklist. It furnishes a finite figure upon which to build your negotiating strategy and it also assists in protecting you from making emotional changes.

A good example unfolds in a story told by Mike Blackstone, the Institute's Sports Practice Leader, who served as the contract negotiator for an NBA team:

Woohoo! We Walked Away!

In the NBA, the free agent signing period is a time filled with long hours, enormous stress, and many dealings with exceptionally difficult people. Our staff did a great deal of work in preparing for these negotiations, which included establishing very clear *Highest Goals* and *Walkaway* positions, both of which, at times, can be hard to stick to. Each free agency period presents only a few players who make real sense for your team at that given point in time. With a limited number of attractive candidates and plenty of competition, the negotiations can get intense and heated at times.

There was one such negotiation that I will never forget. We did our research and gathered every bit of information we could. All of that data was used to develop a strategy, compose scripts for each call, and establish a Highest Goal and Walkaway for this deal. The player's agent came in with what we thought was a ridiculously high offer, but, thanks to our preparation, not one that was unexpected. His "ask" was substantially beyond our Walkaway, so we had no realistic room to adjust. We didn't break off the negotiation abruptly. We "did the dance" for a while, talking and exploring, giving the other side the opportunity to adjust, reconsider, recalibrate, or compromise. In contrast to many people, we created a Walkaway we believed in and didn't submit to negotiating pressure, and therefore stood our ground with confidence.

Of course, the agent was not happy. He did eventually find the player a home with another team, for a deal that was much higher than the largest deal we had thought was reasonable. It would seem the agent got his Highest Goal. But the player did not live up to, or even come close to, the value of the contract. We were content with our decision before that outcome, and that outcome validated our preparation and Walkaway.

---

5. *Strengths and Weaknesses*. Ironically, almost all negotiators overestimate their own weaknesses and the other side's strengths. Try to take an honest inventory of each side's *real* strong points and vulnerabilities. Ask yourself if your weaknesses are apparent to the other side or if you are being overly sensitive to them. The same applies to strengths. Give yourself credit for your pluses. Assess the other side's strengths analytically, not emotionally. Examples of other factors include: The competitor may be bigger but not as market-responsive as your company. They may have been around longer but are they as in-tune with today's demands? Knowing your strengths and weaknesses is vital.

6. *Team*. Create a team on your side. It may consist of co-negotiators, experts in various aspects of the deal, or good cop–bad cop, information sources, and devil's advocates with whom you can role-play. Practice as a team before you go to the table.

Also, assess the other side and the members of their team. Look at their resumes and experiences. Who are their decision makers? How do they make decisions? Have they ever done a deal similar to this one? What was the result? Don't get caught by a higher authority tactic and don't overlook those who may, in fact, influence the decision.

Two Action Planning Steps

7. *Strategy.* Now that you have the known information available to you, write down the questions you want to ask. You need to make some decisions in advance of formulating and making proposals.

How much probing do you want to do? Do you want to control the negotiation or let the other side control the flow? Do you want to lead from strength or react to a lead from the other side? Do you want to start high or low? How many face-to-face meetings do you want to have? No answer is right or wrong. The answer depends on your needs, your goals, the tone and style of the other side, timing, and egos.

Plan your concessions in advance. Where will you give? Where will you stand firm? How will you make a move so that it gives the least and gains the most? Don't be afraid to take a time-out during the negotiation to reassess the situation.

8. *Scripting.* Don't attempt to keep all facets of your proposal in your head. Set forth and write out your proposals in advance. Test them, state them, and restate them until you are comfortable and you have *perfected your pitch.* Don't stop practicing until you are satisfied that you will confidently deliver your message. When possible, have a devil's advocate look over your script to make sure he/she doesn't see an issue or an opportunity you might have missed.

Keep in mind that the information gathered in the Preparation Checklist may be subject to alteration or otherwise be fluid depending on how circumstances unfold. Whenever you have exchanges with the other side, a summary of those exchanges should be inserted in the *Updates Section* at the foot of the Checklist.

Make the Prep Checklist automatic. Get in the preparation habit. Carry the Checklist with you at all times. Follow it methodically, step by step, and create more extensive responses when the time allows.

For those negotiations that come without warning, by phone, by email, or just show up at the door unannounced, you can create an instant version, what I call the "yellow pad checklist." If someone says, *"We have a rush job and need a quote before close of business"* or *"I was driving by and saw your for lease sign,"* by using the yellow pad version of the Preparation Checklist, you can handle the instant negotiation. Tell the prospect you'll call back in five minutes, or an hour, or ask the client to wait in the lobby while you finish up some business. Spend that time with your legal pad. Go through steps one through eight with key words next to each, or your personal abbreviations that cover the hot spots. Build your confidence by briefly scripting, then mentally practicing, your proposals to the other side. Once you have the Preparation Checklist and its steps fixed in your mind, you always have it with you. Hopefully, you will have some time to give yourself the edge of preparation.

Make your use of the Preparation Checklist so routine that you don't feel undressed walking into a meeting without having done a version of it. You'll derive two benefits:

1. You will *be* better prepared by using the Checklist system.
2. You will *feel* better prepared so you'll have the added weapon of confidence.

Preparation Checklist

What follows is a Preparation Checklist form that you can use as a guide before every negotiation.

IMPORTANT: The spacing on the following form is for convenience only. Expand each item as requirements dictate and time allows. A truly complete Preparation Checklist grows with each interaction of the involved parties. Remember that going through the checklist is not about filling in information for the sake of filling in information. If you don't know something, make a note of it so you can go back and write down the questions you will ask or research you will gather to get the information. Knowing what you don't know could be as important as what you do know.

PREPARATION CHECKLIST

Information Gathering

Situation Summary:

Define the situation and objectives for this negotiation:

Include who, what, when, and why:

Precedents:

Deal comparables (for and against you):

Other similar deals or patterns of conduct you can learn from to model your strategy:

Interests:

Wants and needs of the other side (probe for undisclosed interests):

Alternatives:

Various deal structures (including Highest Goal and Walkaway):

Other options that are worth considering if this deal doesn't work (for us and for them):

Strengths and Weaknesses:

Components of the deal, situation, relationship, experience that are/are not in your favor:

Team:

Who are you dealing with on the other side?

How do those people operate?

What does their prior experience tell you?

Roles and responsibilities of the people on your team:

Action Planning

Strategy:

The plan to achieve your goal, including timing and next steps:

Scripting:

Bullet points for message or proposal you want to make, including questions you want to ask.

If possible, have someone act as your devil's advocate:

Updates:

Add conversation notes, with dates, as situation progresses.

If there is any doubt in your mind about the importance of a checklist, consider my partner Jeff Cochran's story about the "Pilot's Checklist."

Pilot's Checklist

After college, I joined the Peace Corps and was assigned to work in Nepal. As you might imagine, traveling in this tiny Himalayan country could be extremely arduous at times. The village I worked in was 200 miles away and was 19 hours by bus to the capital city Katmandu on a good travel day.

However, there was a tiny airport near my village that had flights to Katmandu once per week. This airport was not the kind most people are accustomed to. The runway was a dirt strip in the middle of a field, where goats had to be moved out of the way whenever a plane had to take off or land.

Needless to say, my first flight from there was memorable. The plane was a tiny four-passenger puddle jumper, the kind amateur pilots use to learn how to fly. I walked out across the dirt runway/goat path to the plane, the pilot took my bag and put it in the little hold beneath the fuselage, and I climbed up all three steps to get on and into my appropriately tiny seat.

As I buckled my seatbelt, I saw the pilot reach beneath his seat and take out a clipboard. He started reading whatever was on the paper and I started to panic. If he doesn't have a whole lot of experience and is just now reading up on how to fly the plane, we're in big trouble. I leaned over and tapped him on the shoulder.

Me: "Hey, how you doin'?"
Pilot: "Good, sir, how are you doing?"
Me: "I'm fine. What's up with the extra reading material?"
Pilot: "Ah, it's just my checklist."
Me: "How long have you been flying?"
Pilot: "Over 20 years."
Me: "And you still need the checklist?"
Pilot: "Yes, it has key items about the plane that as pilots we shouldn't overlook."
Me: "And you still need that after 20 years?"
        The pilot turned the clipboard toward me and pointed down the list, "Would you want me to overlook anything on here?"
Me: "Nope. For my money you go ahead and check: Check away!"

Jeff's story always reminds me of how simple but essential checklists can be, no matter how experienced or knowledgeable a negotiator, or a pilot, may be. That pilot's checklist story hit even closer to home for most of us when Sully Sullenberger landed a plane in the middle of the Hudson River in New York after an impact with geese caused a mechanical failure. The most essential point Mr. Sullenberger made about that landing was that they were fully prepared. The pilot's checklist was so ingrained as part of their operating procedure that during the emergency the pilot and crew didn't have to think about what to do, just how to do it.

Now let's take the pilot's checklist concept in other life situations. A sports team practices based on its playbook before every game. An actor or actress reads the script and the director's notes over and over before going on stage. When conducting our business negotiations, many busy people tend to skip information gathering and planning steps and wing it despite knowing better. Why? Because preparation takes time and it isn't fun. So they spend as little time on it as possible and hope that they will still end up with a positive result.

That thought process makes no sense. Preparation is the only aspect of a negotiation you totally control. Everything else is, to a greater or lesser degree, out of your hands. Think like a pilot and go through the Preparation Checklist and you will maximize the likelihood that you clearly understand what you know and what you still need to find out. Use it to make sure you don't walk out of a meeting saying, "I can't believe I forgot to ask them about . . . " or "Why didn't I give them information on . . . ."

The most systematically prepared people have the best chance at negotiation success. Embrace the grid that follows as you pilot your negotiations.

A CASE STUDY: THE SUR-REAL SALES CHALLENGE

To see how practical and helpful the Preparation Checklist can be, what follows is a sample of a Preparation Checklist filled in by participants in one of our seminars, based on the information in the case study below. For another example of following the eight steps of the Preparation Checklist, see the Major League Umpires story in Chapter 12.

The Background

It's June 5th. You're the director of corporate sales for the Virginia Dunkers, a franchise with one of the strongest brands and loyal fan bases in professional basketball. Your job is selling advertising to corporate sponsors for the team's media properties (TV, radio, Internet), special programs/promotions and events, and within the arena (signage, hospitality, in-game features). The Dunkers' fan demographics are highly educated, moderate to high incomes, largely male, ages 18–49. Advertising initiatives directed to the Dunkers' fan base have been very successful at helping companies increase brand awareness and sales, particularly for new product launches.

Here are three success stories: **Shade-O,** ultraviolet transition sunglasses, generated additional revenue of $450K/year for three years to their introductory campaign via the Dunkers venue. **XPlay**, a fantasy league, saw revenue of $575K/year for five years, thanks to its Dunkers-based marketing. Both companies invested in programs utilizing video media, signage, hospitality, and in-game features. **Blasto Chips** invested $120K in a promotion for Dunkers VIP ticket packages through in-store promotions resulting in the company's highest fourth-quarter sales to date.

However, there have been some marketing disappointments. **Home-Game**, mobile phone sports apps, committed to invest $500k/yr for five years, but due to missed deadlines, unacceptable creative materials, and poor early sales results, the client cancelled after one year. **Buzzzz,** the energy drink company, planned to spend $300K for two years on in-arena signage, but has not seen an impact on sales and is now considering terminating its relationship for the upcoming season.

The team owners are putting heavy pressure on you to increase ad sales, generating at least one major new Dunkers marketing partner with a minimum spend of $400K/year. You're thinking, "Where am I going to find a $400K advertiser?" when your phone rings. It's Nick Blitz, president of ADZrUS, a major advertising agency. He wants to explore an ad buy for his new client, **Geek Wilson**, and his latest digital breakthrough, Sur-Real, a virtual entertainment system due to hit the Southeastern market December 7th, one month after the Dunkers' first regular season game. You schedule the appointment and start your research.

Nick Blitz is a 40-year-old ad agency pro, known as "the ad man with the golden touch" for his successful product launches. He has an affinity for highly targeted marketing, sometimes through sports associations, sometimes via other narrow channels such as Internet media. His most recent such success was the rebranding of Metro Bank, introduced during a hockey all-star game about a year ago. His buy for the bank included in-arena advertising, an in-game TV spot, and the offer of a premium incentive for every new account opened. Within two weeks of the intro, the bank opened 2,500 new accounts with deposits totaling $2 million, plus steady increases since (in the face of declines at competition). But this targeted approach (vs. mass media) carries risk as well. Blitz's launch of a recent album by the band, Sludge Factory, via Internet streaming radio ads, fell flat with sales of fewer than 2,000 units.

Geek Wilson is a digital whiz kid, a genius at developing products that consumers become addicted to. Historically he has been reluctant to spend large sums of money on advertising because he can't identify quantifiable ROI. As a result, his products have never been market leaders but he is extremely proud of his latest invention and wants his personal profile associated with it.

Sur-Real is a compact, portable entertainment and communication system delivered by surround-type goggles. Sur-Real can download music and movies, play video games, be used as a cell phone, and utilize business software and email. Target market is primarily male, 18 to 35, moderate to high-income. Geek Wilson is not a great believer in expensive, traditional mass media, feeling its waste coverage cannot justify the costs. Blitz and his agency launched a wireless mobile phone/entertainment product that was considered revolutionary a few years ago (the Mobile Tainer) with a sports franchise in another area of the country. That deal was closed when that sports franchise used all the technological bells and whistles their arena had to offer in a live demonstration.

That's a snapshot of the situation. Now you need to prepare for your meeting with Nick, his client Geek Wilson, and his CFO, **Suzy Slasher**, who always demands a 10 percent proposal reduction. Available Dunker's inventory and pricing:

- Six pre- and post-game radio spots for full season—$25,000 per full season spot
- Three pre- and post-game TV spots for full season—$50,000 per full season spot
- In-arena advertising: One Video Board Rotating Feature, all home games—$100,000
- In-arena advertising: One permanent ad near Jumbotron, all home games—$125,000
- Two game in-arena product demos (includes five booths)—$125,000
- Forty premium Season tickets—$10,000 each (four-ticket minimum)
- Two skyboxes for all home games—$125,000 each

Based on 82-game season—41 home games.

The *Sur-Real* Sales Challenge Prep Checklist

Note: You may not have all the previous information at your fingertips to fill in your Prep Checklist. You'd have to do research, fill in information, probe, fill in more, and so on. The Prep Checklist is a living document, updated as new information is gathered, the situation changes, and the negotiation proceeds.

Information Gathering

Situation Summary: Define the situation and objectives for this negotiation. Include who, what, when, and why. [Incorporate the background facts above.]

Precedents: Deal comparables (for and against you):

For You:

- Shade-O—$450K/year—three-year deal
- XPlay—$575k/year—five years and ongoing
- BlastoChips—$120K—highest Q4 sales using just in-store promotions

Against You:

- HomeGame—$500K—five years, cancelled contract after one year because of Dunker's failures, which included creative miscalculations, missed timelines, and poor sales results.
- Buzzz—$300K—two years ongoing, in-arena advertising program has not seen strong sales results, likely because it only purchased signage and no other inventory (i.e., TV, radio, tickets, and so on).

Related situations/deals that you can learn from in order to model your strategy.

- Nick Blitz and Metro Bank—in-arena advertising, in-game TV spot, and account opening premium resulted in 2,500 new accounts with deposits of $2M in first two weeks of grand opening.
- Nick's client Sludge Factory band sold only 2,000 units of their new release using just ads in Internet streaming radio.
- Suzy Slasher always wants a price reduction of at least 10 percent of the initial proposal.
- Nick Blitz and his agency launched a wireless mobile phone/entertainment product that was considered revolutionary a few years ago (the Mobile Tainer) with a sports franchise in another area of the country. That deal was closed when that sports franchise used all the technological bells and whistles their arena had to offer in a live demonstration.

[Their] Interests: Wants and needs of the other side

Geek Wilson

- Would like to have his own personal profile associated with the product
- Get new product to market, gain high visibility fast, make Sur-Real market leader
- Make sound economic and marketing decisions, quantifiable ROI on ad spend

Suzy Slasher

- Live up to reputation for delivering 10 percent reductions

Nick Blitz

- Maintain status as leading marketing exec with successful track record, insure a hit, avoid a miss.

Alternatives Including Highest Goal and Walkaway

Various deal structures (including Highest Goal and Walkaway)

- Highest Goal—525K total spend
- Walkaway—net 400K after 15 percent discount

Other options worth considering if this deal doesn't work (for us and them)

For us:

- Offer attractive, one-time discount from standard rates
- Do a smaller deal as a test—with commitment to increase if successful
- Create a custom package, created just for this product intro, utilizing variety of Dunkers inventory and opportunities

For them:

- Choose other teams
- Advertise in mass-media, other than sports
- Blend mass-media and Dunkers or other team media buy

Strengths and Weaknesses: Aspects of the deal, situation, relationship, experience that are/are not in your favor.

Strengths:

- Good geography
- Your audience is the ideal target market for Sur-Real: Males 18–49, well-educated, moderate to high incomes
- Dunkers are a powerful brand and have a loyal fan base that has a strong affinity for the team's sponsors.
- Advertising initiatives directed towards Dunkers fan base have a strong track record of success in helping companies increase their brand awareness and sales during new product launches.

Weaknesses:

- No past relationship with influencers or decision makers
- Failure of HomeGame and Buzzz partnerships could hurt if Blitz and Geek Wilson learn of them
- Geek and Suzy Slasher are reluctant to invest large budgets in advertising

Team: Who are you dealing with on the other side? How do those people operate? What does their prior experience tell you?

Roles and responsibilities: Their team

Nick Blitz—will lead day-to-day negotiations

- 40-year-old ad agency pro with an affinity for highly targeted marketing, sometimes through sports associations, sometimes via other narrow channels such as Internet media. Willing to take risks but wants to protect his "golden touch" reputation.

Geek Wilson—Sur-Real developer

- Digital whiz/inventor, a genius at developing products consumers love. Personally not a good marketing communicator, historically reluctant to commit large sums of money on advertising because it is difficult to quantify ROI. Geek's first time working with Blitz and his agency ADZrUS.

Suzy Slasher—Geek Wilson's CFO

- Prides herself on always cutting deals by at least 10 percent of proposal price.

Roles and responsibilities: Your team

- Senior VP & VP, Corporate Sales/your bosses—decision makers on pricing levels and final deal approval.
- Director of Corporate Sales/you—face of the negotiation, handle day-to-day discussions, recommend final deal to your bosses.

Action Planning

Strategy: The plan to achieve your goal, including timeline and next steps.

Initial Strategy

- Find out more about Mobile Tainer product launch.
- Try to learn more about Nick through other sports teams that have dealt with him (if appropriate).
- Research Geek's other products and overall success.
- Work on a program that stresses new product launch advantage of Dunkers' experience and demographics with the variety of media inventory that can be accessed for exposure, both in-arena and broadcasting opportunities. Factor Geek's desire for personal association with the product into the mix.
- Leave room in proposal for Suzy to do her work—at least a 10 percent cushion.
- Arrange for a telephone call or meeting to probe more fully as to their interests, get a sense of their budget, and to fill in gaps, if any.
- The involvement of Geek is important to the success of this campaign. We can facilitate his direct involvement, through personal appearances and hospitality opportunities so he can impact success, to cater to his ego, but to do so in a way that actually delivers results.
- We should open up by asking questions, to see what they (Nick and Geek) have in mind before we make any type of proposal, as we still have some gaps in the Prep Checklist.
- Consider a multimedia demonstration to the client live and in-arena.

Estimated Timeline:

June 5—Today, the day you got the call from Nick Blitz

June 7—Start to gather appropriate materials and compile list of questions

June 10—Meet with internal team to discuss deal

Week of June 15—Conference call with Nick to discuss initial parameters and expectations. Probe for details

Week of June 20—In-arena tour and in-person meeting with Nick and Geek

Week of July 5—Tweak deal points and finalize proposal

July 5–August 7—Negotiation period

August 7—Agreement must be finalized

September 21—Creative/ads must be completed

November 7—Season starts

November 21—Dunkers play rival Shooters (targeted night for product sampling)

December 7—Product launches at retail

Scripts: Bullet points for message or proposal you want to make, including questions you want to ask. Add conversation notes and updates as situation progresses.

Initial Script:

Probing Questions:

- What is your marketing plan for Sur-Real? Product positioning, media plan, PR, promotional plans, timeline, and so on.
- What are your (marketing/sales) goals for Sur-Real? Retail sell-in, brand awareness, presence, sales at intro, sales at holiday season, sales year one, and so on.
- Tell us more about how the Mobile Tainer was marketed successfully. (Note: for Nick only.)
- What are you hoping to get from a partnership with the Dunkers? What else? What's most important to you? Why?
- Do you have any other concerns?

[What follows is an example of a potential script that could be developed after you have finished your preparation and probing and are ready to make a proposal.]

We are glad that you helped us understand what you are looking for from this relationship. The Virginia Dunkers can offer Sur-Real an unparalleled opportunity to reach its target audience: males, ages 18 to 35, well educated, with high incomes, the most likely and influential buyers. The Dunkers can provide Sur-Real with a direct link to its primary target customers through a unique promotion that will allow Geek to cobrand his product with the power of the Dunkers name in an exciting and cutting-edge launch via our home-arena venue.

To create maximum impact and immediate penetration, we recommend the following forms of advertising. This package combines TV and radio pre- and in-game advertising with in-arena signage, utilizing live, real-time presence that will not be delayed by consumers (recorded and deferred for later viewing), as well as a hospitality/entertainment component to impact key retailer relationships (where Geek can meet personally with key accounts to convey his passion about Sur-Real).

- Two pre- and in-game radio spots for full season—$50,000
- Two pre- and in-game TV spots for full season—$100,000
- In-arena product sampling for Sur-Real (five booths, all home games)—$125,000
- Permanent ad adjacent to Jumbotron, all home games—$125,000
- One skybox, all home games—$125,000
- Total Package Price = $525,000

[The scripting portion of Action Planning is a chance for you to get your ideas on paper and, if possible, have someone "Devil's Advocate" your strategy and approach. You don't need to write out a movie script; bullet points are enough, unless you're someone who needs greater detail.]

CONFIDENCE IS THE SECRET WEAPON (BUT THE REAL SECRET IS THAT PREPARATION IS THE KEY TO CONFIDENCE)

If you're prepared, you can go into the most challenging negotiation with confidence. You can accomplish almost anything. As demonstrated in the preceding case study, preparing opens the door to raising confidence and increasing the likelihood of success in the most challenging negotiations. Preparing even works in the context of the reality television world. Witness the work of contestants on the network television show *Shark Tank*. They're out to win over the "Sharks" and gain public support through diligent preparation. It just so happens that the preparation steps the successful contestants took mirror the steps of the Preparation Checklist. The following story is taken from an essay in the Fall 2013 *Wharton Magazine*. (The parenthetical notes are ours.)

Guppies in the Shark Tank

The popular show *Shark Tank* invites inventors to come pitch their products and services to a group of seasoned investors who will each take a turn crushing people's dreams or making them an offer to invest in their business. Don't mind the 7 million viewers that are watching on TV as well!

One such pair of inventors was Ryan Frankel and Kunal Sarda, Wharton alumni, who came up with a language translation community that offered real time access to human translators. They did such a good job in their presentation that Sharks were fighting over who was the best partner for them. Between the Sharks and other investors, they raised $1.5 million in investment capital.

Mr. Frankel wrote in hindsight that the reason they were so successful in getting investors to buy-in (outside of developing a good service) was due to their incredible level of commitment to *preparation*.

"We asked questions to understand what was important to each investor [*Interests*]. Before the negotiations, we researched their past investments and interests [*Precedents*]. We looked at past comments made by the Sharks and talked to people who worked with them so we could understand what factors made a deal attractive. . . . We determined the least we would accept and were prepared to walk away [*Walkaway*]. . . . We tried not to focus solely on the money [*Alternatives, Interests*]. In case we received competing offers, we evaluated the nonmonetary assets each investor could add, such as areas of expertise, business contacts, and specific skills [*Team, Alternatives*]."

This is preparation excellence. They set out to understand who they were dealing with and what made them tick instead of simply thinking about themselves and their own interests. They took the time to think about their walkaway position as well, so that in the heat of the moment, they didn't make a bad deal.

On top of that, Mr. Frankel proactively decided that they would not let emotions get in the way and cause them to become victims of deal fever [*Strategy*]. Deal fever is when people think they are getting closer and closer to making a deal, they push way past their walkaway position and make bad deals because even if it's a bad deal, it's somehow better than no deal.

And lastly, Mr. Frankel and Mr. Sarda very astutely realized that the only way to maximize their chances of keeping their emotions in check was to "practice, practice, practice, and more practice [*Scripting*]. We called on many of our friends for mock negotiations, and while we're still working on this aspect, we felt the practice significantly improved our mental readiness for negotiation."

SOURCES OF INFORMATION

Access to information has increased exponentially since the 1990s when the Internet began to gain prominence. Think about how buying a car has changed. We used to walk into dealerships blind; now we have pricing information from Kelley Blue Book, TrueCar, and Cars.com, reviews from *Car and Driver* and *Consumer Reports*, and myriad other websites and resources that allow us to learn almost everything we want to know about a car before we enter the showroom.

Now, think of your negotiation. You may know what information you need in order to be prepared, but *where* do you go to find it? There are three basic routes to information.

1. *Reference Sources*. Start with generic information and work your way to the specific. Depending on the category of your negotiation— buying, selling, or leasing, bidding and awarding contracts, royalties and residuals, personal services, dispute resolution, business succession, divorce, or family decision making—you want to hone in on the data most relevant to your deal. Begin with search engines

such as Google or Yahoo!. They will point you to relevant websites, news, images, publications, and so on. Then, use these same search engines to find social media pages for the organizations or people you are dealing with. You may be surprised by how much you can learn from a LinkedIn, Twitter, Facebook, Pinterest, or Instagram account. Finally, consider trade publications, industry reports, blogs, and other reference sources available both online and offline.

2. *Networking*. You're surrounded by experts. First, there are experts from inside, that is, those on your team—business partners and investors, coworkers from your own company. Do not forget to leverage their experiences. Then, there are experts from outside—corporate lawyers, real estate lawyers, tax accountants, stockbrokers, financial advisors, insurance and investment advisors, advertising and marketing practitioners, lobbyists, any of the myriad professionals whose advice you heed. Think about all they know about you and your business. Then multiply that by all the clients and businesses they serve. These and other experts comprise your personal knowledge network, a human library. Use it. Your accountant may have direct experience in the industry in which you're negotiating. Your investment advisor may have heard about shakeups in the boardroom of the company across the table from you. A great place to start is LinkedIn. Who do you know? And who do they know?

3. *The Other Side*. There's another party in your network, one so obvious that it is often overlooked. Don't forget the one with whom you are negotiating—your boss, your investors, your potential client, whomever. Who knows more about the situation than the other side? Don't ignore this obvious source of knowledge. Probe them to learn more. But, be careful of the information they provide as it comes with a potential bias. Some negotiators fear that probing the other side makes them look weak. If done where appropriate, it can not only help gather important information, it also acknowledges that the other side is knowledgeable, which is an important reality to keep in mind whenever negotiating.

With each source of information and the information provided, turn back to the Preparation Checklist for the questions to answer and fill it in as you get the information.

Sources of Information Checklist

Reference Sources	Network
___Online/Offline	___Business Partners and Investors
___News	
___Articles	___Coworkers
___Blogs	___Clients
___Company Websites	___Suppliers
___Press Releases	___Competitors
___Videos (YouTube, Vimeo)	___Professionals (Accountants, Lawyers, Investment Advisors, etc.)
___Social Media (Twitter, LinkedIn)	
___Subscriptions (D&B, Hoover's)	___Friends

Everybody Has an Arnie in San Diego: A Real Estate Story

I was involved in a property negotiation that turned almost 180 degrees as a result of tapping into one source of information. One day, out of the blue, I got a call from a real estate client from my days practicing law. He opened with, "Ron, I need your help." He reminded me of a piece of property between Baltimore and Washington that he'd bought for $3 million six or seven years earlier. I had assumed he'd sold it long ago. Well, he would have but, unfortunately, a real estate slump had set in shortly after he bought. On top of that, he'd sunk $600,000 to $700,000 in taxes, insurance, and other expenses. In all that time, the land never moved. He got no offers, no inquiries, not even a lukewarm feeler.

But the day before he called me, he had gotten a call. Somebody was interested. He said, "I'm so excited, I just don't want to blow it. Will you help me make the deal?"

I said, "You know, I'm not the one to do the legal paperwork anymore, but I'd be happy to negotiate the deal."

"Great," he said, "What do we do now?"

I said, "We talk," meaning, we get prepared.

I asked what we knew about comparable land prices in the area. Since only a few parcels had been sold in recent times, we got a thorough history, none of it indicating an upturn in prices. We knew that my client had his parcel on the market for $4.4 million. But he'd held it a long time and that was, in effect, his negotiation weakness.

I asked him everything I could about the prospective buyer. To protect everyone's privacy, we'll just call them the San Diego Electronics Distribution Company. I asked him what he knew about them.

"Not much."

I said, "Okay, let's find out what we can."

The San Diego Electronics Distribution Company was a public company, which was good news. It meant we had immediate access to information—annual reports, earnings statements, press releases—the works. They had only gone public a few months earlier so they had a lot of cash on hand from the stock sale. We looked at their locations. They not only had a distribution center in San Diego but they also had them near Chicago, in Texas, Mississippi, and Florida. They had expanded across the country and their literature said they planned to expand further, into the Mid-Atlantic region, which is the corridor from Philadelphia south to Northern Virginia. More good news: Baltimore/Washington sits squarely in the middle of that territory.

Little by little, we were gaining information and, therefore, strength. I said to myself, what else can we learn? And *how* else can we learn? That's when I thought of my friend, Arnie, who had moved to San Diego to run a network affiliate television station. TV general managers have a way of knowing lots of people in a town, whether it's by selling to, buying from, or serving the community with the important players. So, I called Arnie—one call to one person. I'm not advocating shortcuts. But I do want to emphasize the power of using your network. In this case, all it took was one call.

I asked him what he knew about San Diego Electronic Goods Distribution Company.

He said that since they were a wholesaler, they didn't buy advertising time, so he didn't know them as a customer. "But," he said, "it's amazing that you'd ask me about them right now."

"Why?" I asked.

Arnie said, "The executive vice president of the company sits on the board of the Chamber of Commerce with me. At the last meeting, he leaned over to me and said, 'since you're from Baltimore, can you give me the names of some residential real estate brokers in the area?'"

I couldn't believe what I was hearing. The executive vice president of our prospective buyer wanted the names of realtors in our area. Somebody from his firm was contemplating a move, maybe several somebodies. In a very short time, we'd gone from knowing nothing to knowing a lot.

My friend added, "Oh yeah, Ron, the exec VP also asked me for the name of a good lawyer in Baltimore. I told him I didn't know any but I gave him your name instead." (I don't have to add that Arnie is a bit of a wise guy.)

My client and I went to the meeting. Instead of being desperate, we were prepared. (Well, my client was still a little on the anxious-to-sell side.) The other side walked in and started by telling us our asking price was ridiculous (which it wasn't, based on comparables). We reminded them that our property already had railroad sidings leading in and easy access to highway truck routes. They reiterated that our price was out of line and added that their company may just concentrate on expansion in the Deep South, rather than in our geography. That statement didn't leave us feeling good about them from the standpoint of integrity. Their own literature and our information indicated otherwise.

But, do I call them liars? Never. We set our defensive strategy but we don't poke holes in their story because, to do so would just make communication all but impossible. This was, evidently, their idea of shrewd negotiation. Instead of challenging them on it, I simply said that we respected their business needs. In fact, we too were considering alternatives such as subdividing the property (which, in our case, was true). So, they should do whatever they have to do. Just let us know, in case we haven't already sold our property, if they should decide to pursue moving into our area.

At that point, I was losing circulation in my leg due to my client squeezing it so hard he cut off the blood supply. Obviously, he didn't feel quite as cool about this as I did. But he did keep quiet; I should say, he kept quiet until we walked out of the room. "Ron, Ron, Ron, why are you taking such a risk? They were my one and only buyer!"

I said, "They still are. Yes, we took a risk. But given what we know, it's a low-to-medium risk, not a high one."

You always take a risk when you negotiate. But the more prepared you are, the lower the risk. In this case, we knew there wasn't an appropriate additional location in the Deep South. They were already there. They needed to expand north, to the Mid-Atlantic. And we knew they were house shopping for their people in our area.

We waited. And we waited. To my client, every day of silence was proof of his worst nightmare, a blown deal. He'd heard nothing on this property for years and now he was hearing nothing again. On the eighth day, the San Diego Electronics Distribution Company called. They wanted to talk. No, they wouldn't pay $4.4 million, but they did make an offer. We countered and eventually settled on $3.9 million. It was only a little more than what my client had sunk into the property. But it was at fair market value. And it was more than he had expected.

The deal was done. My client was ecstatic. All because of one phone call to one source of information in our network. Sometimes the key source will leap to mind; sometimes you have to dig for it. But before you sit down to negotiate, when you're preparing, ask yourself, "Who's my Arnie in San Diego?"

REFRESHER

Chapter 5: Prepare . . . Or Else

> By failing to prepare, you are preparing to fail.
>
> —Benjamin Franklin

How do you feel when you're unprepared?

Scared, outmatched, overpowered, anxious, angry

How do you feel when you're well prepared?

Confident, like a winner, strong, calm

What are negative results of being unprepared?

Embarrassment, a bad deal, no deal.

> If you do not have time to do it right, when will you have time to do it over?
>
> —John Wooden, UCLA basketball coach

Why People Don't Prepare

- *I know it already. I don't need to prepare.* Beware of surprises. Everyone needs to prepare.
- *Not enough time.* Preparation is a time saver. The more you know, the less time it takes to explain or understand or correct mistakes.
- *Don't know how to prepare.* Valid but unacceptable. Use prep time to maximize exposure to relevant data.

> It's what you learn after you know it all, that counts.
>
> —Harry S. Truman

A Systematic Approach—Eight Prep Steps

Six Information Gathering Steps

1. Situation Summary
2. Precedents
3. Interests
4. Alternatives (Highest Goal/Walkaway)
5. Strengths and Weaknesses
6. Team

Two Action Planning Steps

7. Strategy
8. Scripting

Confidence—The Secret Weapon

The more prepared you are, the more confident you feel, the better you negotiate.

Sources of Information

1. *Reference Sources*: online digital, industry publications, libraries, public data.
2. *Networking*: who you know, lawyers, CPAs, brokers, marketers.
3. *The Other Side*

"*See? I told you the negotiations would be a lot more fun without a battery of lawyers.*"

CHAPTER 6

Probe, Probe, Probe

> Research is formalized curiosity. It is poking and prying with a purpose.
>
> —ZORA NEALE HURSTON, ANTHROPOLOGIST
> AND AUTHOR

THE OTHER SIDE IS TRYING TO TELL YOU HOW TO MAKE THE DEAL

In addition to the knowledge gathered so that you are prepared, you need to dig for information behind the other side's position. Determine their real interests or needs. That's what probing is all about. Too many people succumb to the temptation to jump to their bottom-line stance—to make proposals—immediately, without taking full advantage of what they could learn about what drives the other side. The more you know about the other side's position—their motivations and expectations, their wish-list and must-list, soft spots and desperate needs, personal aspirations and psychic rewards, stated goals as well as real interests—the better equipped you are to negotiate.

If you ask the right questions and listen intently, the other side may give you the input you need to make the deal you want.

Really? Then how come more negotiators don't know how to make the WIN–win deal they want? Because they don't ask questions (fearing it shows weakness or stupidity) and even when they do, they don't really listen (thinking they know the answers already).

How Well Do You Probe When You Negotiate?

When I negotiate, I . . .	Circle One		
• Spend more time listening than talking.	Always	Sometimes	Never
• Check assumptions made in preparation.	Always	Sometimes	Never
• Ask "why" to learn the other side's interests.	Always	Sometimes	Never
• Use "hypotheticals" to gain information.	Always	Sometimes	Never
• Answer questions with questions.	Always	Sometimes	Never
• Ask the other side to restate a point if it is not clear.	Always	Sometimes	Never
• Take notes, review at end of conversation.	Always	Sometimes	Never
• Tally up issues before going on.	Always	Sometimes	Never

If five or more of your answers were "Always," you have good probing habits and this chapter will hone them further. (If all of your answers were "Always," c'mon!)
If four or more of your answers were "Sometimes" or "Never," this chapter will immediately improve your next negotiation.
If three or more of your answers were "Never," read this chapter as fast as possible!

Here is one of the great historic examples proving the value of probing, of getting beyond stated positions, of listening and discovering the real interests of each side.

The Middle East Peace Talks (It Wasn't the Talks, It Was the Listening)

In 1979, I attended a dinner under a tent on the back lawn of the White House, celebrating the signing of the Camp David Peace Accords. I was filled with awe as I watched Anwar Sadat, the President of Egypt, and Menachem Begin, the Prime Minister of Israel, follow Jimmy Carter to the head table. That evening, I saw these two courageous leaders shake hands, engage in warm, friendly discussion, and express their sincere hopes for a peaceful Middle East. I sat next to my friend, Jim Rouse, the renowned visionary of urban development, who, with tears in his eyes, said to me, "Our President is a quiet man, but he's a man who knows how to get to the heart of the problem."

It was an indelible moment. The following is a condensed and simplified telling of a long historical process that demonstrates how President Carter used the second P—probe (though I doubt he called it that)—to unlock an apparently irresolvable situation.

The peace process started in 1977 when Anwar Sadat made one of the bravest gestures of the twentieth century. He called Menachem Begin and suggested they talk peace. After literally thousands of years of anger and war, this was momentous. Even the usually unflappable *New York Times* ran headlines slightly larger than usual. Amazed commentators noted that if Egypt and Israel could talk peace in the 1970s, by the 1980s or 1990s maybe the Americans and Russians could be at peace.

The talks began with Sadat bravely taking his life in his hands and traveling to Israel to meet with Begin and address the Israeli Knesset. The evening news was riveting as we watched scenes we could never have imagined: Anwar Sadat and Menachem Begin being hosted by former Israeli Prime Minister, Golda Meir, for tea and cookies. Talk of their grandchildren living in peace, visiting one another's countries. To anyone who had lived through the post–World War II years of the fierce resistance to the formation of the State of Israel and the promise of its demise by neighboring nations, this was emotional stuff.

The talks went without incident at first. The two leaders seemed to like each other. Eventually, Sadat told Begin that they must talk about the Sinai. Menachem Begin was stopped cold. To him, these were peace talks, not discussions of giving away key territories. In effect, he said, "You provoked us in 1967 and we pushed you and the rest of the Arab world back and we took the Sinai. Then, in 1973, on our holiest day, Yom Kippur, you attacked us again, to take the Sinai. Again, we pushed you back. We have established settlements in the Sinai and we are not giving them up."

It was push and pull. Sadat said, "We want the Sinai."

Begin said, "No, we want the Sinai."

Suddenly the optimistic headlines turned negative. "Israeli-Egyptian Peace Talks Break Down." Worldwide hopes were in jeopardy. Would all the promise go unfulfilled?

That's when Jimmy Carter stepped in. He felt too much progress had been made to abandon the process. In August 1978, he invited both parties to neutral ground: Camp David, Maryland. They could each have a cabin (not your average cabin) and perhaps resume the talks. They agreed.

But what was Carter going to do? Was he going to try to play Solomon and divide the Sinai in half? Was he going to simply talk one side or the other out of its adamant stance? After 2,000 years, it was clear there was no simple solution.

Although he didn't call his process "The 3 Ps," Jimmy Carter did a great deal of Preparing, Probing, and Proposing. Of course, when you're President of the United

States, you get plenty of high-powered help, particularly in the first P—preparation. Carter didn't spend the weekend at the Library of Congress cramming for the talks. He had a book under his arm that summarized the background. He had notes. He had advisors.

So, he was prepared. But he didn't just leap to the third P—propose—and suggest, "You fellows ought to do this or that with the Sinai." He went to the second P—probe. He got behind the information, behind the facts, behind the rhetoric of positions. He asked why.

In essence, he went to Sadat and asked, "Why do you want the Sinai?" Sadat might have offered many reasons from "Israel took it from us" to "it is part of our heritage." But many countries had lost territory in war and, in this case, the heritage belonged to the "holy land" more than to one nation or another. And Carter suspected these were not the real reasons. He asked more questions. He listened. Finally, Sadat revealed Egypt's real reason for wanting the Sinai. He told Jimmy Carter, "I have risked my life for this mission" (which turned out to be tragically prophetic). "I have made the gesture of offering peace, which many in my country, and the Arab world, see as a sign of weakness, not diplomacy. I must gain something back, a symbol of fair exchange, for the Egyptians—the return to sovereignty of the Sinai. They have to feel they're not just giving, but getting as well." Carter heard Sadat. This was Egypt's real interest that had to be addressed at the negotiating table.

Then Carter went to Begin and, in effect, asked, "Menachem, why do you want the Sinai?" Begin may have offered reasons ranging from "we need the Sinai's oil" to "we won it" to "it's part of our heritage." But Carter knew Israel had agreements to assure their oil supply, that other countries had given up land won in war, and that the Sinai didn't historically belong to one country. Again, these weren't the real reasons.

Carter kept questioning and kept listening. Finally, Begin identified the real reason Israel wanted the Sinai: Security. Begin explained to Carter, "You've been to the Middle East. You can see that we are surrounded on all sides by enemies. The Sinai gives us early warning time. With troop movements, we gain hours to mobilize. With air strikes, we gain critical minutes to defend ourselves. We can't give up that security." That was Israel's real interest and Carter heard it.

The following excerpt from Jimmy Carter's memoirs, *Keeping Faith* (New York: Bantam Books, 1982), is the retelling of the moment at Camp David when President Carter's keen listening skills found the opening for pursuing the Sinai issue:

[Begin] stated emphatically, "I will never personally recommend that the settlements in the Sinai be dismantled!" He added, "Please, Mr. President, do not make this a United States demand." I [Carter] noted with great interest, but without comment, the changes in his words and was heartened by it. "Never personally recommend" did not mean that he would never permit the settlements to be removed. The change was subtle but extremely significant. If others in Israel could be made to assume the onus for the decision, then finally there was at least a possibility for resolving this vital issue.

Carter could now offer a proposal that met the parties' needs. He convinced Begin to give up the "land" of the Sinai but not the security. He promised to provide Israel with an early warning system as good or better than the buffer of the territory. If Arab troops so much as marched a step or one Arab airplane took off, Israel would know instantly. Then Carter told Sadat, Egypt could have the Sinai but only with conditions. The Sinai would have to be demilitarized; buffer zones and monitoring stations would have to be established in order to give Israel the security it needed.

The night of the White House celebration, I saw a sight I thought I would never see, both Israeli and Egyptian troops marching together, instead of against each other. I saw history as a result of successful negotiation. Begin wanted security. Sadat wanted a symbol. The world wanted peace. All the interests were met because Jimmy Carter knew how to probe.

But that's international relations. We know that political leaders have to contend with war and peace and the weight of history. But what about regular people who just want a pay raise to compensate for high quality labor? Like welders, teachers, or tuba players: Their needs and drives aren't mysterious or unknown; they're obvious. Nobody has to probe deeply to find out what their real interests are, right? Well, let's take those tuba players, for instance.

Harmony: Conducting a Symphony Orchestra Mediation

In the summer of 1982, the Baltimore Symphony Orchestra had gone on strike. Strikes always come at the wrong time, but it would have been hard to find a worse time for this one. The city, the state, and a benefactor family were just completing a state-of-the-art concert hall at a cost of $35 million (about $100 million today). The building was dramatic inside and out. The acoustics were superb. The sight lines were flawless. The season was sold out. They had everything but an orchestra.

The strike was over a variety of issues but eventually came down to salary. The symphony board, a nonprofit civic group, offered the players a base pay of

$580 a week. The players wanted $620 a week. That makes the difference $40 a week, significant but not a world of difference, even 30 years ago.

The board and orchestra representatives talked and talked and got nowhere. Relations deteriorated. Federal mediators were brought in; they tried to split the difference and made no meaningful progress. The strike stretched to the fall of the year. First the rumors and then the newspaper articles appeared, talking about members of the orchestra being courted by other orchestras. The Baltimore Symphony had recently risen from the ranks of a good regional orchestra to a truly national one. They were drawing high praise, signing recording contracts, and being invited on prestigious tours. But our nationally ranked orchestra could be cherry-picked by competitors, thereby losing their "national sound," before ever moving into their new home.

I had been part of a volunteer group organized to look for ways to raise money for the future. It seemed all we did in our meetings was lament the never-ending strike. Wasn't there some way to bring the parties together? Somewhere along the way, I'm not even sure how or when, I found myself as a go-between. I was able to talk to both sides, the orchestra committee and the orchestra board. My first official act was to send the parties home for a Christmas break. We agreed to meet on January 4.

I had worked through the holiday period trying to get myself prepared. While I loved symphony music, I knew very little about it. I didn't know how many members there were in a full orchestra, what instruments made up the horn section, that cellists get carpal tunnel syndrome like ballplayers and stenographers, or the difference between a concert and a concerto. I read everything I could. I called on a member of our citizens' committee, Leon Fleisher, who had become a phenomenon as a left-handed pianist due to a medical impairment to his right hand. I did research through another friend connected with the Pittsburgh Symphony. I prepared right up through the New Year's weekend.

Unfortunately, by January 4, nothing miraculous had occurred. The board was still at $580 and the orchestra was still at $620. At the meeting, I put one group in my own office and the other in my law firm's conference room and stocked both with lots of snacks. I went to our law library and finished the last of my preparation.

Then I "shuttled" from one group in the conference room to the other group in my office, back and forth, for hours. I had to find out the real needs of each side. I went to the symphony board representatives and asked the critical question: why. "Why is $580 as high as you will go?" Is it because the board voted on the figure? Is it because the board has to show the players who's the boss? Is it because the board has funds earmarked for other purposes? The symphony board opened its books to me and showed me why: $580 was truly all they could afford. They were at their financial limit. They had exhausted their corporate contributors. They had committed all of their subscription money.

Then I asked the orchestra representatives, "Why must you be paid $620? Is it because you can't live on what you're making? Is it because of inflation? Is it because you have to show the board that they need you more than you need them?" It took a while and a lot more probing, but the answer came out. Sure, they'd like more money to live on but most supplemented their incomes with teaching. In fact, they respected the board. But the Baltimore Symphony was now an orchestra of national rank and the minimum pay for a national orchestra was $620 a week. It was status.

Hank Aaron once said that he could have hit 60 home runs, 150 RBIs, and batted .350 but none of it would have been as important as the day he earned $150,000 a year. Why? Because, in those days, that's how much Mickey Mantle and Don Drysdale were making. It was a recognition of his level of accomplishment, his status in the game.

The orchestra wanted $620 a week. It signaled their status in the game. The board had $580. After that, they were broke. I had identified the needs of each side. But how could they be met? We had to find a way to allow each side to realize its real interest, not just its stated position.

On Day Four of our negotiations, before I left home, one of my kids asked me, "Daddy, when will we see you?" I said, "5 A.M. tomorrow." (Actually, it turned out to be 5:30 A.M.)

That day, as predicted, we worked nonstop. We kept at it into the night. It got to be the early morning hours. But we were making progress so we kept going. I asked the board representatives hypothetically, "If we found new sources of money, would you agree to pay $620?" They responded "yes" but made it clear that they felt no such sources existed.

At 1:00 A.M., I had a thought. I called a colleague who was the general manager of the leading TV station in the city. He had a constant problem holding onto his number one–rated news anchor who was continually wooed by bigger market stations. (His news anchor happened to be my client.) It so happened that the news anchor had a weakness for, of all things, orchestras. The anchor had a fantasy of conducting a real symphony orchestra. I said to the station manager, "I can make you a hero with Jerry (the anchor)."

The manager said, "It's one o'clock in the morning."

I was undeterred. "Here's how it works. Your station donates the airtime for a telethon for the Baltimore Symphony. Jerry gets to conduct the orchestra and host the telethon."

The manager is now fully awake. "I don't even have to call New York. You've got five hours on the air and here's the date. Done."

Well, not quite done. Now I go to my secretary who is also there at 1:00 A.M. (and not too happy with me) and I have her prepare a contract which I am going to read to both the board and orchestra reps gathered in one room. In essence, the contract says, the players will be paid $620 a week (at which point the board members look like they want to kill me but the players look like they've won), *provided,* however, that the difference between the $580 and the $620 is made up by the funds raised through the telethon. Now both sides look at each other and realize it worked for both of them. The two sides bought in because we had brought Jerry, the anchorman, into it, and had introduced an idea that met the interests of both parties.

Throughout the process we had been dogged by the press, but we'd managed to keep most of the negotiations confidential. At this point, though, I purposely let the story out to the newspapers and TV stations. They brought their reporters and cameras and we were all over the morning news and the next day's paper. That created an added pressure on all parties to make the deal work.

The players got $620 a week . . . with a condition. They achieved national orchestra status with a contract that said they would be paid $620 with the proviso that the money be generated through telethon fundraising. The board lived up to its fiscal responsibility by not exceeding their budget of $580 a week and only paying more *if* additional money was generated *from new sources.*

As it turned out, the telethon raised almost all of the money and the anchor, who conducted the orchestra, spent the rest of his career at the station.

The need to be understood is universal. If you take the time and make the effort to understand the person you're facing in negotiation—if you really probe—you'll be able to shape a deal that addresses their interests and yours. That's how you build relationships. (By the way, probing works in personal relationships as much or more than business.) Relationships lead to good deals. Good deals echo—they lead to more deals. It's not conjecture, it's history, proven over and over.

Probing to understand the other party is your goal. But how do you do it? How do you get to the answers you want? The best way to get answers is with a question.

W.H.A.T.? THE PROBING TECHNIQUE

W.H.A.T. is a question to *remind* you to probe and it's an acronym for *how* to probe.

- W represents a collection of key Ws: **What, What else, Which,** and **Why.** First statements in negotiations tend to be positions. The other side says, *"We must own 50 percent of the new company."* That's a position. What you want to discover are their interests. But positions are easier to state. When the other person makes a statement contrary to your interests, your tendency is probably to defend and argue. *"No way. No deal. We're the majority or there's no deal."*

Their demand to *"own 50 percent of the new company"* may be their position, but what interests does it camouflage? **What** is really important to them? Dig to find out. Is it that they feel entitled to half of the profits? That may be easier to live with than having them own half the stock in the event of a possible sale.

Keep going. Find out **What else** is important. Maybe they aren't comfortable unless they have an equal say in all decision making. Again, that may be easier to swallow than splitting profits, or equal stock ownership, particularly if your investment, industry performance, or both are stronger. Get behind the position to the substance.

Then, determine **Which** is the most important interest to them. Not all of their wishes will be of the same value to them. Nor will they be to you. Perhaps, to them, sharing decision making is more important than sharing profits. That may or may not be acceptable to you, but first you want to know where they stand. If you don't uncover priorities, you may do battle over secondary issues.

And always, always probe to find out **Why** an interest is important to them. Why do they feel that way? Is it because of a past deal gone bad? Is it a worry that doesn't apply in this deal? Is it an issue that can be satisfied another way? Must all decision making be equal or just major events such as a merger or sale?

We preach using a systematic approach in all aspects of your nego-tiations. The following four-question sequence is a simple systematic way to get the information you need:
- What is important?
- What else is important?
- Which is most important?
- Why is that so important?

It is important, however, that you not ask the same questions in the same way every time. You can use slight variations to obtain the same information throughout a negotiation. For instance, when you find out they are interested in a low price, keep asking questions. *"Is there any-thing besides price you think is important?"* (**What else** is important?)

You might find out that the quality of goods and services after the sale are important. Or you may find they want fast delivery. Then, follow up with a summary. *"Just so I can make sure I have it straight, of the factors you've mentioned: Price, quality, service, or delivery date—what is your order of priority?"* (**Which** is most important?) You may discover that fast delivery is equally important to price, and you can then ask, *"What makes that such a high priority?"* (**Why** is that important?) Although you should be systematic, you should not become robotic. You goal is to gain information. By using this four-question sequence or variations of it, you will be on your way to gaining the information you need in all of your negotiations.

- **H** stands for **Hypothesize.** Good negotiators are cautious about disclosing information. You ask a direct question. But they decline or sidestep. A nonthreatening method to encourage the flow of information or to break a deadlock is to get hypothetical. *Let's pretend . . . Just suppose . . . What if? . . .* Now you can discuss topics that were previously off limits. This conversation doesn't create an absolute condition or obligation from either party, but rather advances a hypothetical solution—one that might or might not work—strictly for consideration.

  For instance, we conducted a mediation for a statewide association of CPAs. One chapter had become so alienated from the parent organization, because of what they called "philosophical differences," the chapter threatened to pull out and form an independent body. That would have weakened the statewide association, created a vocal splinter group, and fomented bad feelings within the profession. After exploring the nature of the philosophical dispute, it became apparent that the greatest offense to the chapter had been in style rather than substance. The president of the state body had expressed his opinion in a manner deemed offensive by the chapter. So, hypothetically, we asked the head of the chapter, *what if* the president of the state body apologized for the way he had expressed himself? We had no authority to promise he'd apologize; we could only offer up the possibility. The chapter members were skeptical of the president's willingness to do so, but said, *"If he would, we would agree to sit down and talk out our philosophical differences."*

  We took the same *what if* to the statewide president. *"What if, rather than retract your stance on business philosophy, you revised the way you stated your disagreement and apologized for any unintended offense?"*

"Hmm," he considered the possibility and said, *"If the chapter would agree, he would agree."* The hypothetical led to the real. The chapter and the state body met, talked out their differences, and remained a united body.

You can even hypothesize about something as seemingly finite as budget. Have you ever had someone say, "Well, it's not in the budget"?

Rather than argue why it should be in the budget, respond by saying, "But if it were in the budget, would you be okay with the project?" From this you can gain information—if they say yes, then (fill in blank); if they say no, then (fill in the blank).

Modifications lead to conversations. And when you're talking, you're not in a deadlock; you're negotiating.

- **A** stands for **Answer.** (Answer questions with questions.) The other side asks you a question to gain facts, to get background, to compare with what they know of the market, to test the water. If you just respond, you have no idea what other information they have, how your new input may compare, favorably or not, with industry data, whether you will look smart, gullible, cheap, expensive, or reasonable.

But since they asked a question, they have demonstrated interest. Mine the interest by asking another question that probes further into the same subject. They ask, *"If your company agrees to be merged into ours, how many of your employees can be laid off to achieve economies of scale?"*

You'd like to protect as many jobs as possible so, instead of responding directly, you dig deeper, asking, *"Which of our branch offices would you be keeping and which would you close?"* You now have the beginning of real information gain. You can start to learn whether your company will be merged or submerged. You can learn what the other side perceives are your assets and liabilities and even overall value.

In our seminars, we often reference a scene from the television show, *News Radio,* which demonstrates how not to answer questions with questions, but carries the point to absurdity. The scene goes something like this:

News Radio[*]

The Questioner Scene

An employee has just been clued in that shrewd negotiators never actually answer a question with a direct answer, but always with another question. The Shrewd Employee then walks into the Boss's office to try out the new technique but gets a little carried away.

BOSS	What are you doing in here?
SHREWD EMPLOYEE	What does it look like we're doing in here?
BOSS	(baffled) What?
SHREWD EMPLOYEE	(on guard) What—what?
	(The Boss is suspicious of this weird behavior, looks for a reason.)
BOSS	Is this about the raise?
SHREWD EMPLOYEE	(not about to be fooled) Is what about the raise?
	(The Boss is totally confused by all these questions.)
BOSS	Why are you answering every question with a question?
SHREWD EMPLOYEE	Why not?
BOSS	(shaking his head) I don't know. Congratulations. Now you've got me stumped.
SHREWD EMPLOYEE	(victorious) Thanks!
	(The Shrewd Employee is totally delighted, but isn't sure over what.)

---

[*]Courtesy of Brillstein Grey Entertainment.

As this scenario demonstrates, you can go too far even with a good tactic.

- **T** is for **Tell Me More.** Sometimes people feel uncomfortable probing. They feel that they are being nosy or that the other side will feel as if they are being interrogated. One way to make the probing process seem more like a conversation is to use the phrase "tell me more" or "is there anything else?" Most people like to hear themselves talk and by inviting them to "tell me more" you will discover additional information they may have originally omitted. Additionally, "tell me more" can be used to guide the conversation in areas of your interest.

For instance, if a potential employer says that they are interested in people who are willing to work hard, at a low salary, but bring prior experience to the job, you might respond by saying: "Tell me more about your desire for industry experience . . . ." As they tell you the problems they have had in the past with people coming into the organization without the necessary skills, you can begin to gather information to justify your higher salary based on your higher level of industry experience. The beauty of using "tell me more" is that it is an unobtrusive way to gather additional information and extend the probing process. By pushing one step further, following **W.**, **H.**, and **A.** with a reprise of **Tell Me More,** you may learn the other side's key interest at the very end of your probing. The real lesson is, probe, probe, and probe again.

Overcoming Probe Resistance

What happens when you deal with someone who enjoys being probed by your questions as much as being poked with a stick? You ask "Why?" and they say, "Because." You hypothesize and they say, "Get real." What do you do then? Don't give up. Try these tools when dealing with the probe-resistant negotiator:

- Try the *Restatement* technique. "Can you restate that?" It's amazing how often the restatement is different from the original. People tend to explain more each time they state their position, to give more detail, to soften, and even offer options to what seemed like a hard line. Now you can pose questions, ask for clarification and details. You're probing again.
- Use the *Show-Me-How* technique. The other side may make what seems like an unreasonable or unfair demand: *You must pay on delivery, not 30 days after.* Instead of reverting to a reflex rejection, ask the other side, *"Can you show me how that would work?"* As soon as the other side walks through the process in your shoes, they have to think about the challenge. *"Simple. You order merchandise and as soon as we receive your payment, we ship. You order as much as your cash-on-hand allows . . . which will be less than it would be if you had another 30 days to resell the merchandise to your customers . . . so then we'll be getting smaller orders from you than we used to . . . hmm, maybe there is another solution we could try."* Now you can begin exploring alternatives. Why do they have to have cash up front?

How much do they have to receive before shipping? Is there a compromise between order date and ship date? Does the size of the order change the terms? You're probing again.

- Employ the *Says Who?* technique. If the other side simply makes an arbitrary demand—*it has to be done this way!*—thereby seemingly shutting the door on further probing, try asking them *"Who requires that it be done that way?"* You may discover the individual behind the demand is not the one sitting opposite you at the negotiation table. It may be someone higher up, a boss, or an owner. It could be a lawyer or accountant. The person at the table is merely the messenger. All the persuasion in the world can't sway the unempowered representative. See if you can get the real demander to the table. At least then, you'll be talking to, and perhaps probing, the right party.

By now, you should have a good sense of the other side's interests. You know what means a lot to them, what means less, which issues are emotional and which are rational, which are deal-sweeteners and which are deal-breakers. You know how they view your side, what they perceive as your strengths and weaknesses, values and liabilities. Utilizing the W.H.A.T. method, you have probably probed more effectively than they have, enabling you to initiate and control the interest satisfaction process. By also honestly assessing your own real interests, you should be able to see how you can give to get. You should begin to see how you can satisfy some of their interests while satisfying most of your own interests.

THE DON'TS—HOW NOT TO PROBE

Here are three warnings—don'ts—to keep in mind when you go digging for information:

1. *Don't mindread.* Don't assume you know what the other side is thinking and simply proceed on that premise. If you base your thoughts and proposals on your assumptions, you run a high risk of being wrong. You may assume your position is stronger than it is and make an aggressive but naive offer. You may assume your position is weaker than it is and back yourself into a bad deal.

   Let's say you're negotiating a merger between a manufacturing facility based in LaCrosse, Wisconsin, and a distribution center in

Atlanta, Georgia, and a key issue is which city will be the new head-quarters. You say to the third generation owner of the manufacturing plant, "Since you want to live in a cold climate . . . ." Do you know that or just assume it? Maybe she's been dying for an excuse to move south or maybe she'd like to get away from her smothering family or perhaps her husband is from the south. Don't assume: ask. "Do you want to remain in Wisconsin?" "Where do you see the future of the company?" "Should we consider a different location altogether?"

It is natural to make assumptions. It's even acceptable, *if* you don't act on those assumptions. Test them first during the probe phase. Ask questions, explore, find out if your assumption is valid, close, or off the mark.

2. *Don't offend the other side—interrogation versus interview.* You are not a prosecuting attorney. The other side is not compelled to cooperate and answer you. If you interrogate, that is go after them with an aggressive attack, expect them to shut down. When they do answer you, let them. Don't interrupt before they finish. Always ask yourself how you feel when you're being interrogated or interrupted or worse, both.

On the other hand, if you approach the probing process as an interview, there's almost no limit to what you can learn. Show an interest in their side. Soften your inquiries with lead-ins such as "So I can understand where you're coming from . . . " or "Let me see if I have this right . . . " or "Tell me more about . . . ." When you want to answer one of their questions with one of your own, be careful not to come off as one-upping them or transparently ducking their question. Don't evade the question; embrace and explore it. "I'm glad you asked me that because it makes me think about . . . ."

3. *Don't get off track.* The other side may try to rush you through the process. They may try to skip steps. After all, they're not following the same agenda as you. Make sure you get the answers you need before you move on. Don't hesitate to slow the process down by saying, "Let's hold off on that for a moment . . . " or "Can we go back to something you just said?" And don't let your side (you) rush you through the process. Sometimes we get impatient with the pace and try to shortcut before we have answers. Impose the same slow-down techniques on yourself.

Listening skills are an essential piece of completing the circle of effective probing.

LISTENING

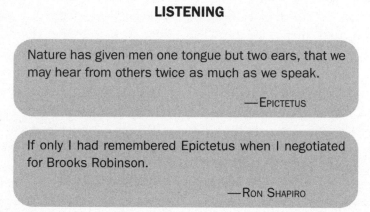

Nature has given men one tongue but two ears, that we may hear from others twice as much as we speak.

—EPICTETUS

If only I had remembered Epictetus when I negotiated for Brooks Robinson.

—RON SHAPIRO

Shh! (That's another secret to negotiation.) People like to talk. Resist the urge. The other side is human, so they want to talk, too. Encourage them. Then listen. As many of the previous stories illustrate, the other side is often trying to tell you how to make the deal. Did you ever notice how the party opposite you may think what he or she has to say is more important than what you have to say? That's okay. Give them a chance and they'll likely tell you much of what you need to know: What they hope for, what they'll settle for, what the real pressure points are, where they can move, and where they can't. They may tell you directly or subtly. Ask questions. Listen more. Every moment you're *not talking* is an opportunity to learn what it takes to make the deal. *The best negotiators aren't smooth talkers; they're smooth listeners.*

No Wonder It's Hard to Be a Good Listener

The *Wall Street Journal* has reported that "Overwhelmed by the incessant, intrusive babble of the modern world, the skill of listening has fallen on hard times." It has been estimated that most people speak at a rate of 120 to 150 words a minute. That sounds fast, but the human brain can process more than 500 words a minute. Because of this gap, many people engage in mental fidgeting, letting your mind drift off the subject, making you a poor listener.

Talk So Others Will Listen—Listen So Others Will Talk

The less you say, the more you can concentrate on what others are saying. Think about it. How much can you learn from what *you* say? Not much. You already know it, so by speaking, you're repeating yourself to yourself. But *everything* the other side says is potentially valuable. (Most negotiators spend too much time on what they're saying, or on thinking of what they're going to say next.)

Make what you do say count. The most effective things that come out of your mouth are those that shape and guide the conversation, particularly well framed questions. When you frame the issues, when you ask a good question, when you nod in agreement or feed an encouraging word that fuels the speaker to go on, you are giving the other side a path to follow. That path should lead to the key subjects of the negotiation—timing, competition, pressures, price, terms, and other interests.

Be an "active listener." Focus your energy on what the other person is saying. Make eye contact. Take notes. (It tells the other person that what they're saying is important and it lets you write down your ideas without interrupting.) If you don't understand, say so. (It's better to ask for clarification than to structure a deal or a proposal on a misassumption.) Repeat and confirm. ("What I hear you saying is . . . ") Repeating makes sure you understand each other and it confirms that you're listening. And if you haven't understood, you'll get things cleared up immediately. Pose candid questions. ("What will it take to make you happy in this deal?") Or try hypothetical questions to ease into a subject. ("If you had it in the budget, would you support this project?") Listen between the lines to what is said and what is omitted. (You hear gross sales figures instead of profits; price is emphasized but quality is glossed over.) Listen for nuance and emotion. (The mention of delivery dates makes him or her nervous.) Listen with your eyes, not just your ears. Where is he or she looking? At you? At papers? Around the room? Respond, laugh, frown, nod. (Receiving information well begets more information.)

The less you say, the more others will remember. It's simple math. Say a lot and they're bombarded and overwhelmed. Say a little and they can retain every word. And, of course, the less you say, the more you can focus on what they say.

> This is the problem with dealing with someone who is actually a good listener. They don't jump in on your sentences, saving you from actually finishing them, or talk over you, allowing what you do manage to get out to be lost or altered in transit. Instead, they wait, so you have to keep going.
>
> —SARAH DESSEN, AUTHOR

Listening Isn't Just Waiting to Talk

Do you think you're a good listener? Some people are, but they are the exceptions, not the rule. Most of us love to hear the sound of our own voices. We know the answers. We have the most informed opinions. We had the most interesting days. We tell the best stories. (Ask a golfer about his last round. Then prepare to hear a shot-by-shot travelogue of every hook, slice, and shank, from tee to rough to sand trap to green, each birdie, par, and bogie, each coulda, mighta, and shoulda, times 18.) The fact is, most of us aren't good listeners. We're interrupters. We just can't wait until it's our turn to speak. *Conversation interruptus*.

What Is Your Interruption Quotient?

How often do you let the other person *completely finish* a thought? If you interrupt in mid-thought, you've lost a valuable information opportunity the other side was giving you. You'll never know what you didn't hear. Do you mentally shut down instead of really paying attention? When was the last time that you simply sat and *contemplated* what was just said.

Do you want to really know if you're a good listener? Or a chronic interrupter? Don't ask people you work with: Ask your spouse or significant other. Ask your kids. (And don't interrupt when they answer you.)

In the very next conversation you have, make a deal with yourself to not interrupt at all. You'll be amazed at two things: (1) How hard it is and (2) How much you'll learn.

A Listening Test

Try this test and see just how good a listener you are. DON'T read the following paragraph. Have someone read it to you out loud. Twice. Listen as carefully as you can. Then take the test that follows.

"A long and extremely busy day had just come to an end at the Scoot-In-Scoot-Out Convenience Store. A shopkeeper had swept the floor and just before the door was locked, a man rushed in and demanded money. The safe was quickly opened and the owner removed the money. After the day's receipts were gathered up, the man drove off. Within minutes, the police arrived."

Test Questions

Do not look back at the text. Answer these questions.

Circle T if the statement is true.
Circle F if the statement is false.
Circle ? if you can't tell from the story.

1. A man appeared just before the owner locked the door.

   T   F   ?

2. The man demanded money.

   T   F   ?

3. The owner opened a safe.

   T   F   ?

4. After the man gathered the day's receipts, he ran away.

   T   F   ?

5. Not much money was taken from the safe.

   T   F   ?

6. The police responded within minutes.

   T   F   ?

7. The robber was a man.

   T   F   ?

Answers

1. A man appeared just before the owner locked the door.

T   F   [?]

The story never identified who locked the door. It is stated that the shopkeeper swept the floor and the owner opened the safe, but it does not indicate whether the shopkeeper and the owner are the same person, or, if they are two different people, which one was about to lock the door.

2. The man demanded money.

[T]   F   (?)

In fact, "a man rushed in and demanded money."

3. The owner opened a safe.

T   F   [?]

The story states the owner removed the money, but doesn't indicate who opened the safe.

4. After a man gathered the day's receipts, he ran away.

T   F   [?]

It is unclear who gathered the receipts. Also, the story states that the man "drove off." Did the man "run away" before he "drove off?" It is not clear.

5. Not much money was taken from the safe.

T   F   [?]

It says the owner removed the money. It doesn't state the amount of money that was removed.

6. The police responded within minutes.

T   F   [?]

It is not clear whether the police "responded" to a call or just happened to be patrolling the neighborhood.

7. The robber was a man.

T   F   [?]

We do not know if there was a robber or a robbery. While a man demanded money, a safe was opened, receipts were

> gathered, someone drove off, and police arrived, the same
> information could be true if the owner simply came in at the
> end of the day and took home the day's earnings.

How well did you listen? Did you hear "in a hurry"? How much did you hear what you *wanted* to hear, or hear what you *thought* was said? Were you influenced by a familiar scenario and did you then mentally fill in the blanks? For instance, when we hear words like "a man appeared and demanded money," "safe," "the man drove off," and "police arrived," we may assume a crime of robbery. There are, in fact, twenty or more different incidents that could account for the facts you were given. (By the way, did you take notes or did you *assume/hear* that because this was a listening test, you weren't allowed to do so?)

There is no trick to this test, no special way to beat it. The problem is, we tend to hear what we listen for. There's a famous old story that illustrates the point well.

THE ZOOLOGIST

Two men were walking along a crowded sidewalk in a bustling business area. Suddenly one man exclaimed, "Listen to the lovely sound of that cricket." But the other man could not hear the sound. He asked his companion how he could detect the delicate sound of a cricket in the midst of the din of traffic and humanity. The first man, who was a zoologist, had trained himself to listen to the sounds of nature, but he did not explain this. He simply took a coin out of his pocket and dropped it on the sidewalk, whereupon a dozen people responded to that sound by looking all around for money. "We hear," he said, "what we listen for."

—FROM *THE DISCIPLINE OF TRANSCENDENCE*
BY BHAGWAN SHREE RAJNEESH

The modern-day version of that story was told in our office one day. Our marketing director at the time, Kelly Harris, took an aerobics class at a health club. During her workout, she would put her baby in an adjoining room that served as a nursery for club members' children. Kelly said, even when the exercise music was blasting, when the instructor was chanting a cadence, when the whole class was grunting and panting, she could hear the cry of her baby over all that noise. Not only that, but Kelly could tell her baby's cry from all the other babies' cries. She, like most of us, can hear precisely what she's listening for.

Some of the most important applications of these lessons aren't in business, they're in everyday life, relationships with close friends, and—especially—with family.

Pavlov's Restaurant Bell

I negotiate for a living. I ought to know how to listen. But even after practicing and teaching, I've sometimes committed the most basic mistakes, and where I'd least want to have them occur, with my wife, Cathi.

Some nights we go out to a neighborhood restaurant for dinner just to escape from life and get back in touch with each other, to communicate what we're thinking and feeling. I really want to hear what she has to say. But one restaurant we liked had one of those bells that rings every time someone walks through the door. And I usually sat facing the door.

So, like one of Pavlov's dogs, I'd developed a conditioned response. Every time I heard the bell, my eyes shifted to the door for a split second, which was just long enough to miss a key signal in the conversation. I may have gotten the drift of the conversation, but I missed a shading, an emotion, or phrase. Losing eye contact is more than a shift of visual focus; it's a loss of mental focus as well.

Worse yet, my wife sensed my lack of attention. Being the patient soul she is, she allowed me several dings before giving me my wake-up call. "Ron," is all she'd say, one word that I hear loud and clear. It means, "I want to be heard. I'm more important than a door bell or who's walking into the restaurant."

Now I not only avoid restaurants with entry bells, but I purposely sit facing away from the door. And I also remember the lessons of the bell when tempted (as is most of the world) to gaze at the screen of my smartphone when I'm supposed to be engaged in conversation with someone else. I create habits that help me overcome bad ones. And since we've all been there, I remind myself of what it feels like when you're on the other side, not being heard.

LEARNING TO LISTEN

Listening is not a God-given talent. You can train yourself, by simply practicing, to be a better listener. You can learn to tune in the important and tune out the extraneous:

- First, think how it feels when you're not being listened to. You feel ignored, unimportant. Instead of liking the other person, you think he or she is rude or self-interested. Conversely, people who feel they're being heard are easier to deal with.
- Look for signs of not listening in others and in yourself. Wandering eyes, distractions, side conversations, boredom, interruptions, doing two things at once. Practice concentrating. Work at listening. Make the person and subject at hand the most important focus in your mind. Above all, make consistent eye contact.
- Don't talk. Just make a promise to yourself to not say a word for 30 seconds. Or a minute. It doesn't sound like long until you try it.
- Don't react, listen. As soon as the other person says something, you'll want to say something back. An answer. A comeback. A correction. Wait. Take brief notes. Resist even formulating your response until the other person is finished. Then think back. Most times, what you would have said a moment ago isn't what you will say now that you've absorbed the whole thought.
- Eliminate distractions. Close your office door. Silence your smartphone. Forward your phone calls. Or, when you're on the phone, cover up the distractions on your desk such as mail and your computer screen.
- Ask questions that lead the other person to talk more, not less. For example, "Can you explain what you mean by this . . . ?" You'll frequently gain information.
- Let listening be an end in itself. Sometimes, simply hearing the other side's issues may not only enable you to find a solution, it may *be* the solution. People want to be heard. *"The pipes in the building are leaking." "The interest rate is high." "Goods are late." "The boss is mad." "There's time pressure."* A surprising number of disputes disappear once they're aired.
- Never stop listening. Everything you hear is information. All output is input.

By employing these techniques, you can create a better listening environment, one that is focused and free of distraction, much like a church confessional. There is a scene in the movie *Moonstruck* that memorably illustrates how the setting of a confessional, while subdued and almost hushed, actually enables the listener (priest) to hear through the distractions, that is, attempts by the speaker (confessor) to gloss over, or minimize, the real issue (sin). As the scene opens, Loretta enters the confessional, genuflects, and, routinely recites the familiar lead-in to what would seem to be familiar transgressions, "Forgive me father for I have sinned . . . " Then, again as routinely possible, she rattles off her sins—taking the name of the Lord in vain two times, once sleeping with her fiance's brother, once bouncing a check . . . due to a math error. The priest seems unfazed, as if these are, in fact, familiar, even modest issues, immediately forgiving the check error. But just when she thinks she pulled one over on him, he asks her about "that 'other thing' . . . " Sheepishly, she asks if he means the one about sleeping with her fiance's brother. Yes, he says, that's a pretty big one. Rather than the hushed tones of confession hiding her real sin, the quiet allows him to hear it, loud and clear, even sandwiched between two minor infractions.

Take a lesson from professional listeners—people like psychiatrists, counselors, and priests. Create your own confessional—a distraction-free environment—when you listen.

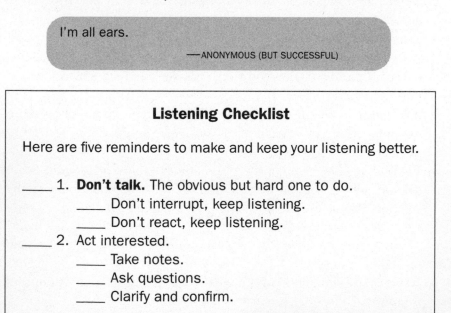

> I'm all ears.
>
> —ANONYMOUS (BUT SUCCESSFUL)

Listening Checklist

Here are five reminders to make and keep your listening better.

____ 1. **Don't talk.** The obvious but hard one to do.
    ____ Don't interrupt, keep listening.
    ____ Don't react, keep listening.
____ 2. Act interested.
    ____ Take notes.
    ____ Ask questions.
    ____ Clarify and confirm.

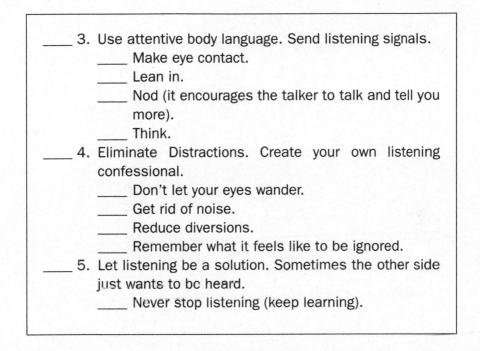

____ 3. Use attentive body language. Send listening signals.
    ____ Make eye contact.
    ____ Lean in.
    ____ Nod (it encourages the talker to talk and tell you more).
    ____ Think.

____ 4. Eliminate Distractions. Create your own listening confessional.
    ____ Don't let your eyes wander.
    ____ Get rid of noise.
    ____ Reduce diversions.
    ____ Remember what it feels like to be ignored.

____ 5. Let listening be a solution. Sometimes the other side just wants to bc heard.
    ____ Never stop listening (keep learning).

You're prepared. You've probed. And if you don't need more preparation or probing, you're ready to propose and negotiate. Not quite. Actually, you're ready to get ready to propose. Then, you'll be ready to negotiate.

REFRESHER

Chapter 6: Probe, Probe, Probe

> Research is formalized curiosity. It is poking and prying with a purpose.
>
> —ZORA NEALE HURSTON, ANTHROPOLOGIST
> AND AUTHOR

WHAT: The Probing Technique

W. What is important? What else is important? Which is most important? Why? When the other side takes a position, don't counter, ask "why?"

H. Hypothesize. This nonthreatening approach is to pose "what if . . . ?" ideas.

A. Answer questions with questions. The best answers may be questions. They could lead to more answers.

T. Tell me more. Take inventory on what you know. If you need more, go back and probe.

Overcome Probe Resistance

Restatement. "Could you give me that again?"

Show Me How. "How do you see that working?"

Says Who? "Who requires that it be done that way?"

The other side is trying to tell you how to make the deal.

If you ask the right questions and listen intently, they will give you the input you need to make the deal you want.

The Don'ts—How Not to Probe

Don't mind read. Don't assume you know the other party's position or response.

Don't offend. Don't interrogate; interview.

Don't get off track. Focus and slow down.

Listening

> Nature has given men one tongue but two ears, that we may hear from others twice as much as we speak.
>
> —EPICTETUS

- Talk so others will listen. Listen so others will talk.
- The less you say, the more you can concentrate on hearing.
- Make what you say count.
- Be an active listener—focus, take notes, ask questions.
- Eliminate distractions like the phone—and especially the smart phone.
- The less you say, the more others will remember.
- Listening isn't waiting to talk.
- What's your Interruption Quotient?

We hear what we listen for—Learn to hear through the noise.

Listening applies to friends and family as much as it does to business.

"Okay . . . I'll trade you Cal Ripken's agent and financial advisor for Kirby Puckett's marketing rep and stock broker!"

By permission of Bob Gorrell and Creators Syndicate.

CHAPTER 7

Propose–But Not Too Fast

Getting the Other Side to Go First

> Make them an offer they can't refuse.
>
> —DON CORLEONE, *THE GODFATHER*

> Patience accomplishes its object, while hurry speeds to its ruin.
>
> —SA'DI, *GULISTAN*

ROLE PLAYING

The Publisher-Agent Game

It's the year 2025. Gray-haired former politicos Al Gore and George W. Bush have retired from public life and are looking for a project to fill their days and make a few bucks. Bush has been spending time at his ranch, while Gore has been teaching stand-up comedy.

In an effort to supplement their government pensions, Al and George W. have decided to join forces and pursue an activity in which each has past experience. Not politics, but book writing. Earlier, Gore had authored *It Was All Bill Clinton's Fault*, for which he got a $1 million advance. Bush had received a hefty $2 million advance for his post-presidency autobiography, *Wow, Did My Life Turn Out Cool!* Both books had big publicity but rather disappointing sales, although each publisher was able to earn back the advance.

Now the two have agreed to collaborate on a self-help book for retirees titled *Learning to Drive—And Other Stuff You Have to Do for Yourself Now That You're Not a World Leader Anymore.*

It's up to you (a.k.a. Swifty McGuire), as the literary agent representing both Gore and Bush, to negotiate the largest advance you can get from the preferred publisher, Pretentious Press. If you and the publisher cannot reach an agreement (deadlock), the public "buzz" on the book will fade, which is bad for the authors, the agent, as well as the publisher and, ultimately, any sales.

Agent or Publisher

In our seminars, we pair up members of the audience, one as agent, one as publisher, give each guidelines, and let them play out the negotiation. You can do the same, taking the part of the agent and recruiting a friend or colleague to play the publisher. As the agent, read the section below, but not the one that follows. Your colleague will read only the instructions on the next page.

Instructions to You, the Agent, a.k.a. Swifty

You realize that while a bipartisan book collaboration is news, you have a short window in which it will remain *the* big story. (There are already daily rumors that Chelsea Clinton is about to announce her intention to seek the presidency.) You have to make a deal fast. Your clients have told you that they don't expect to make the kind of huge killing they did with their first books, but really want to share their wisdom with the world . . . and wouldn't mind making a few bucks while they're at it. Gore and Bush have said they will accept an advance as low as $250,000 each, for a total advance of $500,000.

Being a canny negotiator, you've reached an agreement with your clients that you will not receive one penny of commission for an advance of $500,000 or less. However, you will split any amounts over $500,000 on a 50–50 basis with your clients. And your entire fee will come out of the advance monies, so you will receive nothing from royalties earned by book sales.

Additionally, there is the issue of your professional reputation. If you don't close this deal, your career will be in jeopardy. To ratchet the pressure up a little further, you've just learned that your twin daughters have been admitted to the prestigious Harvard–Yale combined Med School–Law School Program with a total annual tuition of $100,000, due shortly.

Before you begin, you write down on a piece of paper (for your eyes only) the lowest advance you would accept: $_____.

Good luck.

Now have your colleague read the instructions below.

Instructions to the Publisher's Rep from Pretentious Press

You have been chosen by your employer, the publisher, to negotiate the advance on the Gore–Bush book. This is your chance to redeem yourself since you lost out on the last three coauthored blockbusters, the Jay Leno–David Letterman book, the Mark McGwire–Sammy Sosa book, and the Justin Bieber–Miley Cyrus book. Each book went on to be a runaway success, each one you had in your grasp but weren't authorized to spend big money, and you watched each get away. If you do not get this book, you think that you will be looking at a pink slip.

This time, your publisher has determined, they're not about to be beaten. They will pay top dollar for the Gore–Bush collaboration. They have given you free rein to spend up to $3 million on the advance, but not a single cent more than is absolutely necessary. To inspire you to make the best possible deal, the publisher is offering you an incentive bonus of 50 percent of every dollar below a $3 million advance.

(continued)

(*continued*)

You have your personal pressures, as well. Your twin sons have just been admitted to the combined Harvard–Yale Med School–Law School Program at a total annual tuition of $100,000, due immediately.

Before you start, write down on a piece of paper (which you will put in your pocket) the most you'd be willing to pay: $_____.

Good luck.

Okay, you're ready to play. You have 10 minutes to make this deal.

Check Your Results

1. What was the final amount of the advance paid for the book?
2. Who made the first offer, agent or publisher? How much was the initial offer?
3. Was the first offer accepted quickly? If so, what impact did this quick acceptance have on the person who made the first offer?
4. Where did each party set their sights before beginning the negotiations? Why did each of you choose that particular figure? Did you each consider the precedent of the prior advances ($2 million for Bush and $1 million for Gore)?
5. Did the two of you discuss issues other than money? For example, was there any talk regarding timing of publication, publicity obligations, book signings, or other sales promotions or incentives?
6. Did you consider pressures the other side might be facing? Did you feel your side had more pressure than the other side? If so, why?

Conclusions

- *What was the final amount paid for the book?* In our programs, the final amount paid range from $550,000 to $2,950,000. That's a $2,400,000 difference between the highest and the lowest, even though every participant goes in with the same set of ground rules. (And to think, some people say that negotiation skills don't matter.)

- *Who made the first offer, agent or publisher? How much was the initial offer?* We've discovered that the person who makes the first offer does not usually do as well in the negotiation. Many people tend to aim too low in negotiations and in this exercise, if you aim low and make the first offer, you are in trouble.

- *Was the first offer accepted quickly?* If so, what impact did this quick acceptance have on the person who made the first offer? Sometimes an agent will go through the following thought process: "I know I can accept as little as $500,000, but I am really going to go for it and make my first ask an astronomically high $600,000. I am sure we will negotiate down to $550,000 and that will be fair."

  When the agent makes the offer of $600,000, however, the publisher jumps across the table, shakes the agent's hand excitedly and says, "Wow! I'll take it. You have a deal!!" How does the agent feel at that very moment? Not very good. While the agent got $600,000 when prepared to accept $550,000, the agent has a feeling of aiming too low. The next thought the agent has is "How do I get out of this deal?"

- *Did each party set their sights "high" before beginning the negotiation?* Why did each party choose that particular figure? Did each party aim high? Did each consider the precedent of the prior advances—$2 million for Bush and $1 million for Gore? Precedents are powerful. Agents who do the best are those who "aim high" by using the prior book advances as precedents in the negotiation. "I want to be fair," says that kind of agent. "I do not want to ask for too much, because we want to work with you. We will just take the same amount that the authors were each paid for their last book—a total of $3 million." With that starting point, the agent usually settles well north of $2.5 million.

  Publishers do well by looking at the precedents in another way in order to "aim high" (or low as in the case with the publisher). "I want to be fair," says this type of publisher. "Gore's book only earned $1 million, and I do not see how this book can outearn that last one, so I would be willing to go as high as $1 million for this book." People often ask us, how high should we go? We tell them to aim *reasonably high*. What is reasonable? Any offer that is supported by a past precedent. Find the precedent that best supports your goals and use that to justify your aiming high.

- *Did the two parties discuss issues other than money?* For example, was there any talk regarding timing of publication, publicity obligations, book signings, or other sales incentives? Although the agent and the publisher are only compensated on the advance, other issues such as royalty payments, timing of the book's release, and marketing budget are often brought into the negotiations. These may not be the main deal points, but effective negotiators know how to get what they want at the table; it is often good to put many more things on the table.

- *Did you consider pressures the other side might be facing?* Did you feel your side had more pressure than the other side? If so, why? Sometimes after the exercise, the agent will say, "It is not fair. All of the pressure was on me!"

The publisher typically responds, "What do you mean the pressure was on you? The pressure was on me!" What they then realize is that both of them had the same amount of pressure: Both of their jobs were in jeopardy. Both had kids in college. Both tended to think the weight of the world was on their shoulders and never thought about what pressures that might exist on the other side.

Remember, in negotiations, we tend to overestimate our own weaknesses, and we fail to think about the difficulties faced by the other side. In your preparation, you should think about what weaknesses the other side might face, and then, during your probe, you should seek to clarify what these weaknesses are.

PROPOSING FOR REAL

Dean Jernigan, Then-Chairman, STORAGE USA—National Self-Storage Company—Tells This "Make the First Offer" Story

STORAGE USA had abandoned plans for a storage site on the Mississippi River and put the piece of property up for sale. Its original purchase price had been $3 million. But since then, the property had sat, unused and undeveloped, for years. One day, a potential buyer from a Los Angeles entertainment company asked for a meeting. Dean Jernigan sent the company's lawyer to negotiate the deal with explicit instructions. "Let them make the first offer, but take nothing less than $4 million."

> The prospective buyer started the meeting with a simple statement. "We are not going to negotiate. Our offer is $20 million and if you are not willing to accept it, we are prepared to walk." It turned out, the entertainment company was betting on a future legalized gambling boom to increase land values and, therefore, thought $20 million was a "fair" price. Of course, so did STORAGE USA's lawyer who only had one regret. He hadn't handled the case on a contingency basis.

Here's a book negotiation in which I was the real agent making a deal with real world publishers.

The Cal Ripken, Jr., Book Deal

As Cal Ripken's consecutive game streak started to edge toward record levels—after he passed 1,200 games, then 1,500, and 1,700—people would approach Cal, through me, to ask if he would write a book about his career. Each time they asked me, I asked Cal. And each time, he said, "No, Ron, not yet." He didn't want anything to interrupt his full concentration on his job or detract from his ability to perform on the field, game after game.

After he passed the 1,800-game mark, I asked him about a book again. Again, he said, "No, Ron, not yet." The last thing he wanted to do was write about a consecutive game streak because he didn't play for a streak. He played every game because, in Cal's own words, it's "the only way I know." Even after he played in 2,000 games, and people came to me to ask about the book, Cal still said, "No, Ron, not yet."

Then, on September 5, 1995, Cal Ripken, Jr., played in his 2,131st consecutive baseball game, breaking Iron Man Lou Gehrig's record. When the streak was formally announced, in the fifth inning, the sellout crowd at Camden Yards rose spontaneously and erupted into a 50,000-fan cheer. (The notables and celebrities in attendance are too numerous to list, but among those standing and cheering was the President of the United States.) After 10 solid minutes of ovation, Cal's teammates literally pushed him out of the dugout and onto the field to fulfill the fans' need to see their hero. Still, they wouldn't quiet down. Finally, in an effort to satisfy the roaring, clapping, stomping crowd, Cal lapped the field, waving and smiling to the fans. When he came around the third base side of the field, just above the Orioles dugout, he leaned over to my box, hugged me, and whispered in my ear, "Okay, Ron, now."

Okay, maybe I embellished a little when it came to the whispered statement. Just the same, it was after Cal's record-breaking feat that we began to pursue the book in earnest. First, we narrowed the field of publishers down to the two we thought best.

We had a favorite but we wanted a solid alternate candidate to strengthen our position and increase our bargaining power. I made appointments in New York with both, scheduling the favorite first thing in the morning and the other for a lunch meeting. I wanted to be able to honestly say to the first publisher, "We have to leave for a meeting with another publisher."

Before the meetings I prepared, researching precedents of the advances paid to sports figures and other superstars for this type of mega-book. I found that for sports stars, the up-front money for such a book was in the $500,000 range. We knew, in Cal, we had someone who was a star even among stars so we set our sights high and decided to ask for $700,000.

But rather than walk in and say, "We want $700,000," we went to the meeting, asked questions, listened, and waited for the publisher to put a figure on the table. We followed the first rule we'll deal with in this chapter: *Don't make the first offer*. We said, "You're the experts; you know the market. We just know baseball. You tell us." *The first publisher's initial offer was $750,000.*

Imagine if we had gone first. What if we had crossed our fingers and said, "Gee, we want $700,000." We'd have already left $50,000 on the table and this was only their opening offer. So, when they said $750,000, did I leap across the table, shake their hands, grin from ear to ear and say, "Deal!"? No. We followed the second rule we'll talk about in this chapter. *Don't (immediately) accept the first offer.* If I had jumped at that first offer, what do you think the publisher would have thought? Buyer's remorse. "Uh-oh, I paid too much." And if I had jumped at the offer, I also might never have learned what our potential was. I took a lesson from Hank Peters when he sat across from me in the Brooks Robinson deal. I said to the publisher, "I'll get back to you."

We went to the second meeting, with the second publisher, and learned that it too, had a high interest. It appeared they would be willing to pay as much or more than the first publishing house. But, since we maintained our leaning toward the first, we didn't even push for a detailed offer from the second. Instead, we used our time to think and plan our next step.

When we got back to Baltimore from New York to take stock of our situation, we discovered that Cal's endorsement and licensing value was skyrocketing daily. Hundreds of inquiries and offers were pouring in. Realizing that Cal Ripken's market value was reaching extraordinary levels, we revised our goal to a $1 million book advance, double what the precedents had indicated.

It so happened that the editor from the publishing house was an old friend. I suppose I could have said to her, *"We know each other. Let's not play games. Let's* *not beat around the bush. We want $1 million.*" But I recognized human nature, even among old friends. (And I didn't succumb to the temptation to go right to the bottom line, which we too often do out of fear of rejection.) Instead, we formulated our counteroffer to their opener of $750,000 and asked for $1,250,000. And we never forgot the proverb that says, "Many things are lost for want of asking," and followed the third rule of this chapter: *Aim high.*

Eventually we signed a deal with the $1 million advance we wanted (plus some assistance to the Ripken Foundation). The negotiation for Cal's book was a textbook example of the third P: Propose. We didn't make the first offer. We didn't grab their first offer. We aimed high.

THE THREE RULES BEHIND PROPOSE

Try Not to Make the First Offer

When the other side does make the first offer, you can learn from them going first. You have a goal in mind. You expect to have to work your way up to it. But, the other side may meet or exceed it with their first offer. You might even be able to revise your expectations further upward as the negotiations continue. If you had gone first, you might have set your sights too low.

If you get a low offer, even if it's far less than you hoped for, now you have a floor, a minimum from which to build. In fact, a low offer may suggest you try to achieve your goals creatively. Let's say you wanted to sell a business for a given price but the other side's initial offer is so low it's apparent, no matter how much you can inch it up, the purchase price alone won't be enough.

Maybe you should pursue different or faster payment terms, retaining ownership, noncash remuneration such as in-kind services or other goods, or other imaginative ways to reach your goals. The knowledge you gain by the other side opening the bidding is invaluable in determining the course of the negotiation.

Don't (Immediately) Accept Their First Offer

If you grab the first offer, the other side's first thought is likely to be that they offered too much, too good a deal, too high a price, too something.

Since you are in the process of negotiating, they'll start finding ways to "unoffer" what they offered, to add conditions, subtract payment, to work their way down to where they're more comfortable.

How Well Do You Propose When You Negotiate?

When I negotiate, I . . .	Circle One		
• Encourage the other side to make the first offer.	Always	Sometimes	Never
• Resist jumping at the first offer in my acceptable range.	Always	Sometimes	Never
• Aim high (doesn't hurt to ask).	Always	Sometimes	Never
• Try to increase the pie so everyone gains.	Always	Sometimes	Never
• Try not to make concessions just to get the deal done.	Always	Sometimes	Never
• Avoid reflex reactions to rejected offers.	Always	Sometimes	Never
• Negotiate points totally, not individually.	Always	Sometimes	Never

If five or more of your answers were "Always," you have good propose habits and this chapter will hone them further. (If all of your answers were "Always," c'mon.)
If four or more of your answers were "Sometimes" or "Never," this chapter will immediately improve your next negotiation.
If three or more of your answers were "Never," read this chapter as fast as possible!

And chances are, their first offer is not their best offer. Wait a little. Let the negotiations play out. Ask questions. Suggest alternatives. Counter. You'll soon see how far they are able to go. You'll learn which parts of their offer are flexible and which are immovable. The very worst you can do, assuming their offer is still on the table, is end up where they started. You can accept their first offer later, not immediately, after you know it's the best you can do.

Set Your Aspirations High

If you expect little, you are liable to reach your goals. *I'm losing money on this building. If I could just get what I paid and get out, I'd be relieved.* Fine. But what if the building is worth more to someone else than it is to you?

If you set your expectations higher, you'll often reach them. Say you're selling ad space in a program and the deadline is approaching, but you still have one page unsold. Aim low and you're just looking for anyone who's willing to buy that last page at any reasonable price. Aim high and you have a virtually sold-out program with only one page left. Who will pay enough to get it? Negotiators who ask for more, get more.

Caution: It's not enough to aim high; you must *ask* high—not arbitrarily, but with reason (use precedents). Have you ever set a high goal in your mind, only to reduce that goal the moment you got to the negotiation table because you were afraid of rejection? We all have. When faced with this situation, write down on your Preparation Checklist the old English proverb, "Much is lost for want of asking." When the time comes to make your offer or "ask," reread that statement and bolster your confidence. There's no reason to fear that rejection. At worst, you'll be where you are now. At best, who knows? And, further build your confidence by scripting.

Scripting—the 3 Ds

Experience has taught me that no matter how well I know what I want to propose, a little extra effort in Scripting, via the process of the **3 Ds**—Draft, Devil's Advocate, Deliver—is a real difference maker.

I remember as a young agent being prepared but winging a proposal. And after doing so, echoing the mental refrain that many of us have heard, said: "*Why did I say that?*"

I knew about aiming high—to get a $1 million contract I had to make an ask of $1.25 million. The other side was going to counter and allowing that negotiating room was essential to protecting my bottom-line number. Yet when I sat at the table with other side, whether because of fear of rejection or desire not to be viewed as overreaching, I would end up saying something like, "We can do this deal for $1.25 million . . . but certainly not a penny less

(continued)

(continued)

than $1 million." Because of my verbal retreat the other side was already contemplating a number less than $1 million. So I ultimately developed a process of "drafting" what I wanted to say, letting my associate or partner "devil's advocate" and ultimately practicing my "delivery."

As a result, I became comfortable with the message and made the ask with a level of confidence and conviction so that the other side didn't sense a retreat.

Having learned from my mistakes, I trained myself to speak confidently, especially when making a high request, by developing and adhering to an "aim high" script. I wrote down what I wanted to say, made corrections with the help of associates, studied my notes, rehearsed them, and then delivered the ask confidently with the comfort gained by my preparation and empowered by scripting utilizing the 3 Ds.

I scripted myself out of feeling the regret of "why did I say that." In fact I came to feel so strongly about the power of scripting that in 2013 I wrote a book on just that topic: *Perfecting Your Pitch: How to Succeed in Business and in Life by Finding Words That Work* (New York: Hudson Street Press, 2013).

Encouraging the Other Side to Make the First Offer

How do you get them to go first, especially when they want you to go first? And how do you do it without ending up in a verbal standoff?

"You go first!"

"No, you go first!"

"No way. I asked you to go first, first!"

- *Defer to the other side's expertise.* They may have more experience in the category than you do. Instead of being intimidated, use that to your advantage to gain knowledge. *"You're in the real estate business. I'm a manufacturer who happens to own one piece of property that my business no longer needs. You tell me what an industrial park site of this size is worth."* Use their experience as a basis for fairness or objectivity. *"You've done more deals of this type than we have. What are the going terms in similar deals? What's fair?"*
- *Turn discussions into offers.* Once you start talking, the other side is likely to give enough information to suggest an offer even if they don't

make one formally. Probe their thoughts, fleshing out more and more details. Then paraphrase what they've said as an offer. *"What I hear you saying is that you would be willing to pay in the neighborhood of $2 million if all the conditions were acceptable. Is that about right?"* Or ask them to restate what they've said in terms that constitute a proposal. *"You've mentioned a lot of interesting possibilities and options. Can you summarize them for me?"* By requesting help and putting it in the form of a question, you've created a nonthreatening "offer." The other side has a way out if they're uncomfortable but a way in to start negotiations in earnest.

- *Force a counteroffer bid.* If it appears there's nowhere to go in the negotiations, ask the other side where they *want* to go. *"You say the list price is too steep. What price can you afford?"* If you have to make the first offer, don't bid against yourself. Try to extract a counteroffer from the other side. *"I hear you saying you're not prepared to meet our terms. Is the problem in the area of overall price, payment schedule, or delivery?"*

- *Make a tangential first offer.* Offer something important the other side wants in exchange for something more important to you. *"We know your company wants to ship fast while the produce is fresh. We can take delivery immediately, if the price per pound is right."* As response to your tangential offer to accept delivery, you're now in a position to hear from the other side what amounts to the first real offer, price.

- *Engage in exploratory conversations.* Use exploratory conversations to learn what the other side expects. *"Say, I've heard houses in this neighborhood sell for as little as $200,000."* No risk. It's just what you've "heard." See what kind of response you get. *"Yes, but we put a $25,000 kitchen in ours."* Suddenly, your nonoffer, conversation-starter may result in the other side making an opening offer of $225,000.

Now that you've gotten the other side to either make the first offer, or communicate the elements of that offer, how do you respond? How do you counter?

MAKING COUNTERPROPOSALS

Once the other side states their position, it's frequently difficult to get them to move. Abandoning a position looks like weakness. It feels like losing. If you have determined their real interests during the probe phase, you can focus on those interests and demonstrate why it's in their best interest to modify their position. That may sound like sleight-of-hand but it's not a matter of fast-talking or putting one over on the other side. If it is not in their interest to change their position, they won't change. If it is in their best interest but they don't know it is, they won't change. Only if it is in their best interest and they come to believe that it is will they change. That's not easy to accomplish, but you can **Trade, Remove,** and **Increase.**

- **Trade.** Look for an interest to trade with the other side. Consider two basic types of trades you can make:
  1. *Horse trading* is when you exchange items, terms, or deal-points of similar worth.
  2. *Value swapping* is trading something you value less for something you value more.
     Your perception of value will not always be the same as the other side's perception. You may place great importance on something that is insignificant to them and vice versa. What's important when you trade is that you have something they want which you give up for something you want. You both gain.
     Let's say you sell Szechwan Drive-Thru franchises. The prospective franchisee wants an exclusive territory for its units. You don't want to give exclusivity; you want as many franchisees with as many units in an area as possible. But this particular dealer is well capitalized and requires no financing. She'll either buy ten of your units or, if she can't get the terms she wants, five of yours and five of your competitor, Hunan Drive-Thru. You offer her territory exclusivity in trade for her promise of franchise exclusivity to Szechwan Drive-Thrus only.
- **Remove.** Try to identify barriers you can remove to help the other side. Again, consider two forms this may take:
  1. *Remove pain*. If the other side is currently being harmed, seek ways to ease or stop the pain.
     You represent a limited partnership trying to buy a breathtakingly beautiful mountain resort from a visionary architect-developer teetering on bankruptcy. Your group has the assets to make the deal but needs time simply because of the number of members in the partnership who have to agree. The visionary is under pressure from

his lenders and is paying exorbitant interest on a short-term loan. He has to make a deal yesterday. Your group can't act that fast. But they can put up the cash to pay off his short-term loan, thereby taking the time pressure off the deal.

You've removed the pain, allowing the deal to go forward.

2. *Reduce a risk*. You may obtain a more favorable deal by removing a risk facing the other side.

A grand old civic theater wants your professional stage management company to take over the booking and running of the house. They're willing to give you a share of the profits when you bring in touring shows. But, as a civic organization, they can't gamble on shows that can lose money. In exchange for a higher share of the profits, when and if they occur, you offer the theater a no-risk, no-loss management contract.

- **Increase.** If you can increase the rewards of a transaction for the other side, you can increase the chances of making the deal. Two routes to greater rewards are:

1. *Provide potential*. Increasing potential rewards of a transaction may help close the deal. Instead of just making a deal for today, you may consider a deal in which both parties stand to make more tomorrow. You can agree to become partners and share the future payoff when it comes.

For instance, you're interested in a high-priced piece of speculative property—supposedly due to triple in value when the new highway goes through and retail zoning passes. You offer to pay 75 percent of today's asking price but agree to give the seller 25 percent of any profit you realize from the greatly increased selling price of the property after the highway and rezoning. The seller gets less than they wanted now but the possibility of much more later.

2. *Increase pie*. Finding ways to make the entire pie bigger may entice the other side.

You own a minor league baseball team. Across the table is the owner of an empty stadium. Together, you two can do business. But the city, whose land the stadium leases, has a restriction against night games. Without night games, you can't draw as many fans so the stadium owner can't get as much rent. Instead of the two of you driving a harder and harder bargain with each other, bring the city in as a third partner and perhaps you can all make out better.

Sometimes in counterproposals, as in life, you have to make concessions.

How you do it can make all the difference. When you are proposing or counterproposing, the fact is, sometimes you have to concede something. Nevertheless, rather than 'giving the farm away' we use a technique for getting something in return when you give up something. It is a three-step process, defined by three rules based on human nature.

Rule 1. Cochran's Law of Deflation

The first rule, developed by my partner, Jeff Cochran, is that Satisfaction equals Reality over Expectations (S=R/E).

S, or Satisfaction level, can be manipulated by the equation of Reality over Expectations. Unfortunately, we cannot control the other side's Reality, but we can deflate their Expectations.

Application:

Let's say you have some wiggle room on price and the customer demands a discount. You can lower their expectations for that lower price by saying something like:

"Gee, that will be tough," or "I don't know if I will be able to do that,"
or "A discount may be hard in this case."

Rule 2. Transition to Munger's Law of Justification

Once you have deflated their expectations, you will want to give them a reason behind the lowering, so we move to the second Law—Munger's Law of Justification.

Charlie Munger, Warren Buffett's business partner, once gave a speech in which he discussed a university study that was simple in nature but profound in its result. The study had an actor approach a line of people waiting to make copies at a copier with various reasonings for his cutting in line.

1. The actor said: "Can I cut in line?" and no one let him do it.

2. The actor said: "Can I cut in line *because I need to make copies*." Some people let him cut even though, obviously, everybody in that line was there to make copies.

3. The actor said: "Can I cut in line because my boss is late and needs these copies now?" and several more people allowed him to cut in line.

4. The actor said: "Can I cut in line because I only have to make one copy and my boss really needs the copy now?" almost everyone let him cut in line.

Munger's Law of Justification is that people are willing to accept bad news as long is there is justification for it (even weak justification rationalized by simply using the word "because"). The better the justification—the more likely it will be received positively.

Application:

If you started by deflating the customer's expectations, *"That will be tough,"* you would follow that statement with something like:

> " . . . because I have a very thin profit margin to begin with . . . ," or
> " . . . because our pricing is well established on this product . . . ," or
> " . . . because we have to be equitable with other similar customers who pay our set price . . . ."

Rule 3. Cialdini's Law of Reciprocation

"The final step is to ask for something in return"—Cialdini's Law of Reciprocation.

Robert Cialdini wrote a classic book called *The Psychology of Influence,* which described another simple experiment that proves that people are more likely to give you something if they have already received something first.

The experiment was to send 1,000 randomly selected people a holiday greeting card. Of those 1,000 people, how many people would you think then sent a return card even though they did not know who Cialdini was? Ten percent? Twenty percent? In fact, more than 400 people sent him a card, over 40 percent, proving that people are more likely to give you something if they have already received something from you.

Application:

So you have Deflated their Expectations ("That will be tough . . . ") and Justified why lowering the price will be hard for you to do (" . . . because I

(continued)

(continued)

have a very thin margin to begin with . . . "). Now you are positioned to Ask for a Trade:

> " . . . but if I were able to drop the price somewhat, would you be willing to sign a longer term contract . . . ," or " . . . would you do your own engineering . . . ," or " . . . would you accept a higher price on the ???"

Tie All Three Laws Together in a Model

Tie them together with language like this:

Customer (to you): *"Joe, thanks for calling me back. I need a quote from you by the end of the week."* (Note: It may be normal and possible for you to give them the quote by then, but they do not know that so use that as leverage.)

You (to Customer): *"Fred, that's going to be difficult for me to do (deflation) . . . because we are trying to give the best response possible to your RFP and that may take longer than the end of the week . . . (justification) . . . but if I am able to pull the resources together on my end to get the response to you, would you be willing to consider giving me the last look if we are not one of the finalists?"* (Ask for trade.)

REFRESHER

Chapter 7: Propose—But Not Too Fast

Three Rules of Propose

1. Try not to make the first offer.
2. Don't (immediately) accept their first offer.
3. Set your aspirations high—with reason.

   Script—*draft, devil's advocate, deliver*

> Remember: Much is lost for want of asking.

Encourage the Other Side to Make the First Offer

- *Defer to their expertise.* "You've been in this business much longer than we have...."
- *Turn discussions into offers.* The other side often gives enough information to constitute an offer. Listen, then paraphrase what they've said as an offer.
- *Force a counteroffer.* If they think the terms are too steep, ask what they'd like.

Don't bid against yourself.

- *Make a tangential offer first.* Offer something important to the other side, but not so important to yours.
- *Engage in exploratory conversations.* Explore highs and lows and look for a response.

Making Counterproposals

Trade: Look for an interest to trade with the other side.

Remove: Try to take barriers away. Remove pain and reduce risk.

Increase: Find ways to increase the rewards of the deal. Provide potential (upside). Increase the pie (more for everyone).

When considering concessions, don't forget the Three Rules: Cochran's Law of Deflation, Munger's Law of Justification, and Cialdini's Law of Reciprocation.

"So now we deal mano a mano, as it were."

CHAPTER 8

Difficult Negotiators

> Whenever two people meet, there are six people present. There is each man as he sees himself, each man as the other person sees him, and each man as he really is.
>
> —William James, psychologist

We've all dealt with difficult negotiators. In the movie *Swimming with Sharks*, Kevin Spacey played the classic, arrogant Hollywood mogul, Buddy Ackerman. In a scene that begins as a simple office conversation/negotiation by his assistant, Guy, wishing to be treated with a bit more civility (following an alleged mistake), Ackerman escalates it into a verbal dismemberment of his underling. Ackerman sarcastically offers that everyone is entitled to make a mistake, and now that Guy made his mistake, he has used up his quota. When Guy has the temerity to suggest that he didn't actually do anything wrong and doesn't think he should be yelled at, again Ackerman continues his scorching derision—a mock apology for hurting Guy's feelings and an equally hollow compliment to Guy for fostering office communication. Ackerman then closes the door and finishes shredding Guy, no holds barred. He tells Guy that his thoughts, feelings, opinions, in fact, his very existence on earth, are meaningless; he isn't worth flushing in a toilet; he isn't as important as Ackerman's pencils or pens or paperclips, all of which he throws at Guy's head. Guy finally, meekly backs out the door, Ackerman mimicking (and yelling) Guy's request not to be yelled at, then smugly straightening his tie and returning to work—in power, in control—the poster boy for difficult negotiators.

What a despicable guy! He's so smug, so crude, so cruel. Aren't you glad you don't have to deal with him? But you do. That scene may be from the entertainment business, but difficult negotiators are everywhere. They just have different names, wear different clothes, make different demands, and have different styles. If only they didn't exist, negotiating would be so much more pleasant. But they do exist. You can either ignore that reality or learn who they are, what makes them tick, and how to deal with them effectively.

...AND THE AWARD FOR MOST DIFFICULT NEGOTIATOR GOES TO ...

In the course of a career, you'll deal with so many kinds of difficult negotiators, you'll be hard pressed to name the single most difficult. But to tell you the truth, in my case, it wasn't a sports team owner or a corporate titan or a political power broker. It was an elderly man who owned a farm.

The Old Man and the Farm

A real estate client called me some years ago with a real challenge. He and his partners were well on their way toward developing a new community by buying up large tracts of farmland. They had acquired 172 farms that would comprise the tract. They had made good progress with the local county as far as zoning and planning ingress and egress from the highway. The only problem was the 173rd farm, which they had not acquired, and just happened to be situated on a stretch of highway that would be the link to the entire community.

I asked the obvious question, "How could you get so far along without the key piece of property?"

His response will strike a familiar chord with any of us who've been down the road with a deal and suddenly faced an obstacle we should have seen earlier. "I thought it wouldn't be a problem."

I asked, "Can you change the pattern of the roads leading in and out?"

He said, "Maybe, but it could take another six months or more." Projects like this need momentum. When they take too long, the momentum slows and the project dies. He needed to act now. He asked if I could try to intercede and negotiate to acquire the farm right away.

I started with preparation. I asked him all the questions I could to give me background. Is it an active farm? What's the owner like? Is he well off? How long has the farm been in his family? Is he married? Does he have children? My real estate client told me everything he knew. The farmer was 83 and a widower. The farm had been in his family four or five generations. The farmer had three children but they didn't live on the farm. As far as my client could tell, the farmer did not have a lot of cash and this active farm was his most valuable asset.

I said, "Okay, I'll try to negotiate for you. But if you turn this over to me, I need leeway. I need to have control over what the farmer is paid and the terms of the deal."

My client said, "If you can make a deal, do it whatever way you can." It was clear they needed a deal badly.

Did I go right over to see the man and make him an offer? No. I did more preparation so I could be ready with a strategy. I found out that not only was the farmer an old man who lived alone, but he wasn't the nicest person in the world, either. In fact, he was widely perceived to be a very nasty fellow. He didn't like to talk to people. He was known to throw sticks at anyone who set foot on his land. The word was, nobody could even get near him, let alone sit down and negotiate. I started to get a picture of him and I let it sink in. I identified him as a "situationally difficult" person—someone whose conduct was triggered by circumstances impacting his life. (For a full discussion on identifying the three types of difficult negotiators—situationally, strategically, and simply—see my book, *Bullies, Tyrants, and Impossible People*, Crown Business, 2005.)

I strategized—I wrote a note to myself on my pad: "Four or five visits. Do little or nothing on the first couple of visits." Why did I write that down? Because I could tell this negotiation was going to be like a marathon. I would have to pace myself. My client might be in a hurry, but I'd have to proceed at just the right tempo if we had any chance of making this deal.

Was it worth that kind of time and effort on my part? Yes. My client would lose millions of dollars already invested, as well as the enthusiasm and trust of his coinvestors for future deals. On the other hand, if, somehow, this deal could be pulled off, everyone stood to gain.

I'll never forget the day I finally drove out to see the old farmer. It was thirteen miles north of where I live, many miles north of where most people live, truly the heart of farm country. I came to a long gravelly driveway and made my way down, looking around the whole time for flying sticks. I walked up to this old farmhouse, onto the porch, and there, next to the front door was—yes, I swear—a shotgun. My client told me all kinds of things about this guy but he never mentioned a shotgun. Well, I figured, at least it's where I can see it. (I'm an incurable optimist.) I reached for the bell, which was the old-fashioned kind you turn. It rang but there was no answer. I turned it again. More rings, no answer. I was in about my third midturn when the door flew open and this grizzled old character yelled, "What the hell is going on? Who the hell are you? What do you want? Get off my damn porch." And that's the printable version. He tore me apart for a good five minutes, using every four-letter word I'd ever heard.

What did I do? Did I give it right back to him? No, I counted. As Thomas Jefferson said, when you're upset, count to 10, and when you're really upset count to 100. I got well past 100. But I followed the number one rule in dealing with difficult negotiators. *Don't get emotional.* Neutralize your emotions. Let the other person get emotional, but don't let their emotion get you emotional. *Don't take it personally and don't get personal.* I just kept counting. (By the way, the same applies at home. When your spouse or significant other is upset, it's rarely a personal attack. It may feel personal and it's tempting to get personal back when it feels that way. But usually, your partner is dealing with something or someone other than you and it's carrying over into your life together.)

Back to the farmer: He finally ran out of breath and four-letter words. When he did, I didn't say anything about buying or selling or making deals. I said, "You've got a nice farm here." He laid into me all over again, unloading another barrage of salty language. At his next pause, I said, "I live on a farm, too." I handed him my card and said, "I'll see you again," turned my back, prayed he didn't pick up the shotgun, walked to my car, and drove home.

Four days later, I came back. There was the shotgun next to the door. I rang. He came out. He let me have it again. But he stopped a little sooner this time (unless it was my optimism again). I then said, "I live on a 170-acre farm. Yours is over 500 acres. How do you handle it?" He just looked at me and didn't speak. I repeated my question, "How do you handle it?" He stared at me for a while. Then he told me about this cooperative that existed in the north part of the county that helped him.

What I was doing was "sailing" with the old man, not literally, but figuratively. If you sail, you know if you want to move forward, you can't sail directly into the wind. You have to sail at angles to the wind, from side to side, working your way forward. You're tacking. That's what I was doing with the farmer, not going directly at him with my demands, but moving from side to side, asking apparently unrelated questions. It takes patience and, though tacking is not the shortest distance between two points, it's often a far more effective way to control the encounter than making a direct assault.

The farmer and I talked a little more about his concerns with farming, the pressures, where he needed help, and how difficult it is to run a farm. I was empathizing with him and could understand his problems and he could tell that I did. After a while, I said, "I'll see you again." That was the whole conversation on my second visit.

I came back a third time, continued to empathize and acknowledged some more of his concerns. I said, "I understand this farm has been in your family for four or five generations. I suppose you really would like to give it to your children." He looked at me, wondering where this was leading. I went on asking questions, "You've got three kids and I have seven. My older ones are spread all over the country. Yours are too, right?" I could tell by looking at him, I was touching on something that he felt. We were bonding, only a little, but still bonding. I asked if he thought his kids would come back and live on the farm. He said he doubted it but he still wanted to leave it to them. He said, "It belongs in our family."

That's when I started negotiations. I responded, "I know you own this land, but unless you have a lot of money, you're not going to give this place to your children." He got hot. Who was I to tell him he couldn't leave his farm to his own children? I said, "I'm not your lawyer. Do you have a lawyer?" He said he did. I asked if he had talked to his lawyer about his estate. He said, "I haven't talked to him about anything for years!" I suggested he talk to his lawyer about the difficulty of giving the farm to his children. Then I changed the subject to cattle. I asked him about raising and slaughtering cattle. Shortly after, I left.

On my fourth visit, by the time I got up to the house, he was asking me questions. First, he told me the lawyer said I was right. He didn't have the cash it would take to cover the taxes. I told him I wasn't an estate lawyer and he should consult one. The lawyer, in turn, told him that since his wife was deceased, he couldn't get a marital deduction and if he gave it to his kids he'd be taxed brutally.

That's when he asked me what I'd give him for the farm. Four visits later, after being hollered at, after counting, after talking about farms and children and estate taxes, we were finally talking about a deal. Tacking was paying off.

I told him he'd be paid more than any other neighboring farmer had been paid, "You will get what's called 'most favored nations' treatment." I told him it was because he'd been through tough times and had good reason to hold back in selling. He would get paid a dollar more than the highest amount paid anyone else. His eyes lit up.

Was it enough to just give him more than anyone else? Is that the secret to winning over the situationally difficult negotiator? Just give them a little more? No. You have to give them something else, something that acknowledges their particular concerns or needs. They want to win and the best way to get what you want is to help them get what they want. We needed to enable the old man to recognize the value of dealing with us but also save face—so we could accomplish our objectives.

What could we do here? He wanted to keep the farm and stay in his house. We let him. We paid him handsomely for 570 acres of his 581-acre farm. We gave him the 11 acres surrounding the house and worked around it. My client could develop and build access roads and still leave him alone. Of course, we might need to use his parcel some day but the reality was, he was 83. We leased it to him for five years with a five-year option at $1.00 a year. It was WIN–win. We liked the deal. He liked the deal. He must have because he never once picked up the shotgun.

DEALING WITH THE DIFFICULT NEGOTIATOR (WITHOUT BECOMING ONE)

Let's take a recreation break. If you play golf or tennis and you get angry and then hit the ball, where does it go? Into the net? Into the trees? It tends to go everywhere except where you want it to go. It may feel good for a moment to let your frustrations out on the tennis or golf ball, but the results are usually terrible. The same holds for negotiation. It may feel good to lash out (or lash back) at the difficult negotiator, but if you do, the negotiation tension will likely escalate, possibly to a full-scale war. Remember, in golf, tennis, and negotiation, when you let your frustrations out, the results are usually terrible.

When I'm angry, I count to ten before I speak. When I'm very angry, I count to one hundred.

—THOMAS JEFFERSON

Neutralize Your Emotions: Don't Take It Personally—Don't Get Personal

Difficult negotiators' conduct may seem unfair, inflammatory, provocative, even mean. They use or display these emotional approaches that put you in an emotional—less rational, less measured, more volatile and vulnerable—state. They can cause you to lose focus on your game plan. If you do, you're prone to make mistakes. Therefore, I always remind myself, "Don't take it personally—don't get personal."

A Full Court Emotional and Psychological Press

Former Chicago Bulls and Los Angeles Lakers coach (and current New York Knicks president) Phil Jackson, in a story in *INC. Magazine*, discussed teaching his players to deal with emotional and psychological attacks. Rather than succumb to the temptation to strike back emotionally or physically, he drilled them in the art of refocusing on the game they were playing every time they were attacked. When the Bulls played the Pistons in the late 1980s—a team notorious for their outrageous tactics—Detroit often won because they could incite the Bulls into fighting back, thereby losing concentration. When the Bulls learned to control their desire to strike back and turn it into focus, they changed the outcome of the games. Jackson stated, "Everybody on our team was slammed around . . . players were tackled, tripped, elbowed, and smacked in the face. But they all laughed it off. The Pistons didn't know how to respond. We completely disarmed them by not striking back. At that moment, our players became true champions."

Be Prepared

The more difficult the negotiator, the more prepared you should be. Before I met with the old farmer, I used my research about him to determine the cause of his being difficult and to formulate a strategy for dealing with him—multiple meetings, tacking, finding common ground. Know what to do before the situations occur and you can overcome the most difficult negotiators without reverting to becoming one of them.

Take a Time-Out

People are reactive creatures, not computerized responders. Be conscious of your human tendencies and you've taken the first step toward staying calm in the face of provocation.

Don't respond to emotion with emotion. That's easy to say, not so easy to do. After all, you've just been bombarded, even if only verbally. One way to assure you won't have an emotional response to an emotional prod is to have no response—take a time-out.

Slow Down

Take your time. Again, start counting. Or stop the process altogether and *call a time-out*. Ask for a break. Go to the bathroom. Get coffee. Do anything that interrupts the emotional momentum. Emotion tends to build on itself. Break the chain and the emotion recedes. It's amazing how the expression, the demand, or the challenge that causes a visceral reflex loses its bite even 30 seconds later. It's even less upsetting after a few more minutes. Write it down. That will make it even less emotional. Look at the words and the meaning. Ask yourself what the other side was *trying* to get you to do. As soon as you start to analyze it, you begin to defuse your emotions and move toward rational action.

Controlling a Situationally Difficult Encounter—Tacking

As demonstrated in the story of *The Old Man and the Farm*, tacking can be an invaluable negotiation tool. When sailors meet strong headwinds, they tack, turning the ship at an angle to the wind, moving forward in zigs and zags, rather than confronting the force and being rebuffed. Sailors are patient. They don't have engines, only nature. But they inevitably get where they're going. To get where you want to go in negotiation, use the tools of tacking.

1. *Empathize: Understand their pressures.* Why is the difficult negotiator being difficult? Maybe the person is just plain unpleasant, one of those social misfits who doesn't like anyone and lets it show. Maybe, but chances are there are other forces at work. Someone or something is applying pressure on them: There's an unreasonable but unseen boss in the background. Or they just hate this kind of task. Or they had a deal like this once before and it went bad. Or there's a deadline looming. Or there are financial issues at home. *Something else* is applying pressure.

> I do believe that in order to be a successful negotiator that as a diplomat, you have to be able to put yourself into the other person's shoes. Unless you can understand what is motivating them, you are never going to be able to figure out how to solve a particular problem.
>
> —Madeleine Albright

2. *Ask Questions.* Start tacking by asking questions that may reveal the real reason for their behavior. Instead of attacking the deal or the dealmaker, probe into the surrounding issues. The moment you get an answer, you begin to mute the emotional fervor. You'll find yourselves discussing unpleasant bosses, the negotiation process, other deals, deadlines, or your personal lives.

3. *Respond: Acknowledge their concerns.* Once you know some of the issues or pressure points affecting the other side, continue tacking

by letting them know that you have some of your own issues as well. Joke about those bosses of yours. Share stories about your past deals. Commiserate on the ticking clock of deadlines. Tell them you've got bills to pay, too; who doesn't? Simply acknowledging their concerns may turn the heat down. Then you can return to the issues of the deal as people who share the same or similar concerns.

As you finalize your response, consider letting them save face as a part of the solution. (This is how tacking often concludes.) Just as I did in the situation with the old man, craft solutions that the other side can justify to themselves or those they answer to. Satisfy their need to win by conceding a less significant point. Address the issues behind their issues and they can walk away with a victory or the appearance of a victory. You don't need the trappings of a win as long as you get what you came for.

A Case Study

Fresh feelings, strong wills, and conflicting goals—a story from my career in which I helped control a situationally difficult encounter.

Cal Ripken Wanted Three More Years—The Owner Wanted Two

Just before we were about to enter into negotiations for the extension of Cal Ripken's contract, I'd come out of very tense dealings with the Orioles representing their broadcaster, Jon Miller. In a short time, Jon had risen to national stature, not only as a voice of the Orioles, but also doing play-by-play for ESPN.

Jon wanted to stay in Baltimore but he and I, and the Orioles management, were never able to arrive at an acceptable contract and eventually he accepted a lucrative five-year contract from the San Francisco Giants plus an extension from ESPN.

Coming off the tense Miller dealings, I was now taking on Cal's contract extension. Cal wanted a three-year extension. With him approaching 40, the club insisted on a two-year extension. I was concerned about facing a situationally difficult negotiator—the Orioles management.

From the outset, I felt unusual tension from the Orioles' General Manager, Pat Gillick. In response, I refrained from diving right into the negotiations. I instead told Pat that I empathized with his situation and the tense feelings that existed at the Orioles concerning me. "I have been through similar post-negotiation fallout myself."

After some "asking," during my preliminary dealings with Pat, it became apparent that a good deal of their behavior did in fact stem from residual feelings from the Jon Miller negotiations. Following some back and forth, Pat revealed that club owner Peter Angelos was contemplating personally negotiating the contract.

I "responded" to the situation by informing Pat that Cal would negotiate directly with Peter, and that I would stay out of the negotiations to reduce tensions. I had told Cal, due to the hard feelings, it may not be in his best interest for me to be at the center in the negotiations. (Sometimes the best tactic is to replace yourself.) Peter and Cal had a good relationship and it made sense for them to discuss the contract directly.

Cal and I would meet to strategize, but when it came time for the face-to-face sessions, it was Cal who attended the meetings, did the probing, and, eventually, the proposing. His "power of nice" plus the elements of tacking we'd employed earlier, enabled us to achieve together what might not have occurred through me.

Cal got his three-year contract *and* Peter Angelos got his two-year contract. It sounds impossible but creative solutions often seem that way at first. The Orioles signed Cal to a two-year contract plus a third option year. If the Orioles chose not to exercise the option for year three, the club would make a substantial buyout payment to Cal. And we felt confident that Cal's performance would result in the full three years.

Postscript: How many years did the "Orioles' two-year/Cal's three-year" contract deal end up lasting? Three. The team exercised their option to pay him his full salary for a third year.

EMOTIONAL TACTICS—NONEMOTIONAL RESPONSES

When the other side gets emotional, see their use of emotion for what it may well be: a negotiation ploy or tactic. It may simply be a device by a strategic negotiator to elicit a particular reaction from you, just as an opening low bid is meant to get you to drop your high asking price and eventually meet somewhere near the middle.

Don't Get Emotional Back

Emotional attacks are often negotiation tactics, not personal condemnation. Don't counter personal attacks with personal attacks. Just as the nonemotional response will neutralize the emotional ones, the impersonal approach will neutralize the personal. It takes discipline and a reminder of your purpose. Remember, the best retaliation against being called nasty names is to make the deal you want, not calling them even worse names.

The way to avoid emotional responses is to be ready for emotional tactics.

Tactic: Anger

You've made certain proposals that cause the other side to take offense. They feel you asked for too much. They're furious. Your proposal is unreasonable. They're outraged. They get loud and volatile. You better give in on something or they'll stay angry. They insist you make a concession in exchange for them lowering their rage.

Response: Find Out Why

Do you ignore their anger? No. You respond to it, but *not* to the emotional blackmail. What is it about your request that made them angry? Did they fully understand it? Can you put it another way or explain your reasoning better? Perhaps you can learn information from them as to *why* they're angry and what it takes to put the negotiation back on track. Respond to the anger, not the demand.

Tactic: Insulted

The other side claims to be insulted by your offer. In fact, they're so insulted, they insist you make another, more realistic offer. They're trying to get you to bid against yourself. Don't. Remember, it should be difficult, if not impossible to insult a negotiator with an offer. By definition, an offer demonstrates you are engaging in business conversation. It may be a low number; it may have tough terms; it may have out clauses, but it is no more insulting than the other side coming back with a high number, better terms, and no out clauses. This is the process of negotiation, back and forth.

Response: Learn What Wouldn't Be Insulting

If the other side says they've been insulted, ask them to tell you what kind of offer they would consider "not insulting." By doing so, they're showing what aspects of your offer were unacceptable and are, in fact, countering rather than having you bid against yourself.

Tactic: Guilt

Guilt can be a powerful and effective emotion when employed by a skilled dealmaker. You should feel bad for asking for so much. Just because you have the upper hand, you've put us in a corner. How can you do this to us?

Response: Focus on the Issues

Remember, guilt is a negotiation device, just like anger. It's used to make you feel bad and soften your requests. Isolate the emotion from the issues. Focus on the issues. What would they propose back? How would they proceed with the deal? What do they see as fair? Don't feel guilt (unless you're negotiating against your mother).

Tactic: Exasperation

The other side is overwhelmed, too busy, inundated with problems. They want you to solve this one. They're under immense pressure; their world is chaos. They want you to handle this one and get back to them.

This is just another negotiating ploy. They're taking themselves out of the give-and-take process necessary to making a deal. This forces you to be both sides, making concessions in anticipation of what they might want. It also allows them to come in at the last minute and reject everything you've done (since you did it without them).

Response: Understand

Tell them you understand the pressures they face. Ask if there is anything you can do to help with their immediate problems or if they'd rather wait to do this deal when things have calmed down. Sympathize with their exasperation but keep them in the process.

Tactic: False Flattery

Watch out for anyone who keeps telling you how brilliant you are during the negotiation. We all like to have our egos stroked. Deft negotiators will use this human foible to praise us into concessions. After all, if we've gained every point all day, why not give up a minor one here and there? Some compliments are real, but beware of a flood.

Response: Refocus

Smile. Say thanks. And refocus. Don't be surprised if the compliments ebb as the deal comes to a close.

When You Face Emotional Tactics, Get R.I.D. of Them

- **R**ecognize the emotion as a tactic.
- **I**dentify exactly what kind of emotion is being employed.
- **D**eflect the emotion in order to refocus on the issues.

CHALLENGING PERSONALITIES

Negotiators don't come in just two flavors, difficult and easy. They possess an infinite array of characteristics, in an infinite number of combinations. The first step in getting them to make the deal your way is recognizing the characteristics you're up against.

The Extrovert

Personality Traits. Think of Rodney Dangerfield in *Caddyshack*. Extroverts are outgoing, impulsive, and full of energy. The plus is enthusiasm. The minus is lack of focus.

How Extroverts Become Challenging. They don't prepare because preparing isn't "doing." They'd rather "do." They talk instead of listen. Action is mistaken for progress. Extroverts can be infuriating because you can never pin them down on details. They agree with you one day and then change their story the next.

How to Negotiate with an Extrovert. Let them do what they do best—extend themselves. Their surroundings are often cluttered with trophies, celebrity photos, and mementos. Each one is a story. Listen. Extroverts seek recognition. Give it to them. Let them know how much this deal will enhance their reputation. Then, when it comes time to deal, document. Get promises in writing. Keep the Extrovert focused by using agendas.

The Pragmatic

Personality Traits. Think of Gordon Gekko in *Wall Street* saying, "Greed is good." The Pragmatic always wants to take charge of the negotiation. Pragmatics have lists of deal points or key issues they want to tick off so they can get to the bottom line fast. They're impatient and consider time almost as valuable as money.

How Pragmatics Become Challenging. They play hardball. They want to win and they want you to lose. They lack patience. They abhor loss of control and sometimes revert to dictates and threats. As a result, they cause deadlocks and are rarely willing to expend the effort or time to work it out.

How to Negotiate with a Pragmatic. Know what you want and be prepared to stand your ground. Start off by aiming high. Put additional items in your proposal that you'll eventually give away. After a struggle (perhaps just before a deadlock) give in. Let the Pragmatic declare victory while you go home with the deal you wanted.

The Analytic

Personality Traits. Think of Mr. Spock in *Star Trek*. Everything must be based on logic. Analytic negotiators are very cautious, obsessed with process more than outcome. They try to take the human element out of a human process.

How Analytics Become Challenging. Analytics slow the negotiation process down to give themselves time to study, and restudy, all available information and alternatives. You have a deadline. You want to get the deal done. The Analytic can become a nitpicker whose analysis, or overanalysis stops the deal dead in its tracks.

How to Negotiate with an Analytic. Do not try to jam the deal down the Analytic's throat. The more you push, the more they resist. The more you hurry, the more uncomfortable they become. Force yourself to slow down to their pace. Avoid being unpredictable. Since preparation is so important to them, do your own homework. Instead of trying to convert them to your principles, work with theirs to the extent that you can still get a deal done that works for you. (This may be against your instincts. It will require great self-discipline but may be well worth it.)

The Amiable

Personality Traits. Think of former President Clinton when he "feels your pain." Amiables are relationship-driven. People are more important than facts. They avoid confrontation at all costs.

How Amiables Become Challenging. Amiables are difficult to pin down in their decision-making process. Amiables want so much to be liked that they will tell you whatever you want to hear at the moment, only to change their tune when the next person expresses a different position. Eventually, negotiations break down because the Amiable is unable to make a commitment or decision.

How to Negotiate with an Amiable. Focus on people issues. Let the Amiable play host; be the guest. Avoid impatience. Let time pass so the Amiable can build a relationship. Let the deal unfold.

Combinations and Permutations

Challenging negotiators come in all shapes, sizes, and variations. So do the means to handle them. Realize that your next difficult negotiator isn't likely to be a textbook Analytic or a classic Amiable. You're more likely to run up against a Pragmatic Extrovert, or an Amiable Analytic . . . and you'll have to use a combination of methods. And sometimes, you'll encounter a truly unique negotiator.

Negotiating against God

Charlie Casserly, the former general manager of the Washington Redskins, was trying to sign Sean Gilbert, an extremely talented defensive lineman. Each side had put its best-and-final offer on the table. The Redskins offered $3.6 million per year. Gilbert said he would not take less than $5 million. Neither side would give an inch. Negotiations broke down. No matter what the Redskins tried, they could not get Sean Gilbert's agent, Gus Sunseri, to even discuss reducing his demand of $5 million per year. Charlie Casserly could not understand why this figure was totally nonnegotiable. That is, until he read an AP report in the sport section. Sunseri said, "It's over money, but it's not about money. It's a spiritual thing. Sean feels he's had a revelation from God that this should be the figure" (in his contract). Now that's a challenging negotiation tactic. Charlie ultimately decided that "no deal" was the best deal.

Realize that in order to negotiate successfully, you'll have to employ a combination of the tools provided, customized to the particular challenging negotiation you face. Listen to their stories, flex with their timetable, recognize guilt as a ploy and get to what's behind it, let them save face, brainstorm a menu of alternatives, offer an outside standard of projections, and be prepared to revisit and revise throughout.

REFRESHER

Chapter 8: Difficult Negotiators

Dealing with the Difficult Negotiator without Becoming One

Neutralize your emotions: Don't take it personally. Don't get personal.

Be prepared (for difficult negotiator); have a strategy.

Take a time-out. Slow down, cool off.

Control a Situationally Difficult Encounter—Tacking.

1. Empathize: Understand their pressures.
2. Ask questions.
3. Respond: Acknowledge their concerns.

Emotional Tactics	Nonemotional Responses
Anger	Find out why they're angry
Insulted	What wouldn't be insulting
Guilt	Focus on issues
Exasperation	Understand
False flattery	Refocus

When You Face Emotional Tactics, Get R.I.D. of Them

- **R**ecognize emotion as a tactic.
- **I**dentify what kind of emotion is being employed.
- **D**eflect the emotion, refocus on issues.

"My people will get back to your people."

Negotiating from Weakness

What if you're negotiating with someone who has the upper hand, that is, more clout at the table? Let's say, their side has property you "must" have. Or their company is the "only" customer for your goods. Or, maybe, they know that you're "under pressure" to make a deal. How can you still be a formidable negotiator? How can you achieve your interests? How do you negotiate effectively when you're in a weak position?

PERCEIVED WEAKNESS VERSUS REAL WEAKNESS

> Pretend to have the confidence you don't yet feel.
>
> —SHERYL SANDBERG

The first question you have to answer is: Are you really negotiating from a weak position or is it just your perception? Too often, we exaggerate our own weaknesses, assuming them to be greater than those of the other side. Don't assume the other side holds all the cards. You may have a good sense of what their strengths are, but you don't know what *they* perceive as their own weaknesses or your strengths.

Ask Questions

The best way to determine the other side's state of mind is with thoughtful inquiry. You don't have to ask, "Do you think you have me where you want me?" But you can dig into the subject by getting surrounding or ancillary information by finding out:

- What other deals of a similar nature have they made?
- What brought them to you for this deal?
- What can they tell you about the background of their company or their players?

- Who are some of their references?
- What do they know about your company and/or players and what can and should you tell them?
- How do they see the negotiations going? Timing? Goals?

The content of their answers will tell you how they perceive their side and yours, as will their *style* of answers. For example:

- Are they arrogant? This may be an overcompensation for their own fears.
- Are they confident? Perhaps they are realistic about their own strengths. This will be helpful to you in determining your strategy.
- Are they hesitant? Maybe they are worried about your strengths or their own deficiencies.
- Are they open and friendly or closed and guarded? Again, this will tell you about their self-perception.

Consider the Real Possibility That They Are Afraid of You

Both sides go into negotiations with trepidation. It's natural. You probably don't know each other. You may not trust each other. You have different, perhaps opposing interests.

Take a step back and assess your own strengths. Try to put yourself in the other party's shoes. *How would you like to deal with you?* What would be most intimidating about your position, most influential, least assailable? What do you have that would be most enviable? That's what the other side is seeing.

Now ask yourself, who has the stronger position? Or, more pointedly, does one side even have the stronger position? You may well find yourself better armed than you thought. You may be able to enter the negotiations on even footing, or maybe with the scales tilted in your favor.

Think back to the Publisher-Agent Game in the beginning of Chapter 7. The Agent and the Publisher faced the same pressure, yet did not realize it. They both felt stress at the possibility of losing their job as well as the financial strain of sending twins to Ivy League schools. People tend to presume the weight of the world is on their shoulders and fail to realize there is probably pressure on the other side as well.

But what if, after honest evaluation, you conclude you really are in a weaker, more vulnerable position? Then what do you do?

EXPAND THE GOALS

If you are, in fact, in a weaker position, it's on the basis of the apparent goals of your negotiation: You want to win a contract, but you have to protect your profit margin. You're a seller and you want to get a favorable price. You're a potential merger partner and you don't want to get swallowed up. You've discovered that you lack strength when these are the goals. Don't sacrifice your goals; change or expand them.

Though it may seem so, money isn't your only goal nor is it the other side's. Turn hard-dollar deals into percentage of profit deals where you make more if they make more. Consider joint ventures instead of buy-outs. Change the terms or timing of a purchase to make a higher (or lower) price more palatable.

Look for intangibles that may be important to the other side. If you're joining forces, whose corporate name will prevail? Who will control the press spin on the deal? Do you have other resources valuable to the other side such as customer leads or referrals?

Make the deal bigger than it is. If you're looking at a one-time deal, perhaps there are other pieces to add. Bid on multiple contracts, not just the one at hand. Sell several parcels of land, not just one. Consider joint venturing with the other side. Put renewal or option clauses in the deal, raising the potential upside for both parties. Bring in more partners for an even bigger deal.

You don't necessarily think about creative solutions when you are feeling weak in price negotiations. Yet witness how my partner, Todd Lenhart, was able to overcome a demand that could have led to lost business.

Turning a Perceived Weakness into a Strength

A few years ago, SNI was attempting to enter into a new client marketplace for the firm: pharmaceutical sales companies. We got involved in an opportunity with a global pharmaceutical corporation and were up against several competitors that had more extensive experience working in the industry. However,

(continued)

(continued)

during the sales process we earned the respect of a key decision maker who was willing to position us with the selection committee. We earned a spot in the final selection process, but ultimately found ourselves dealing with a procurement team that used our lack of experience and, hence, credibility in the industry against us. They applied pressure to our pricing model and told us they would simply go with the more proven vendor partner if we did not meet their discounting demands.

Todd and our team explored options and collaborated closely with the key decision maker. Rather than caving in on price or walking away, Todd identified a way to lower our base price but link our training impact to several key business performance indicators that the client agreed to measure. The deal was structured so that 30 percent of our overall fee was contingent on meeting or exceeding the goals identified in the partnership agreement between SNI and the client. If met, attaining those goals would result in additional income, to make up for our initial discount.

In the end, Todd and the SNI team made a significant positive impact on the company's sales. SNI ended up capturing even more revenue than the original proposal provided because of the return on investment gained by the client due to SNI's training. The perceived pricing weakness, and Todd's creative response, ultimately worked in SNI's favor, as SNI established itself in a highly competitive industry and also captured a model that SNI could take to other clients.

LOCATE ALLIES

Even if you can't strengthen your position, there are several ways to strengthen your negotiating team and, in turn, bolster your position.

1. *Add to your team.* Bring in another entity, company, coinvestor, buyer, or partner. You will immediately change the equation. The new player's strength could be in your area of weakness. Let's say you're a high-quality manufacturer selling to a distribution company. They're skeptical of your ability to deliver goods to their various warehouse locations on a timely basis. So they're forcing your price down to compensate for possible late delivery. Bring in an established shipper to partner with you. Suddenly, you've changed the balance.

2. *Find an expert or coach.* These outside eyes will look at the deal through the lens of their respective specialty. You'll get an accountant's view; a stock-trader's view; or a marketer's view. They may assess your vulnerabilities differently. They may bring creative solutions to the table that you have overlooked or taken for granted.

3. *Locate others similarly situated.* Rosa Parks was arrested for refusing to give up her seat to a white passenger and move to the back of the bus. Though her gesture was brave and symbolic, there was little she, or any other individual, could do to end segregation in the South. But Martin Luther King, Jr., knew the power of numbers. Where one individual was powerless, one hundred, one thousand, or one hundred thousand individuals working together helped take African Americans from the status of individual weakness to a position of group strength.

When you feel weak or alone in your position, find others in a related or similar situation, join forces, and gain negotiation clout.

Improbable Allies—Unexpected Impact

Because of my love for the game of baseball, during the Major League's labor dispute in 1994, I found myself in the role of informal mediator. It started with frequent conversations with Randy Levine, the chief negotiator for the team owners, and Don Fehr, the head of the Players Association. Both Randy and Don have extensive backgrounds in labor law. In order to decipher some of the issues raised in our conversations, I turned to some former law school classmates who were experts in labor law. While it was not enough to put me on an even playing field with Randy and Don, at least the expertise of my law school friends gave me a comfortable position on the bench.

As the labor dispute continued, I was spending as many as 20 hours a week talking to various parties. The Players Association and the club owners had teams of negotiators and substantial resources. Being an informal mediator, without official designation, title, staff, or budget, I often felt weak, by comparison, as I reached out to the two sides.

In an earlier story, I told about the ill-fated meeting at the Mayflower Hotel in Washington, D.C.—one of the low points of the baseball dispute. While the principals were not making settlement progress, during my time at the Mayflower, I was able to forge an alliance with Tom Reich, then one of the game's most respected player agents. Following those meetings we, in turn, connected with

Randy Hendricks, Jim Bronner, Bob Gilhooley, and Tony Attanasio, all highly regarded agents who shared my strong desire for a solution to the player-owner battle. By creating this network of similarly situated parties, by working together, the six of us were able to influence the process to a greater extent than any one of us could have, working alone.

Our ad hoc confederation of allies strengthened our position but we knew, as agents, we would still be perceived as primarily representing the players' interests. To broaden and bolster our influence and credibility, we needed a partner whose interests were parallel to those of the owners. Propitiously, Aramark, one of baseball's biggest business partners, providing food, concessions, and other services to a number of teams, also approached me about working on the problem. Joe Neubauer, Aramark's chairman, not only offered profound insights and strategies, but had great respect from Don Fehr, creating another link between the players and the owners. It's no coincidence that Aramark's motto was "unlimited partnerships." I believe it was our own unlimited partnerships that we, collectively, were able to build during the labor dispute that helped us turn our negotiation weaknesses into strengths.

While the official representatives of each side continued their protracted, publicized, and frustrating negotiations, we worked quietly, cooperatively, in the background. The public didn't know of our involvement. It wasn't until the settlement was reached that our influence came to light.

It took a federal judge's order to bring about the resumption of baseball. And then it was eight months after that order that a real settlement was finally negotiated between the players and the owners. While management's chief negotiator, Randy Levine, and players' head, Don Fehr, were the principal architects of the peace, the *New York Times* recognized the impact of our unofficial alliance: "The new labor agreement would not have been possible without the behind-the-scenes initiatives of a group of player agents."

We each played different roles in the game of baseball. As agents, we could be rivals, vying to sign the same player. Then, representing a player, we could be out to get the most money from a club for our client, leaving less for the next agent's client. When it came to Aramark, we were even on the opposite sides of the age-old labor–management spectrum. We were competitors; we were adversaries; but in this case, we had one common interest—the game. And in that, we were similarly situated. Unlikely allies can forge a strong negotiation force. When you look for allies, look beyond the obvious, to those who share the overall goal—the business or endeavor that feeds all of you. If you're successful, afterward, you can always go back to being rivals.

NEVER LET THEM SEE YOU SWEAT

You may evaluate the situation and determine, in all objectivity, that the other side possesses all the leverage. But they may not know it. They may not be as smart as you are. They may not have gone through an objective evaluation. They may assume you have strengths that don't show. There's no reason to give away your insecurity. The way you act telegraphs how you view your pluses and minuses.

Play the role of the sheep and you will get slaughtered.

—ANONYMOUS

If you act weak, you will be treated as if you're weak. Let them know you're not as financially liquid as you'd like to be and they will demand more collateral. Send signals that you have pressure to close a deal regardless of cost and you certainly will pay a premium.

Keep talking. A dead giveaway that you feel less than secure in your stance is cutting off or limiting communication. You're withdrawing. Withdrawal says fear, regrouping, or retreating. It's as loud a signal as yelling, "I surrender."

Continue talking; ask questions; go on negotiating. Keep finding common ground. Keep looking for common interests. Keep getting to know the other side. The other side is much less likely to extract a pound of flesh from a party they've come to know, than from a stranger.

Act confident. Whether you are confident or not, act that way. That doesn't mean act cocky. Conduct yourself with sureness, steadiness, and a sense of control. Two things will happen. You'll communicate that confidence to the other side; they will not sense vulnerability. And you'll actually get more confident by acting confident. It's self-perpetuating. Many deals are won more on confidence than on pure merit.

The Inventor and the Investor

I represented a young man with a great imagination. He had watched athletes in competition—tennis players, ballplayers, bowlers, golfers—constantly wiping the perspiration off of their hands to better grip the racquet, bat, ball, or club. Most of us barely notice such a thing. An inventive mind sees opportunity: *People who play sports need something to keep their hands dry*. He came up with an invention to do just that, a compound that absorbed perspiration on contact. The compound was so effective, the inventor convinced a major superstar athlete to give it his endorsement and become an investor in the company.

The problem came when the superstar's advisors grew impatient with the way business was being run. Unless they were given control of the company, they threatened to revoke the star's endorsement, thereby deflating the value of the company and sending it into bankruptcy, leaving the inventor with nothing.

The inventor didn't have the financial resources to fight back against the advisors or buy out the superstar-investor. Sure that his position was weak, the inventor panicked. I sat with him and we worked through the process of negotiating from weakness. First, we *tested the basic assumption*: Was his position really weak? Yes, on most objective measures. The success of the company was predicated on the superstar's endorsement. No endorsement meant no company. It was that simple. Was the superstar-investor's position truly strong? Yes, because of the investor's deep pockets, he could even buy the company post-bankruptcy and jettison the inventor. But did the investor and his advisors really want bankruptcy? Placing the company in bankruptcy might taint the superstar-investor's well manicured image. That was a big risk just to take control of, and run, such a small company. Therefore, it was unlikely they'd take the fateful steps that might impair the superstar's reputation. That was, in effect, our strength and his weakness.

Next, we *searched for allies*, someone to act as a failsafe. What if the investor's people did put the company in bankruptcy? Who might be willing to replace the investor with fresh funds? We found some interested candidates but frankly, no one who was willing to commit. No strength here.

So, the inventor and I set out to *expand his goals*. The primary issue was control. Who would run the company, the inventor or the investor? I asked my client, "Why do you want control of the company?" He said that he saw the company as the platform for his real goal, to develop and launch more and more inventions. To do so, he would need capital. Therefore, we expanded our goal from complete control to some control and, more importantly, additional capital.

We were determined to *never let them see us sweat*. (We sweated plenty, over our relative strengths and weaknesses, over locating other investors, and over finding ways to expand the goals. But we did it in private.) In front of the investor's people, we appeared calm. Why? Because we had thought through the process and had a plan. We never stopped talking and negotiating. We kept the lines of communication open. We didn't allow animosity to creep in because, if we were able to work out our difficulties, the inventor and superstar-investor would still be in business together, albeit in a different relationship and configuration.

By focusing on the expanded goal of financial reward, we moved past the issue of control. Maybe the investor's advisors *could* run the business better. What the inventor wanted was to be sure that if the product succeeded, he reaped the fruits of his genius, and found a platform on which to create his future inventions. We offered them what they wanted—to run the company—in exchange for a favorable royalty deal—a financial return on each product sold. The needs of both parties were met. The weaker position of the inventor was negated.

BRAINSTORMING

Another ramification of feeling like the weaker party is that you can't see other alternatives that may be available. If you sense your vision has been clouded in that way, you can use the tool of brainstorming to help come up with creative approaches to seemingly insoluble dilemmas.

Few situations can make people feel as weak as facing a government agency. Imagine you walk into a Zoning Board meeting with a proposal to build a shopping center in a booming residential area. You unroll your plans and make your case: It's a state-of-the-art mall offering 200 stores to a community that is drastically underserved for its retail needs. You sit down, having presented your case. But one board member says, 200 stores seems like too many. Another says, as far as he's concerned, they don't have any underserved retail needs. Another says that malls are ugly. The last member adds, shopping centers cause traffic jams. Unless you have something else to say, they're going to put it to a vote. And you're going to lose.

Talk about being in a weak position. The government officials across the table have ultimate power. They can reject your proposal dictatorially, irrationally, close-mindedly, or just plain unfairly, but no matter, it's their door to slam. What do you say? How do you counter? If you're like most negotiators, you don't know. You came with your best argument. Period. And that was your first mistake.

When you're David squaring off with Goliath, it's not a bad idea to bring more than one stone. How? In negotiation terms—brainstorm. Get a partner or two; lay out the problem, and purposely generate a vast array of solutions. Preempt complaints. Offer alternatives. Overcome likely objections. Demonstrate flexibility. Approach the problem differently.

Overcoming Objections

Salespeople feel weak when they face recurring objections from potential customers for which they have no answer. The salespeople need to regain their confidence to rebut competitor claims, unsubstantiated rumors, or customer misunderstandings about the products or services they are selling.

I remember one such instance when we advised the affinity credit card pioneer MBNA. Competitors tried to weaken MBNA's market position with potential affinity partners by floating objections in the marketplace related to diminishing service MBNA provided its partners. They suggested that, among other things, MBNA had grown so large and had so many partners that its potential partners would feel like a small fish in a big pond. They also accused MBNA of turning over account executives so frequently that "it's like a revolving door."

To counter objections such as these and build salespeople's confidence, we recommended a brainstorming session among MBNA's business development leaders; ideas were shared, and ultimately a list of best answers was developed. The result, an Objection Planner, included scripts of solid responses to the preceding objections. The responses included "You should not be concerned with how large we have grown, but rather with the service and compensation we provide; operating in sectors and through regional offices allows us to be close to our customers." And, "Your account executive may change from time to time, but other members of your marketing team stay in place to promote continuity. New account executives bring fresh ideas to your program." We also crafted potential scripts for responses to 34 other objections, all of which empowered the salespeople, after practicing delivery, to give confident responses. The brainstorming sessions were the key to unlocking the salespeople's dilemma of how to effectively respond to potential partner objections.

Back to the Zoning Board challenge: After conducting a brainstorming session, you might come up with the following ideas:

- Prepare a study of the number of households in the residential area, members per household, typical shopping needs, distance currently traveled to shop, cost of travel, time away from home, and other related statistics to illustrate the service and convenience the mall would provide to families.

- Use statistics to demonstrate that the mall will keep businesses and taxes within the community rather than having those jobs and dollars go elsewhere.
- Present an environmental impact plan to show how the center will be sensitive to natural surroundings.
- Answer concerns about parking and traffic patterns before questions are raised.
- Offer to have a community panel for input into the structure and placement of the mall.
- Create a tie-in with local schools to display students' outstanding work in the mall courtyard.
- Show three plans, each with a different number of stores so the Board dwells on what size the center should be, not whether there should be a center.

These are only examples. You could brainstorm many more, then narrow them down and refine the best of them. But most people don't know how to brainstorm. They think negotiation is a one-on-one contest. They think they know all the answers and the input of others would simply be distracting. In our office, we adhere to the saying, "None of us is as smart as all of us." When we face a tough situation, we follow the four rules of brainstorming:

The Four Rules of Brainstorming

1. *Brainstorm in groups of four or less.* You must have two to brainstorm. Two people will have more ideas together than if they each have ideas separately and add them up. One person's ideas spark another's. However, there is a point of diminishing ideas. Groups of more than four tend to stifle ideas. The group becomes an audience instead of participants. Judgments set in. Status can play a part. Such factors tend to inhibit ideas.
2. *Don't criticize ideas. Let them flow.* A great idea can be the first words out of someone's mouth; or the last. Let them all come out without succumbing to the temptation to evaluate, accept, or reject. Nor should anyone feel the need to apologize for an idea either before or after uttering it. Just throw it out there. If it isn't good, or even if it's awful, it could be the seed of an idea that's great. Do the sorting and sifting later.

3. *Keep at it. Creativity is more perspiration than inspiration.* Effective negotiators are creative negotiators. But many people are intimidated by the prospect of having to be creative. They shouldn't be. Everyone has the capacity to create ideas. It is an exercise where you force yourself to think of that which is not apparent. You impose a rule, for instance, that you must come up with 20 answers to a question that seems to have only two answers. Among those 20 are bound to be another one or two creative solutions. Volume begets creativity. Don't worry about the ideas that don't work. You only need to use those that do.

4. *Make it fun.* Like most preparation, brainstorming is not inherently fun. So, make it fun. Sometimes we brainstorm by splitting into two groups. Each side gets a packet of Post-it Notes®. The idea of the game is to write down ideas, one per note, and connect all the ideas into a chain of notes. Depending on the issue, we take from five to fifteen minutes to generate ideas. People become so involved in coming up with ideas, connecting them, and trying to construct as long a chain as possible, they invariably come up with new solutions, no matter how many times we've taken on a problem before. Of course, some of the ideas aren't great (maybe some are even awful) but that isn't the point. Finding one or two good solutions is the goal. By making it fun, we come up with new ideas, ideas we might never have found if we were sitting around a conference table seriously debating the merits of a problem.

Brainstorming Works

A young woman named Shannon called me with a salary challenge. Her employer offered her a promotion from bookkeeper to business manager. The company wanted to pay her a salary of $125,000—but based on precedents for like jobs, and her new responsibilities, Shannon sought $150,000. When she addressed the issue with the managing partner, the partner declined her request: "That is the salary budgeted for this position and we cannot move on it." But recognizing that she was important to the organization, he agreed to talk to her about the issue the following week, adding she should not get her hopes up because there was simply "nothing more available," and that the person she was replacing was paid $112,000.

Prior to her meeting, I advised her to "think outside the box"—to brainstorm ideas that might achieve a satisfactory result for her and allow the managing partner to maintain the budgeted salary. She enlisted two of her book club friends for brainstorming help. Together they came up with a significant list of alternatives to a salary increase. They didn't restrict themselves or their thinking—instead they fleshed out all ideas, both good and bad, and put together a list that looked like this:

- Deferred income instead of salary.
- Same pay but for fewer hours of work, allowing Shannon to use open time for consulting.
- Same take-home pay but have the company make a donation to a charity she supports.
- Childcare reimbursement instead of added salary.
- Change her promotion to a higher title with the salary budgeted for that position.
- Larger office in lieu of higher salary.
- More vacation and personal leave time.
- Additional staff support.
- Enrollment in a 401(k) matching savings plan.
- An education supplement for children when they go to college.
- A company car or other tax-deductible benefit.
- Profit-sharing and/or a phantom stock plan.
- Incentive or performance plan for outstanding work.
- Commission in addition to salary.
- Home office equipment to allow her to work at home.

The best ideas were not uncovered first or last or in the middle of their session. Some ideas grew out of others. Some took them down blind paths. Others were unexpected but creative. Many of the ideas only occurred because Shannon had her friends to play off.

She went to the meeting with the managing partner and reiterated her desire for $150,000. Again, she received push back. Shannon countered by positing a package built on her brainstorming list: A profit-sharing bonus not to exceed $15,000; $10,000 in deferred funds to be paid upon retirement; and a company car.

After further discussion, the managing partner told Shannon that to ensure that he didn't lose her, he would offer a package valued in excess of the $25,000 salary difference that was at issue. He agreed to the profit-sharing bonus and deferred income, but told Shannon the company car would have to wait until she completed one year in her new role. He also said that while he wouldn't put this into a formal agreement, she could count on him that it would happen.

So, Shannon brainstormed her way out of a deadlock with her boss, and into a WIN–win deal.

REFRESHER

Chapter 9: Negotiating from Weakness

Perceived versus Real Weakness

- *Question*, probe, explore.
- *Learn your vulnerabilities* and theirs.

> Consider the possibility that the other side is intimidated by you.

Expand Goals

- *Money isn't the only goal*—percentage of profits, partnerships.
- *Look for intangibles*—control, influence, public relations.
- *Make the deal bigger than it is*—for both sides.

Locate Allies

- *Add to your team*—bring in partners who have strengths you lack.
- *Find an expert or coach*—gain outside knowledge.
- *Locate others similarly situated*—create alliance of common interests.

Never Let Them See You Sweat

- *Keep talking*—keep the deal going.
- *Act confident*—confidence makes more deals than clout.

Brainstorming

1. Brainstorm in groups of four or less—small and manageable.
2. Don't criticize ideas. Let them flow.
3. Keep at it. Creativity is more perspiration than inspiration.
4. Make it fun—create a game of idea generation.

"Frankly, Dennison, this was not the merger proposal I was expecting."

Unlocking Deadlocks

> When an irresistible force meets an immovable object, something's gotta give, something's gotta give, something's gotta give . . .
>
> —JOHNNY MERCER, *COMPOSER-LYRICIST*,
> *SOMETHING'S GOTTA GIVE*

IF NOTHING WORKS, CHANGE SOMETHING

Two parties have been negotiating long and hard. They've stated their respective positions, made offers, heard counteroffers, listened to each other's needs, even traded a few lesser points with each other, but finally have come down to *the* pivotal issue. It could be price or timing or terms or control. But whatever it is, neither side feels they can give any more. They're eyeball to eyeball and nobody's blinking. Now what?

You've reached deal gridlock. Nobody's going anywhere. How do you break it? Who moves first? Who gives without feeling like the loser? What do you do about the egos that may be bruised or need massaging?

As with all impasses, something has to change—almost anything—whether it's at the heart of the matter or tangential to it.

Two left-turning trucks get blocked halfway across an intersection by a crossing onslaught of bumper-to-bumper taxis. Horns blare, cabbies swear, neck veins bulge, and pedestrians can't even walk on the "walk" sign. Who's going to move? How much? When? Truckers won't; it's defeat. Cabbies won't; it's retreat. More horns, more cursing, more gridlock. Finally, a little blue subcompact, 10 cars behind the cabs, inches slightly left and slightly up. The cab next to him pulls a little right and a little forward. Ten cars, one by one, angle off and creep up a little, each opening a few inches of daylight, eventually adding up to just enough of an opening at the intersection. Two truckers scowl. One turns. The other turns.

Gridlock unlocks. All because one element, not necessarily at the heart of the problem, changed. When deals deadlock, look for the little blue subcompact.

What Should You Change?

Change Locations

If you've been meeting at your office, pick a new location as we did when we moved Cal's five-year contract negotiation to my farm (Chapter 3). Or offer to go to their office. Settings can be intimidating, stifling, stale, or negative. Being on your turf may create a sense in the other party that they've already given in just by being there. In addition, either or both parties can get tired of staring at the same walls. Imaginations and energies wane. After too much time passes without progress, the negotiators may subconsciously associate the surroundings with lack of progress. *This is where we don't get anywhere each day.* Just by going to their office or a neutral site, you will change the dynamics of the negotiation. Everyone will sit in different seats. You'll each face different directions. The pictures on the walls will be new. The chairs may be more comfortable. *Moving sometimes feels like movement.* It may not be logical but attitudes shift with locales.

Change Negotiators

Maybe you're the problem. It may not be that you're negotiating poorly, but that the other party isn't hearing you anymore. (You may be guilty of the same thing in reverse.) Nerves may be on edge after being at the table too long. In the heat of negotiation, things may have become personal. When emotions supersede logic, negotiators tune out the substance and let animosity set in. Progress halts.

Do what a smart basketball coach does when his team is being shut down by a man-to-man, full court press, and they need one basket to change the momentum. If the players on the floor are stalled, take someone out—in this case, yourself—and substitute with a fresh player.

Send in your partner or associate. Make sure they're briefed on the status of negotiations, but don't prejudice them as to outcome. The whole purpose of bringing in someone new is to bring in a fresh perspective.

The simple change of bodies, a new face across the table with a new style, is often enough to jump-start a stalled deal. One of the hardest moves to make is to remove yourself. But remember, it has less to do with you than with the dynamics of dealmaking. It's not a failure on your part; it's a strategic move.

Call in a Mediator

This is a more dramatic version of the previous suggestion. Maybe both sides are so entrenched, so mired in the impasse, they're unable to see a way out. Then, no one from your side can bring movement to the negotiations and no one from the other side can, either. Both have become so passionate in defense of their positions they require a dispassionate participant.

Go outside of both parties to a neutral party. Mediators have to possess certain qualities beyond impartiality. They must be respected by both sides and able to maintain total confidentiality so the parties can express themselves freely. Mediators have to be expert in the negotiation process, though not necessarily in the specific business or topic. A good mediator can grasp the fundamentals of the deal well enough—mail order sales, personal services contracts, separation agreements, patent royalties—but not become so consumed by esoteric details that he or she loses sight of the broad goals of the deal, which is often what has happened to the negotiators themselves.

The best mediators are good listeners. They assess both positions, probe for sensitive spots, look for areas of mutual interest, and bring simple conclusions to the table. Their lack of emotional attachment to positions enables them to do what the negotiators couldn't, put the deal ahead of feelings.

We were involved in a mediation that was born of a firestorm of feelings, from name-calling to silent treatments to playing the press against each other. Two men who had to work together, professionals in their field, claimed to dislike each other with such a fervor that each called for the firing of the other. That's when we came in. (It's funny but nobody seems to call in mediators when the parties are only mildly annoyed with each other, before they reach real animosity.)

Stepping between Two Police Officers: One White, One Black, Both Mad

My former partner Mark and I were privileged to present a *pro bono* program to the Baltimore Police Department. We worked with 30 of the leaders of the Baltimore City Police Department, up the chain of command to the very top. No matter how blasé we might have wanted to appear, we were a little intimidated. We had faced tough audiences before, from hostile NFL general managers to hard-charging Manhattan real estate barons. But when the officers walked into the seminar in full uniform, with official firearms on their hips, we realized this was not your average seminar.

At first, the officers were so conditioned by their paramilitary structure, they insisted our lessons did not apply to them. "We don't negotiate," one colonel said, "We give orders." After that daunting start, however, they began to respond to our concept of WIN–win negotiation. They started to see how it could apply not only within their ranks but on the streets, as well. Sometimes when facing a 15-year-old, wannabe tough guy, or dealing with officer issues in the ranks, talking, probing, and listening works better than a threat. By the time the session was over, the officers were thanking us, telling us they were genuinely inspired to put WIN–win to work. We had really gotten through to them. Or so we thought.

A week after the seminar, the newspaper carried a big headline declaring that two of the Police Department's top officers—the commissioner and a colonel— were locked in a very bitter, very racial, very public dispute. Both had been at the seminar. Evidently, they were experiencing a problem more challenging than those we'd dealt with in the seminar. Mark and I felt we had established a rapport with the two men. I called the mayor and asked if we could be of service in trying to bring the two parties together. The mayor took us up on our offer.

The two officers agreed to come out to my farm, during off-duty time, to discuss their differences. Their dispute had grown over time and comprised a collection of complex issues. Practicing what we preach, we spent a day giving ourselves a cram course in those issues. Naturally, we agreed to keep the specifics of those issues confidential but we can share the following matters of public record: The colonel, when he'd been a major, had been passed over for the top job when the commissioner was recruited from another city to take command. However, the two men had worked together for several years, seemingly successfully. Beneath the surface, a rift had emerged between them. Small misunderstandings turned into substantial disagreements, eventually turning into major impasses. Recently, the controversy had made front-page headlines, such as "Racial Tension Stifles Leadership of Police Department." The papers, looking to sensationalize and sell more papers, focused on the racial differences more than the complexity of the issues underlying their battle.

We completed our Preparation Checklist and reviewed our information just prior to the evening's negotiation. We knew both men would come with entrenched positions. We knew we would have to break a strong deadlock. By offering to mediate, by changing locations from the downtown offices of the Police Department to the rural setting of my farm, and by suggesting they dress in casual clothing rather than uniforms, we were already employing deadlock-breaking tools.

We waited for their arrival, wondering who would arrive first, the commissioner or the colonel. Much to our surprise, they came in the same car. The commissioner was unfamiliar with the area but the colonel knew the way, so they'd decided to make the ride together. Two men, who were at each other's throats publicly, shared a ride to the mediation session. Maybe there was hope.

We went into the house, sat down, and began to slowly approach the subject. We listened. We asked questions. Borrowing from the Middle East negotiations, I asked my wife, Cathi, to play Golda Meir and bring us cookies on a break. Like Sadat and Begin, the commissioner and the colonel liked cookies. (Who doesn't?) After more talk, we adjourned until the next day.

We met again. Again, we sat and talked and listened. At one point, Mark sat with one party while I sat with the other, in order to put each at ease enough to deal with the most sensitive subjects. Then we got back together. Yes, sometimes the conversation got heated. And sometimes things got too quiet. But throughout, we were impressed with the dedication that both men had to the city, the police force, and to their jobs. Slowly, we began to see a thaw. Again, without breaking any confidences, we identified areas of agreement, not just those of divergence. The tools of deadlock breaking were working. The location had changed. The tension of one person's office, ringing phones, paperwork stacking up, watchful eyes of other officers, the formality and rank of uniforms were all absent. The view wasn't of teeming urban activity, but of pastoral serenity. The sounds weren't blaring car horns and sirens but quacking ducks and mooing cows. A mediator had been brought in, actually two. The pressure wasn't only on the two principals. Somebody was listening to each of them. Somebody neutral wanted a solution for the sake of the parties, not for a personal agenda.

At the end of the second day, a cautious resolution was reached. The racial aspects had been put aside and the real problems had been addressed. They had found enough common ground to find a way to try to work together. A press conference was called the following day. The deadlock was broken.

As is often the case, the nitty-gritty issues make almost no difference. They vary from negotiation to negotiation. It's the entrenchment that sets in after the issues that creates the impasse. And it's finding a way to change something that gets the process unstuck.

FIND REASONS TO AGREE

This method of unlocking deadlocks is so obvious, it's the one most often overlooked. By the time you reach deadlock and get to the issue that you cannot agree on, you've undoubtedly passed by lots of issues on which you do agree. But that sticky one seems to render all the previous negotiation useless. In fact, you start to feel that the two parties don't agree on anything.

Recount the Points of Agreement

Was the deadline okay? Were the terms? Did both parties complete due diligence? Were your profit definitions the same or compatible? Did you concur on market value? Were the shareholding percentages acceptable? Number of offices? Employees? Benefits? Measurements of success?

In most negotiations, there are many more issues of agreement than disagreement. Unfortunately, we lose sight of them once deal paralysis sets in. All we see is the battle issue: Who gets more board seats? Will the payment be cash or stock? Whose name goes first in the merged entity?

When the sticking point has you stuck, go back to the unsticky points. List every single area of agreement. This accomplishes two objectives:

1. It shows you how close you are to a deal.
2. It reminds you of why making a deal is a good idea.

GET CREATIVE

Dee Hock, the one-time visionary leader of VISA, has said, "The problem is never how to get new, imaginative thoughts into your mind, but how to get the old ones out. Every mind is a room packed with archaic furniture. You must get the old furniture of what you know, think, and believe, out before anything new can get in. Make an empty space in any corner of your mind and creativity will instantly fill it."

Deals deadlock when both sides become too attached to past positions. Six weeks ago, proposals were exchanged. They weren't set in stone then, but positions hardened over time. Now, both parties are negotiating as if their original proposals were carved into holy tablets. Each side has lost the ability to use creativity to look at the situation in a new light. If you have to, clear all of the deadlocked issues off the table and start over again. Agree that without new ideas, the negotiation is over. Get creative.

Wrestling with Deadlocks

Herb Kelleher, the unorthodox but highly successful innovator behind Southwest Airlines, lived up to his reputation when he found his company in a slogan dispute. It seems Southwest was using the phrase "Just plane smart" to describe its no-frills pricing only to discover that Stevens Aviation, an aviation sales and maintenance company, was already using "Plane smart." Instead of each side's lawyers unleashing the usual barrage of letters and litigation threats, Kelleher and his counterpart, Kurt Herwald, came up with a unique solution. They'd arm wrestle for the slogan. They created a media event around the mock battle, charging admission and selling souvenirs. Rather than fight over rights or compensation for use of the line, all proceeds from the publicity event went to charity. The dispute was settled. Kelleher, 61, lost to Herwald, 37, in what was obviously a setup ending by the two bosses. But, in another fixed outcome, both companies got to use the line. Their companies got press and television coverage beyond their wildest dreams. Plus they saved what Kelleher estimated to be as much as $500,000 in legal costs.

As discussed earlier, the way to get new ideas is to brainstorm. But even before you start generating new ideas, follow Dee Hock's advice and get rid of that old furniture. Here are some guidelines to help you clear the attic and make room for new ideas:

1. *Start all over again.* Ronald Reagan and Mikhail Gorbachev were deadlocked in arms talks at a summit in Iceland. Both sides had staked out their positions and neither was willing to budge. After a particularly difficult exchange, Reagan stood up, smiled, told the group they were not going to make any progress, and that they might as well start all over again. Reagan reached across the table and said, "Hello, Mikhail, my name is Ron and I think it's time we talked about the arms race." It broke the tension and got meaningful talks initiated. By "starting over," Reagan made it possible for the parties to see past their entrenched positions and be more open to new ideas.

2. *Keep a secret.* At times, negotiations deadlock because negotiators try to please third parties who aren't even at the negotiation table. The negotiator might fear reprisals if these third parties ever hear that certain taboo secrets were even discussed. Before beginning your talks, obtain an agreement that all information exchanged will be held in strict confidence. With this protection, negotiators' mental attics that are cluttered with worries over absent, third parties can be cleared out to make room for new, productive, dealmaking ideas.

3. *Recount interests.* Don't talk about positions. Don't take stands. Don't mention deadlines. Focus, instead, on each side's real needs, goals to be met, hopes to be fulfilled, both short and long term. Tell the other side, "It's my understanding that you are most interested in salon-quality hairbrushes shipped and delivered to meet your overseas customers' timetable. Am I correct in my understanding?" If the other party agrees, ask them, "What do you think are our main interests in this deal?" By focusing all parties on interests rather than positions (i.e., "We refuse to pay for shoddy hairbrushes"), you create room for new solutions to whatever problems may arise to develop.

4. *Don't stop.* When you're engaged in creative problem solving, if successful, pretty soon the hypothetical blends right into the real. You're addressing interests instead of egos; one or both of you has come up with a new approach; together, you're modifying it to work for your circumstances; you're both finding different ways to "win." You're negotiating again. The deadlock is broken. Keep going.

I had a negotiation early in my sports agency career that was deadlocked, dead-in-the-water, every kind of dead there is. My client was ready to give up. So was I. And so was the other side. Almost.

Eddie, Edward, and 1 Million Dollars

Baseball trivia quiz: Who was the fourth player in the history of Major League Baseball to sign a $1 million per year contract? *Hint*: He's one of only four players to reach both the 3,000 hit and 500 home run marks. *Answer*: Eddie Clarence Murray, who is more affectionately known as "Eddie." I knew the answer because I was the agent who negotiated the contract. One million dollars may not seem like much by today's standard when players sign contracts worth $30 million per year and the average salary is approximately $3.5 million per year, but breaking the $1 million barrier was quite a feat in 1981.

Eddie Murray had already begun to demonstrate Hall of Fame abilities in the years preceding 1981. He was a Gold Glove first baseman. He could switch-hit for both average and power. He was what baseball people call "a complete package." The year before, in 1980, Nolan Ryan, the legendary strike-out pitcher, had signed the first $1 million per year contract in baseball. Superstars Dave Winfield and Dave Parker had also joined those ranks. When it came time to negotiate Eddie's salary, we viewed their contracts as relevant precedents for Eddie Murray. We set out to achieve a five-year contract worth $1 million per year.

The new owner of the Orioles in 1980, Edward Bennett Williams, known as EBW, was a famous trial lawyer known for his courtroom savvy in defending various notorious clients. Larry Lucchino, general counsel of the Orioles in 1980, was a law partner and protégé of EBW. It was Larry who first approached me about Eddie's contract. After a period of negotiations with general manager Hank Peters, the Orioles offer was stuck at $600,000 per year for four years.

I told Larry we were disappointed and asked him why the Orioles were proposing only $600,000. Larry made it clear that, although the Orioles were a perennial winner on the field through the 1960s and 1970s, their attendance and television revenues lagged behind comparably performing teams. For the Orioles to remain a competitive team, stars like Eddie Murray would have to accept smaller contracts than their counterparts elsewhere in the game. The Orioles felt that they could not compete with the escalating salaries of larger market clubs and were determined to keep their payroll down. The Orioles also felt there were many players who wanted to play for a winner so much, they would accept less than they could get elsewhere.

Eddie was clearly worth $1 million per year. We knew he could get that amount from other clubs in a few years, when he became eligible for free agency. But Eddie's heart was in Baltimore. He wanted to stay, but he also wanted a contract for $1 million per year. I labored hard to demonstrate to Larry why Eddie's achievements plus the recent increase in players' incomes justified a $1 million salary. As with the Brooks Robinson contract negotiation, I had done my preparation. I had learned my lesson from dealing with Hank Peters. Rather than just spilling my guts when I negotiated with Larry, I took my time, asked questions, and listened. The negotiation went on and on, week after week. We still wanted $1 million and the Orioles refused to budge from their $600,000 offer. Larry and I had reached a deadlock.

I was frustrated that we were going nowhere and, worse, Eddie wanted to get his contract resolved so that he could focus on baseball. In order to break the deadlock, I started by using two methods previously discussed. I suggested to Larry, "It seems we have reached an impasse. Why not arrange a meeting so that we can bring EBW into the process?" I knew that Larry would want to still be involved in the process, so we could not totally *change negotiators*, but adding EBW to the other side's team served virtually the same purpose. It brought in a fresh perspective.

Next, I *changed the location* of the negotiation. While the talks, up to this point, had been conducted either at the Orioles' offices in Memorial Stadium or at my law firm in Baltimore, I decided to travel to Washington, DC, to meet with EBW. I wanted to put him at ease by going to him, rather than having him come to us. That way, he could feel we were on his turf.

To start the meeting, I used another deadlock-breaking technique by *summarizing all of the deal points* that Larry and I had reached agreement on previously. I did this to show good faith on our part (not attempting to revisit already agreed-to points) as well as demonstrating our willingness to work together. After my summary, EBW demonstrated his negotiating skills by probing me with the following question. "Ron," he asked, "does Eddie really need $1 million per year to survive?" It was a fair question.

"No," I responded, "But remember, a ballplayer's career is much shorter than your average lawyer, doctor, or computer programmer. Eddie has relatively few years to earn his life's income. It's only fair that he try to maximize that income while he is able."

After being probed by EBW, I knew it was time to probe back. I decided to answer a question with a question. I asked EBW, "If Nolan Ryan is worth $1 million and only plays once every four or five days, do you think that Eddie, performing at an All-Star level, is worth $1 million playing every day?"

"I certainly think he is worth it," countered EBW. "It's that the Orioles just cannot afford $1 million right now."

Again, practicing what we preach, I probed, "Why can't you afford $1 million right now?"

EBW explained that, while he had plans to improve Orioles' attendance and television revenues by marketing the club in Southern Pennsylvania and Washington, DC (before they had their own team), as well as other cities and towns in the Mid-Atlantic region, that was an investment that wouldn't pay off overnight. "I think we'll have one of the most successful franchises in baseball, but it will take both time and money. While we're trying to transform this local team into a regional team, we need every penny we can get to bolster that marketing plan."

At that point, I knew (1) they wanted to keep Eddie and (2) they would pay him the money if they had it. It was time to use some creative problem solving to break the deadlock. We approached the problem from the standpoint of finding ways to increase Orioles attendance immediately and, if they could be found, exploring whether these efforts could fund Eddie's salary. Both sides agreed it would take at least two years to see the results of this aggressive marketing effort. For Eddie to be paid $1 million per year, the Orioles had to come up with the money now.

The Orioles needed an immediate source of cash to fund the contract. Or did they? EBW's question stuck in my mind, "Does Eddie really need $1 million to live on?" As I told EBW, no, Eddie did not need the money now, but he would need it later in life, either after his performance declined or after he retired from the game. I huddled with my partners and we engaged in a *brainstorming* session. Finally, we came up with a solution often used by lawyers when negotiating a settlement to a lawsuit. Rather than paying the $1 million per year, the club could pay Eddie approximately $700,000 per year, and the remaining $300,000 would be put off, or deferred, to a later date. This was one of the earlier uses of deferred compensation in a Major League contract.

The solution was creative, as it had to be in order to fit the needs of both Eddie and EBW. Eddie now had a contract with the stated value of $1 million. He didn't need the final $300,000 immediately, so the club would owe it to him. The Orioles got what they wanted. They were obligated to pay Eddie $700,000 per year in the short term. That left money available to increase their marketing efforts.

In the end, EBW and Larry Lucchino were visionaries. By tapping into the regional market, they were able to take Baltimore from a town that had trouble getting significantly past the one million fans in attendance, even in a playoff year, to a team that drew over 3 million a year win or lose. By the time Eddie's remaining $300,000 per year was due, there was plenty of money available.

OBJECTIVE MECHANISMS

The single biggest roadblock to successful negotiation is people. If people weren't involved, deals would be objective. They would add up or not, deliver profits or losses, meet timetables, create cash flow or tax write-offs, result in mergers or spin-offs. Deals would be measured against absolute criteria.

But people are subjective beings, fueled by feelings, not just facts and conclusions. Humans don't have strictly objective needs in their deals; they have subjective *wants*. One negotiator *wants* to achieve the highest sale in the company's history. Another *wants* to show the other side who is stronger. Still another *wants* to make the deal that no one else could make. In fact, more deals are made because humans—with wants, drives, and other emotional motivations—are involved than if deals were determined only by cold, quantifiable measurements. But many deals are lost or stalled because of those same human factors.

When deals become too personal, negotiation runs into trouble. Egos enter; logic leaves. Once that happens, personal success is on the line, not just the success of the deal. Ego is now bigger than the merger, the buyout, the price, the savings, the growth potential, the lease, the contract, the bid, or the bottom line. Ego is everything. The deal isn't. Which negotiator's ego will prevail?

The deal comes to a halt. Deadlock sets in. Ego vs. ego. In order to restart the process, you need to depersonalize it. Someone has to introduce *objective mechanisms.* An objective mechanism is a standard that exists apart from one party or the other's prejudice. It is purposely nonhuman, nonemotional, unfeeling, impartial—no winners, no one to blame.

Remember, the process is *ne*-gotiation, not *ego*-tiation.

Here are some examples of objective mechanisms to depersonalize deals:

You Cut—I Choose

This is a variation on the old parental trick to keep kids from fighting over the last piece of cake. No matter how carefully Mom tries to divide the cake evenly, when she hands one piece to Sam and the other to Samantha, one of them is sure to cry foul, "She got the bigger piece!" So, Mom hands the knife to one (Sam) to do the cutting and lets the other (Samantha) have first pick of the slices. It makes Sam try his best to cut evenly (with no one to blame) so he doesn't give Samantha (with no one to blame, either) a chance to select the lion's share.

Let's say two negotiators are at a standstill. They each represent partners who must liquidate the assets of a company. Each partner wants to retain certain assets, sell others, and put the remainder up for auction. Therefore, they must first divide everything in half. But the division isn't easy. The company's assets comprise a variety of goods, from manufactured inventory to tooling machinery, as well as real estate, short- and long-term investments, partnerships, contracts, and patents. After countless unsuccessful attempts at an equal split, one negotiator suggests that he or his partner divide the assets and the other negotiator or her partner select which half she would like. No one can complain that the other got the bigger piece of cake.

Sealed Bids

Where "You cut–I choose" works because both parties see what's happening and nothing is hidden, the sealed bid approach works for the opposite reason. Neither party sees what the other is doing, but they both don't see equally. Each side submits a bid or a number or a date or a name, the envelopes are opened and each has agreed to outcome rules they determined in advance.

Open the Envelope

I had an experience with a real estate developer and an investor where we used the sealed bid method to solve an otherwise unsolvable dilemma. The two had a falling out and the relationship simply had to come to an end. In fact, that relationship end was the last thing they agreed on. They tried to split up the total properties owned, with one taking certain parcels and the other taking different parcels. As soon as the investor wanted a site, so did the developer. When the developer was willing to part with a piece of land, the investor was sure it was worthless.

After months of fighting over who would get which parcels, it became obvious that one had to buy the other out. But that presented its own problem. How much would one party, suspicious of the other, pay for the other's interest? Each thought the other was trying to steal the property. Neither wanted to "lose" to the other. I represented one of the two, the developer who asked me to try to intercede since they were getting nowhere. My first observation was, they're right. They were getting nowhere.

I suggested my client and the other party, the investor, each call their respective accountants, have separate meetings with them, and each determine the value of the total holdings. After that, I said, each of them should submit a sealed bid to the other with an offer to buy out the other side and own all of the properties. In other words, what would the investor pay the developer for the developer's half? What would the developer pay the investor for the investor's half?

The key rule: *The lower bidder would be bound to sell the property to the higher bidder for the higher price.*

They agreed and each submitted a sealed offer. We opened the envelopes. My client, the developer, offered to pay $ 1.2 million for the investor's share. The investor offered $2 million for my client's share. The investor "won." My client was thrilled with the $2 million payment. He got more than what he thought half the property was worth so he was happy to sell. The investor ended up with all of the property for what he thought was a fair price, so he was happy to buy. Both parties benefited from taking emotion out and going to a "blind" method.

External Criteria

When parties can't agree, maybe they shouldn't try. Sometimes they should turn to outside measures and standards.

A landlord wants to raise the tenant's rent 8 percent every year in order to cover anticipated increases in overhead, but the tenant thinks an annual increase of 4 percent is more than adequate. Maybe they should turn to external criteria such as government figures on the inflation rate. Let the rent increases follow neutral data, not the landlord's or the tenant's.

Use the Consumer Price Index, the Dow Jones Averages, Standard & Poor's, published market values, gold prices, OPEC, census data, interest rates—any information that comes from *outside* the negotiating parties and therefore stands as objective.

Arbitration

As the word says, it's arbitrary, meaning determined by an individual at his or her absolute discretion. Arbitration by an outside party is effective when all methods that directly involve the negotiating parties have been exhausted. At that point, additional perspective is necessary to bring the deal to closure. Arbitrators (and mediators) are professional deal-makers with no vested interest on either side. All the negotiating parties have to agree on is who the arbitrator will be. In some cases, they've decided in advance, just in case they reach a stalemate. In mediation, the opinion is a strong suggestion but is not obligatory. In arbitration, the judgment generally carries more weight. In binding arbitration, the settlement is mandatory.

For instance, in Major League Baseball arbitration, it's an all or nothing binding arbitration. The arbitrator must take either the player's figure or the club's figure and nothing in between.

In labor-management strikes, frequently arbitrators (lawyers, former judges, professors) are brought in because the two sides can't agree and the longer they disagree, the more damage they do to their industry.

Arbitration, particularly binding arbitration, is drastic but in true standoffs, very effective. Sometimes the mere specter of arbitration works to close deals. Both sides know that if they can't settle their deal, a third party will, and it's possible that neither of the two sides will be happy. So, they try harder to find a solution of their own.

SOMETIMES NO DEAL IS THE BEST DEAL

We've all suffered from "negotiation fever" at one time or another. That's where you get so caught up in the heat of making a deal that you lose sight of the quality of the deal. If you weren't involved and you were just an observer, you'd whisper in your own ear, "Stop! It's not worth it." But it's hard to remind yourself to be objective. Some deals just aren't worth making. The trick is knowing which ones and when.

> Don't let the thrill of the hunt lead you to a bad deal.

IF DEAL FEVER PERSISTS, KEEP SAYING "NO"

How bad does a deal have to be to be worse than no deal at all? In an episode of the 80s television show *Ned and Stacey*, there was a scene that carried negotiation demands to absurd extremes and showed the equal absurdity of how far people will go once they're caught up in the fever of a deal.

Ned and Stacey, saddled with a money-losing muffin shop, finally find two business sharks ready to buy the property and level it for their own development. Just before the deal closes, Ned is overcome with guilt. He can't bring himself to take the shop away from the dedicated, elderly couple who lovingly run it. In order to get out of the deal, he tries to raise his demands on the buyers to their breaking point. Both sides have already settled on a price but Ned arbitrarily ups it. The buyers are so caught up in the chase, they agree. Desperate, Ned gets creative, "*I want . . . a monkey. A huge monkey.*" His own partner, Stacey, looks at him in shock. But the buyers can't stop themselves. Again, they agree. Ned has to go further, "*And I want to meet Kristy McNichol.*" Amazingly, the buyers acquiesce. Ned reaches for the totally absurd, "*And I want a sponge bath.*" Finally, enough is enough. The buyers walk.

It may have been a sitcom, but don't think deals haven't been made with terms as ridiculous or more so. Deal fever makes people forget they have the option of no deal.

During years of corporate law practice, I never gave a sponge bath to get a deal done, but there were a few times when I took a bath by doing a deal I simply should not have done. I'd have been better off with no deal.

Sometimes negotiators get so enthralled with the process, they lose sight of their goals. Remember, you came to the table to buy, sell, invest, sign a contract, place an order, or merge. You didn't come to buy for too high a price, sell too low, invest with a lousy return, sign a punitive contract, or merge yourself into oblivion. You didn't come just to make a deal, no matter how adverse the conditions of the deal. The goal isn't the deal. The goal is the fruit of the deal. Don't pick rotten fruit.

Unfortunately, the negotiation engagement takes on a life of its own. Working out Paragraph 4 on Page 9 becomes so daunting and so challenging that, when and if it's finally agreed upon, your focus simply moves on to Paragraph 5, instead of stepping back and asking yourself if you're still heading toward the achievement of your overall objectives. That's how bad deals get done.

The best deals occur when you remain emotionally objective (much easier said, than done) about the result. If you could really not care about closing the deal, and assume another deal will always come along, you'd probably make better deals every time. Recognizing that detachment is hard if not impossible to impose as a self-discipline, you can employ the tools we've already explained to take ego, pride, fear, anxiety, greed, revenge, and other common deal-related emotions out.

But, perhaps the best way to make a good deal is to remind yourself throughout that "no deal" is a viable, reasonable option.

When Is No Deal the Best Option?

- *When the other side forces you below your bottom line.* If you've pre-pared before sitting down, you know your starting point for a deal and you know your ending point: the level, price, timing, terms, or what-ever, below which you cannot go. This is the walkaway point, which you not only don't want to go beyond, but should not. That's why it's called the bottom line. Any lower (or higher) and the deal no longer pays out, has a return, works, or makes sense for your side. Don't get sucked into going beyond that point and convincing yourself that somehow circumstances will change and maybe it will still work out. If it didn't work out in your calm calculations before you sat down, it most likely won't work out when you've signed under duress. Just stop.
- *When you have better alternatives than the one proposed.* Never stop evaluating the quality of the deal. Remind yourself, at given junctures (every two hours or every two days depending on the length of the

negotiations) to look at the big picture. How good is the deal that's on the table? Is it good by absolute standards or merely as good as it's going to get with the other party? What else can you do? Where else can you go? If you know there's another buyer, seller, landlord, tenant, supplier, shipper, or partner with whom you can make a better deal, don't get drawn into a lesser deal just because it's the one at hand. Stop.

- *When you're confident the other side cannot abide by the terms of the deal.* Don't think you're the only one who can get seduced into making a deal just because it's the one on the table. The other side is just as susceptible to temptation. In fact, in their quest to make the deal, they may agree to specifics they can't meet. They might wish themselves into a price they cannot afford, dream themselves into an overly ambitious profit, or just hope to get lucky enough to meet an unrealistic timetable. Again, you have to step back and take a reality check. Can they really do what they say? Can they deliver? Or will you spend as much time and effort enforcing the deal as you have in making it? If the answer to the last question is "yes" or even "maybe," don't make it. Just stop.

- *When long-term problems can outweigh short-term gains.* Either side may be guilty of falling for "instant gratification" instead of eventual satisfaction. It happens with deals just as it happens when you down that fudge brownie sundae because it's in front of you and hate yourself in the morning when you get on the scale. You may opt to partner with an investor you don't really trust because together, you and Mr. Slippery can land a contract you couldn't otherwise get. However, after the contract has come and gone, you're now the partner in Slippery & Partners. Or you agree to deliver your No-Stick Zippers to Global Trousers, Inc. on a 52-week-a-year schedule that will practically kill your drivers, just so you can beat out your arch rival, Slick-Zip. Okay. You got the deal. Slick-Zip loses. But, now you have to deliver. And deliver. And deliver. Who really got stuck? Before you make a deal right now, take a break, and force yourself to look at the future. If tomorrow doesn't look as good as today, don't sign. Just stop.

Another $10 Game

Since we rarely give away $10 when we play the $10 Game, we often give our seminar participants a second chance to win the money. We tell the participants we're going to "auction off" $10 to the highest bidder.

We then tell them that the only rule is, the top two bidders must *both* pay us the full amount of their last bid.

At that point, the bidding starts. Most people are cautious at first, but pretty soon, someone says, "Okay, I'll bid one dollar," (since I can get $10 back). We look for the second bidder, asking, "Does anyone offer $2? You can make $8 with a winning bid of $2." Another person inevitably joins in and the horse race is on. We turn back to the first bidder. "You don't want to lose, do you? Bid $3 and you still end up making $7." After the first bidder raises the bid to $3, the second bidder goes up to $4, and, in no time, one of the two has bid $9. This is where it gets interesting.

Now we tell the other bidder, "You can bid $10 and break even. If you don't bid $10 and you come in second, then you still have to pay us the amount of your last bid which was $8." That bidder usually ups to $10, as a defense. Then we tell the $9 bidder, "Right now you're the losing bidder and you have to pay us $9 as your last bid. Of course, if you bid $11, you will win the $10 and only end up $1 in the hole." Suddenly the bidding escalates *beyond* the value of the prize, just to avoid losing. On occasion, the bidding has escalated past $20 before we stop the auction. (No, we don't make the bidders really pay us.)

If we had asked the people, before we began the exercise, if they would bid $20 to win a $10 bill, they would have said, "Absolutely not." But once they get caught up in the competitive atmosphere—once they seek to "cut their losses" by bidding more—the participants begin acting irrationally and making bad deals.

Although not as stark an example as the exercise, the same kind of irrational behavior sometimes takes over in corporate deals.

Economies of Scale versus Deal Fever

Not long ago, we were hired to consult with a corporation that was acquiring various medical practices, which, as a consolidated entity, would benefit from economies of scale. As a part of our preparation, we worked with an accounting firm to establish a precise formula for setting prices to pay for each practice. The formula took into account revenues, number of physicians and employees, all relevant business factors. What the formula did *not* take into account was the Founder's "acquire at all costs" state-of-mind, once the negotiation or "bidding" process began.

It was a $10 auction atmosphere except for the decimal point. The medical practice auction was in increments of millions of dollars. Time and again when the bidding got out of hand, we would tell the Founder, "Walk away from this one. No deal is the best deal." The Founder was unswayable. The carefully determined price formula was disregarded because of the Founder's irrational acquisition frenzy.

The Founder had raised $20 million, projected to acquire 10 medical practices. Because the bidding got out of hand, the money ran out after the purchase of only five practices. As a result, those efficiencies and economies of scale of the consolidated practice were severely diminished. Several years later, I talked to the Founder and he told me that he learned from his mistake. "I let my emotions overrule our planning and lost sight of the big picture."

Not only is "no deal" sometimes the best deal but, as demonstrated by the story of "The Pizza Sauce Salesman," at times it may lead to a better deal.

When Pizza Hut Sliced the Price of Tomato Sauce

I was flying cross-country, woke up from my nap, and discovered I was traveling next to a tomato sauce apostle. This fellow was the director of national accounts for Hunt Wesson, a division of Con Agra and the makers of Hunt's Tomato Sauce. You may think sauce is sauce. Wrong. He believed in his product. He lovingly and painstakingly told me about the tomatoes, the spices, the recipe, the care, jarring, the shipping, the quality control. He told me more than I really needed to know since I had no plans to compete in the business.

But, as I often do, I asked about recent deals or negotiations. He said he'd just been through one of the biggest of his career. It seems that Hunt's was one of the largest of six tomato sauce suppliers to Pizza Hut, providing the sauce for 30 percent of all their pizzas (which is a lot of pizzas). He swore that his sauce is so good, you could tell, just by tasting a Pizza Hut pizza, if it was made with Hunt's or not, which is to say, Pizza Hut was a satisfied customer.

Nonetheless, one day he got a call from the purchasing agent at the pizza chain. She informed him the company had decided to put the sauce contract out for bid to all six suppliers and select the two best bidders to divide the entire business.

I asked him how he felt given the quality of his product and his long-standing relationship with the customer. He said, he just took it as another bid on another contract, another negotiation. He followed the disciplines he always followed.

First, he called his team together. He elicited opinions from the quality control people, the production people, the sales department, and, of course, the financial people. They reanalyzed their current pricing structure at current order levels and then reanalyzed what they could offer given the possible increase in order level. They did a form of a preparation plan. Then they arrived at a bottom-line financial analysis to determine how far they could reduce their price, while maintaining a reasonable profit margin, and without any sacrifice of product quality—their lowest, best number. That was the number they had to write down on a piece of paper. They didn't think they even had the usual opportunity of making an offer, getting a counteroffer, then countering the counter. They had been told, "submit your final bid first."

So, they did just that. But they also submitted a value analysis along with the price. They reminded Pizza Hut of why dealing with Hunt Wesson is worthwhile. Quality is assured and guaranteed. There's virtually an unlimited supply of product. If you suddenly need more, you can get it. Should there be a service or delivery question, Hunt Wesson has distribution centers dotted across the country. They sent in the document and the price and they waited.

Ten days later, he got a call from the purchasing agent. Since she worked on practically a daily basis with each supplier, she was confident she knew each of their bids even though the bids had not been formally opened yet. Before that happens, she told the Hunt Wesson man, "You should submit a new bid." He asked, why. She said, "We agree, your product and service are excellent, and we want to continue doing business with your company, but I'm pretty sure your bid is $2\frac{1}{2}$ cents a barrel too high. So, you're going to finish third."

I said, "Boy, what a break. So, you lowered your bid and got the contract, right?" "No," he said, "we didn't change our bid at all." They regrouped, thought about it, reviewed their analysis, and decided they'd come to the right conclusion in the first place. He called the purchasing agent and reiterated their quality story, reminded her of the long-term relationship, and explained that their bid was the lowest possible number at which they could make a reasonable profit. He even apologized to her for not being able to go lower.

A few days later, he got another call from her. As she had predicted, Hunt Wesson had finished third. She discussed a wind-down period of two and a half months, after which the relationship would end.

Did he let her have it? Did he tell her what a huge mistake she'd just made? No. He shifted back into "sales mode." He thanked her for being a good customer and wished her the best. He offered to help out as much as possible during the wind-down. Why? Because he knew something, anything, could happen down the line, and she and/or Pizza Hut might once again become a customer. Not long after that, he wrote a letter to her and her boss, the executive vice president, thanking Pizza Hut for a great relationship and wishing them well.

The best deal was no deal. The man from Hunt Wesson didn't take it personally. He took it as business. He had analyzed the situation in his preparation plan. He knew his bottom line. He didn't go below it. He even developed alternatives. He knew it wouldn't be easy to replace a customer as large as Pizza Hut, but he saw a growing chain on the horizon called Macaroni Grill. They would be his first call should the Pizza Hut negotiation fall through. He weighed the short-term victory against the long-term burdens. He resisted today's deal for tomorrow's profit squeeze. In the end, he didn't make a deal just for the sake of making it.

Is that the end of the story? Not quite. Remember, he kept the relationship intact even as it was winding down. About six weeks after that, he got a call from his old customer, the Pizza Hut purchasing agent. She had a crisis: Runny pizza. (Evidently, one of the supplier's sauces wasn't worthy of their dough.) That may not seem like a tragedy to you, but you don't have Domino's, Papa John's, and Little Caesars breathing pepperoni in hot pursuit of your customers. Suddenly, Pizza Hut had to turn to their best source, not their cheapest. She told the Hunt Wesson man that Pizza Hut would give his company the lion's share of their business and he could virtually name his price.

What a turnabout! I asked him how much he raised his price. He said, "It was a good price when we bid and it was still a good price." In fact, all they did was adjust slightly to cover the costs of short-term delivery demands. Hunt Wesson went from 30 percent of the sauce business to 70 percent. In this case, no deal turned into a bigger deal.

Chapter 10: Unlocking Deadlocks

If Nothing Works, Change Something—(Moving Sometimes Feels like Movement)

- Change location.
- Change negotiators.
- Call in a mediator.

Find Reasons to Agree

Recount the points of agreement—two benefits:

1. Shows both parties how close they are.
2. Reminds both parties why the deal is a good idea.

Get Creative

1. *Start all over again.* If you're stuck, start fresh.
2. *Keep a secret.* Confidentiality minimizes worry about what a third party would think, allows room for new ideas.
3. *Recount interests.* Don't talk positions, talk real interests.
4. *Don't stop.* Keep talking, go from hypothetical to real.

Objective Mechanisms

Remember, the process is *ne*-gotiation, not *ego*-tiation.

- *You cut–I choose*: the kids' method.
- *Sealed bids*: fair and honest.
- *External criteria*: for example, government, industry data.
- *Arbitration*: neutral outsider.

When No Deal Is the Best Deal

When the other side forces you beyond your walkaway.

When you have better alternatives than the one proposed.

When the other side can't abide by terms of the deal.

When long-term problems outweigh short-term gains.

"Guess who took over the company?"

CHAPTER **11**

Building Relationships

> When you need a friend, it's too late to make one.
>
> —MARK TWAIN

> Well, the thing I learned as a diplomat is that human relations ultimately make a huge difference.
>
> —MADELEINE ALBRIGHT

TODAY VERSUS TOMORROW: HOW LONG IS THE LONG RUN?

Who is the real dealmaker: (a) The hit-and-run Hollywood producer who scores a fast profit on a script he options on Tuesday and resells to another studio on Thursday? or (b) The development executive who, instead of turning a fast buck, invests in a writer-director's idea, gathers funding, puts together a crew and stars, negotiates foreign distribution and streaming video rights, and has an option on the writer-director's next two ideas as well? The answer is, both. One is in it for the moment (the deal on the table) while the other is counting on the future (all the deals that may emanate from the deal on the table). Neither is right or wrong. But even if you successfully make several one-time deals, you have to start over each time.

If you pursue deals that have the potential to lead to more deals, your *return-on-effort* will pay out longer with larger rewards. Studies by Bain & Company, a Boston-based consulting firm, have suggested that a 5 percent increase in customer retention rate could double the profits of a small to midsized business. Bain also found that the average

Fortune 500 company could double its revenue growth rate with that same 5 percent increase in customer retention.

If you deal as if there's no tomorrow—classic win–lose—your deals won't lead to more deals. If you burn bridges, destroy the other side, squeeze the last buck out, "take no prisoners," you can't expect the other party to want to do business with you again. They'll run from the negotiating table, let alone consider returning to it. That's why so many hit-and-run negotiators have conveniently adopted the philosophy that each deal is a one-time event. Go in, score, get out.

On the other hand, if you follow the principles of WIN–win—if you set out to get most of what you want by helping the other side get some of what they want—**you'll build relationships that can spawn additional deals**, ad infinitum. As a matter of fact, people are willing to work through more difficult negotiations and even pay more where there is an existing relationship and trust. That's getting the highest return on effort. That's getting the most from the Power of Nice.

From the Pennant in 1979 to the World Series in 1983 (With Help from the Power of Nice)

The Orioles fell one game short of winning the World Series in 1979. It was a team that had all the makings of a World Series winner, if the players could be retained. But keeping a team of that caliber together, during the dawning of free agency, was a real challenge. Hometown heroes were leaving daily for big bucks in other markets. It so happened that, in the rarest of situations, I represented 15 members of that team. We had negotiated very hard on behalf of every one of them, but we and our clients also tried to understand the other side, the team.

So, when it came time to renegotiate contracts, how many of the players opted to leave Baltimore for greener pastures? How many did the Orioles decide just weren't worth the price? None. Eddie Murray, Ken Singleton, Rich Dauer, Scott McGregor, Doug DeCinces, Rick Dempsey, Dennis Martinez, among others, all stayed. They each achieved WIN–win. They stayed with the team and in the town they wanted and got paid market or near-market value. That was and is, unprecedented in modern sports. It wasn't because one side caved in to the other. It was because bonds had been forged, relationships had been built, and deals had been made that led to more deals.

In 1983, the heart of the 1979 team was still there and went on to win the 1983 World Series. It was a long-term dividend of the Power of Nice.

Coincidentally, 20 years later, I, along with our team at SNI, had the pleasure of forming a partnership with another franchise that was impacted by the Power of Nice philosophy and systematic approach and reaped its benefits. This time, we were involved from the team side. The San Antonio Spurs management, whom we have trained and consulted for over a decade, had the good fortune of drafting Tim Duncan in the 1997 draft. They have fully capitalized on Tim and their other talent by winning five championships from 1999 to 2014. Most importantly, the Spurs were able to draft and retain Tim Duncan, Tony Parker, and Manu Ginobli—their core players—throughout their unprecedented streak of playoff appearances. The Spurs are a small market club that has been successful by negotiating with the 3 Ps and doing WIN–win deals, which take into account the interests of the other side.

A RELATIONSHIP TOOL: BONDING

Every negotiation takes place in an environment. That doesn't just mean the physical setting, the conference room, or the office. It means the feelings, sensitivities, tensions, fears, and hopes that comprise the atmosphere of the negotiation. They make up the environment as much, or more so, than the four walls, table, and chairs. *Bonding*—finding what you have in common with the other party, rather than where you're at odds—can create a more positive negotiating environment and help build a relationship where there has been none previously.

Just as negotiation is a process, not an event, so is bonding. Bonds are built. You find a link that leads to conversation, that leads to another link, and more conversation. Pretty soon, you have a chain that stretches from one party to the other, like a bridge. The more you travel it, the more familiar with it you become. After enough travel, your bond becomes a shared set of experiences—a relationship.

When you reach an impasse with someone you don't like or simply don't know, you're more likely to let the impasse stand. When the same situation occurs with someone you've come to know, understand, and even like, you're going to look for ways to get past the deadlock. It's just human nature. *A good negotiating environment can carry you past bad negotiating moments.*

The value of relationships is immeasurable. Ask a manufacturer who's been under the gun to deliver by a date certain, who turned to the supplier they can always count on to help meet that delivery deadline. Ask the giant developer who gets three bids on every set of drawings but one bid is always from the builder that took a chance on his company when it was starting up. Ask the stockbroker whose clients swear her word is the Dow Jones gospel.

Relationships can accomplish what acquaintances can't. Relationships make for not just one deal, but deals that lead to deals, repeated deals, subdeals, offshoot deals, renewing deals. Why make only one deal when you can make several?

THE MEET-AND-BOND STYLE

The opposite of the hit-and-run style is *meet-and-bond*. When you encounter the party with whom you'll be negotiating, instead of focusing on your differences, look for connectors ... and you are bonding. Purposely search for things you may have in common, shared interests. After all, you already have a pretty good idea of where the two of you will be opposed. Whatever your asking price, they're likely to want a lower one. If you want cash terms, chances are good they'll want to stretch out the payments. The deal itself is bound to be full of push and pull. To minimize animosity and to appreciate each of your points of view, it helps to see each other as people, not just positions.

Bonding is finding links between two parties. The link may be familial, social, business, political, or recreational. It's anything you and the other person share, from the most common ones such as both having young children, to the most specific, such as being collectors of vintage French wines. The bonds you discover may have to do with the deal directly, indirectly, or, seemingly, not at all. Both of you may have been charged by your respective CEOs to come back with deals that will impress the board of directors, not cost much, have low risk, and high return—all goals in which you can sympathize with each other's pressures. The bond may appear to have nothing to do with the deal and yet everything to do with getting it done. Perhaps you both do have young children and you've both promised your families a vacation *if* you can get the deal done by spring break. In either case, if you don't bond, you'll never know what you might share.

Start the Bonding Process

Gather Information

Remember the Prepare phase of negotiation? Before you actually meet with the other side, look back at the research you did on them. Chances are, within that data are cues about the background, interests, and habits of the person or people you're facing. Look through social media profiles, biographies on company websites, interviews, articles or blog entries, or countless other resources available online. Chances are, you have something in common. Where did they grow up? Where did they go to college? Were they part of a fraternity or sorority? What are their hobbies? When you do come face to face, you already have a base of bonding information on which to build.

Observe

Bonding clues will be all around you. If you meet in the other side's office, look at what's on the desk, floor, and walls: vacation pictures, inspirational quotations, those yarn-wrapped pencil holders made by a kid in arts and crafts, running shoes tucked under a credenza, a paperweight made from a sailboat pulley, celebrity photos, family pictures, a doubles team trophy. If you meet in neutral territory, study the other person: style of dress—conservative or bold; jewelry—lots, little, flashy, crafty, or antique; shoes—Italian, sensible, or beat-up boaters; college ring; diver's watch; body type—jock or couch potato.

Talk

Ask questions. Make the first gesture. Bonding is the difference between "Hello, here are my five key issues. What are yours?" and "Hi. It looks like you do a little practice putting on the carpet. Are you a golfer too?"

Use the cues and clues you observe to start the conversation that creates bonds:

"I have a pencil holder like that only mine is in green and orange yarn. How old is your artist?"

"What island are you on in this photo? I'm looking for a getaway this winter."

"I couldn't help but notice your watch. Do you scuba dive?"

Once you make the gesture of building the bond, it's likely to build on itself. Ask about a vacation, a child, a college, or a hobby, and you'll get a response. After all, the other person put that picture on their office wall because it's a favorite. You're asking them to tell you about something they like. If you have similar interests, you two may not be archrivals after all. You may be two people who could be friends and just happen to have a job to do. You now have something negotiators need but rarely recognize, empathy. You understand the other person and their personal interests, and they, yours. Once you do, you're both bound to be more open to understanding each other's interests in the deal.

It's easier for strangers to practice win–lose negotiation. Once you've bonded, you have a better chance to achieve WIN–win results.

Here's a bond I built at the eleventh hour, just in time to turn the deal around.

School Ties

I had been working long and hard on a deal to get multimillion-dollar funding for a biotech project. We had found our investor. We had a commitment for the money. We had gotten to the last step, drafting of the contract. At that point, the chairman of the board of the investing company told me to deal directly with their lawyer. "You're a lawyer. He's a lawyer. You two get it done."

It sounded good to me. After all, the hard part was done. We had the funding committed. Then I got the first draft of the contract. It was 95 pages. I got on the phone with the lawyer. We talked about the preambles for almost three hours. That was not the first real page of substance, just the "whereas" clauses that precede the substance. He was rock-hard, immovable, mechanical, and anything but human. Three hours later, I knew his position. He knew ours. We had gotten nowhere.

I hung up and sat there thinking. I have to find a way to bond with this guy. *If there's a way*. There's bound to be a way. *Maybe not this time*. Everybody has something. *Maybe not this guy*.

We had another telephone call scheduled for the next day. Instead, I got up early and drove two hours to Philadelphia to meet with him face to face. I figured if we're going to bond, we're going to do it in person.

I walked into his office and it was as if the connection between us jumped off his wall. There was a framed diploma from a small, Eastern college. It just so happened to be the same small, Eastern college from which I had graduated. I said, "You went to Haverford?"

He said, "Yes, I did. Where did you go to school?"

I said, "Haverford."

There we were, two Haverford grads. We'd had nothing in common the day before and today we had four years in common.

I enjoyed my years at Haverford, but activities on its behalf didn't occupy much of my life. But they were very important to his. He lived not far away, so he could visit often, support the school, and he could volunteer. He was involved with the Alumni Association and annual giving. He asked for my donation on the spot. I gave. The hard, immovable, mechanical, anything-but-human lawyer was human when it came to his alma mater. He even smiled when he said, "Haverford."

We finished the negotiation in less than a week. Bonding didn't change the basic issues. It changed the tone with which we approached the issues. It enabled us to find solutions to problems.

REBONDING

Bonds are like muscles. If you don't keep them active, they weaken. Often people do a great job of bonding right up to the time they close the deal. Once the deal is done and the check has cleared, many people forget the power of bonding. Several years later, when it's time to renew the contract, the customer can't tell the incumbent vendor from the rest of the competition. Bonding was allowed to disintegrate—a true relationship was not established.

Even long-term relationships need to rebond from time to time. Remember, "It's not the sale, it's the relationship that counts." We make it a practice to keep track of the people with whom we negotiate during the times when we aren't negotiating. A phone call to say hello. A holiday card. An e-mail congratulations on a promotion. The Internet has made maintaining bonds easier than ever. Today, there are countless, simple, and sincere ways to bond once the relationship has been established.

When negotiations break down, or appear that they might, look for opportunities to rebond. Get away from the negotiation table. Do something social. Bring in new parties, spouses, other partners, people who share personal interests, not just business interests. Of course, the best approach is to keep bonds active and they will be strong when you need them most.

Here's a situation where I literally went out of my way to rebond with the other party.

Double Delight

For several years, there was a general manager of a ball club located in the Midwest with whom I'd had dealings from time to time. However, to say we had any kind of relationship would go beyond the bounds of exaggeration. I knew where his office was. He had my phone number in his Outlook. That was the extent of our rapport. He had a reputation as a pretty cool customer and he was living up to it.

I figured it was time to try to build a relationship. Did this just occur to me like a bolt out of the blue? Hardly. I had an ulterior motive. Someday, perhaps soon, I was going to have a major transaction with him. When "someday" came, and it always does, I didn't want to deal with an adversary or a stranger. I wanted to deal with someone I already knew, someone I could talk to, someone with whom I shared something other than a contract we would be shoving back and forth at each other.

So even though, at that moment, we had absolutely nothing to negotiate, I decided to go see him. Like everyone else in business, the one thing I don't have to spare is time. But I felt this was an investment worth making. To use my time as economically as possible, when my next trip to the West Coast came up, I booked a stop in his city.

I called the general manager and asked to see him. I flew out, got in a cab, went to the stadium and showed up for my appointment with nothing on my agenda. Why did I have to be there in person? Why didn't I do it over the phone? Because I wanted to see him, see him in his habitat, see him when he talked to me, see how he talked, when he smiled, if he smiled.

I wanted him to see me, as well. I wanted to meet face to face. You can't do that over the phone, by an e-mail, or text. But once you have done it in person, phone calls and e-mails can be much more effective.

I walked into his office. I looked around. I was searching for links, human connectives between him, the cool general manager and me, the client advocate. I scanned the room and saw: Autographed baseballs. Baseball books. Game day programs. A team jersey. A couple of team hats. Photos of him with players, past and present. Photos of him with the team owner. Endless baseball paraphernalia. Basically, I disregarded all the baseball-related items in the room. We'd known each other through baseball and so far had never really bonded that way. It wasn't as if he grew up in my hometown of Philadelphia and we shared fond memories of watching the Phillies from the bleachers. We hadn't each played minor league baseball, collected baseball cards, or had the same baseball heroes. For both of us, baseball was business.

So, I looked further: More photos. Pictures of his family. Pictures of his wife. Pictures of his children. I stopped. I have kids, love kids. That's a link. But, lots of people have kids. Some people are close to theirs, some aren't. Some people are proud, some aren't.

Then I noticed two more photos, one on either side of a family shot. Pretty prominent placement, I thought. Only these weren't pictures of children or even pets. These were roses. A light bulb went on in my head. This man has pictures of roses on his desk in front of him all day long. He loves roses.

I said, "That's the most beautiful Double Delight I've ever seen."

He looked at me and said, "How'd you know it was a Double Delight?"

I said, "Do you grow roses?"

He said, "Yeah, I grow roses. Do you?"

I said, "Yeah."

We both grew roses! That was our link. Outside of baseball, it's his passion. And it's mine, too.

For the next hour and a half, we discussed organic fungicides, pesticides—pro and con, weather, colors, varieties, how many leaves to cut under to make them regenerate. We traded problems and we swapped secrets. We didn't talk baseball or business but the whole tenor of our relationship changed then and there.

I called him during the winter when it got unseasonably warm and asked him what he does for his roses when that happens. He did the same with me during a cold snap. We talked about special diseases that threaten roses, particularly in the East. He told me that, if he was in Baltimore to see a game, he would love to see my rose garden.

When "someday" came and it was time for us to make a deal, we knew each other. That doesn't mean he collapsed and gave in to every request I made, or that I acquiesced to his demands. It means we listened and talked and heard each other. It means hurdles didn't turn into stonewalls.

Did we become friends? Yes. Is he my best friend in the world? No. But we've bonded. We're two parties who negotiate as people, not just positions. As a result, we make better deals, and I stress, *deals,* plural, not singular. Because just as "someday" always comes, so does the day after, and the deal that goes with it.

NO FAUX BONDING

There's a very important point to make about bonding. It's not a ploy. It's real. You can't pretend to share something with the other person. First of all, it's likely to blow up in your face. If you don't really love Persian cats, don't know the first thing about Greek cooking, or never hiked the north face of the Rockies, you're bound to give yourself away.

Secondly, the whole idea of bonding is to genuinely invest in the relationship. Find the link, don't fake it.

There's a sequence in the movie *Used Car*, where a salesman attempts to bond with every customer. It goes something like this: A shopper walks onto the lot and the salesman strides over, sticks his hand out and says, "What's your name?"

The innocent shopper says, "Mr. Polanski. I'm looking for a Buick."

The salesman breaks into a mile-wide smile and says, "Really? My name is Kowalski and I sell Buicks." Wow! They're both Polish. Who says you can't trust a used car salesman? Coincidentally, when the next customer is Swedish, Spanish, Irish, Scottish, or Jewish, the salesman will be whatever "ish" is called for.

Don't pretend to be what you aren't, like what you don't like, or play what you don't play. Look for the real link. Look for the true common interest. And, if you don't do it early in the negotiation, which is better, do it late, which is better than never.

Three Bonding Rules to Keep in Mind

1. *Meet face to face.* You can't bond with a stranger. If you cannot meet in person, try a videoconference before resorting to phone and then e-mail, in that order. The richer the communication medium, the better the ability to form relationships.
2. *Go to their turf.* You can learn more about someone in his or her own lair than in neutral territory. Don't be afraid to play an away game. On their own terrain, their office, their club, they'll be comfortable, just comfortable enough to let you see them, know them, connect with them.
3. *If negotiation breaks down, rebond.* Have another bonding session. Get away from the negotiation table. Do something social. Bring in new parties, spouses, other partners, people who share your interests, not your business.

PRACTICE MAKES BONDING

A participant in one of our seminars came up to us during a break to talk to my cofacilitator. She was in business in the United States, but wasn't American, and most of her customers were younger. She was older and she was Spanish. Therefore, she didn't know American television shows or movies, didn't follow American sports, couldn't share growing up stories, had no family here, and would seem to have no connections with any of her customers except business. She asked how she could bond with customers with virtually no links available. The facilitator and she engaged in a bonding exercise right then and there.

Bingo! We Bonded!

He said to her, "You're from Spain?"

She said, "Yes."

He asked her, "What part?"

She replied, "Barcelona."

He said, "I love Barcelona."

Interested, she said, "You've been there?" Right away, she softened. He liked her hometown.

He explained, "Yes, after I graduated from law school, I traveled all around Europe. I spent three days in Barcelona. It's a beautiful city."

As soon as he said it was beautiful, she got a nostalgic look in her eyes. "Ah, yes, I grew up there. It's so beautiful."

He asked her, "What do you remember doing there when you were growing up?"

"Well," she said, a little sheepish but willing to share this with a fellow Barcelona-lover, "one of my fondest memories is playing bingo."

He smiled knowingly, as it seemed he had a connection to bingo.

She went on, "They had bingo parlors everywhere. You see, after the regime fell, the government allowed the bingo parlors that had been closed to reopen. So I remember my mother taking me to play bingo when I was a little girl." He could see in her eyes, she was reliving those times with her mother.

That got him thinking back, "You know, you may not believe this but here in Baltimore, my mother used to take me to play bingo all the time at the local Catholic schools. They all had bingo parlors to raise money for the parish. You see, my mother took me, too."

She smiled at him. Memories of bingo in Barcelona. Memories of bingo in Baltimore. Bingo, they had bonded.

A Bonding Exercise

First, pick a bonding partner

It can be anyone you don't know, a stranger. A worker in your office from another department, number 63 when you're number 62 at the deli counter, somebody else in the dentist's waiting room, the passenger next to you on a plane.

Next, observe

Check out your co-bonder. Look for cues. What's she reading? E-reader or book? How is he dressed? What's in the shopping bag? Short hair or long? Manicured nails. Serious face or ready smile? Looking at her watch. In a hurry? Carrying a briefcase or backpack? Constantly checking his iPhone? Or does she prefer a Samsung Galaxy? Ear buds in her ears? Pens in pocket? Something in his contact lens?

Now, find a link

That magazine article on fishing. You fish, too. Nice necktie. What time is it? I'm a big book reader, and I just switched to an e-reader. What'd you get at the outlet stores? Need any contact solution?

Add links to your links

Keep going until it's time to go back to work, the deli man asks for your order, the nurse calls your name, or the plane lands.

A Quick Guide to Bonding

Start with Interests, cued by something they say or have—that is, the picture on their desk, the college on their LinkedIn profile, and so on. These start the bonding process but are not too intrusive.

Once you feel it is appropriate, dig a little deeper into their Goals, Struggles, or Stressors. Start professionally first and move into personal life if it fits the flow of the conversation.

According to UCLA professor and human communication expert, Albert Mehrabian, only 7 percent of communication is verbal—so how you say it should receive as much thought as what you say.

Do not try to move too quickly. Bonding is not a race. Only dig into topics that make sense.

Make sure that the communication is <u>two way</u>. Most people love to talk, so the conversation doesn't have to be exactly even. But people do not like to be interrogated. Be prepared to answer the same questions you are asking of the other person.

Don't only call or contact when you need something. A relationship is a <u>balance</u>. Every favor does not have to be counted and returned, but people do keep a general tally in their minds. Try to reach out at least as often to check in, share news, or do a favor for someone, as you do to ask for something.

THE VALUE OF RELATIONSHIPS

I can't stress enough the values, both measurable and intangible, of building relationships (instead of just making deals one at a time). Nor can I overemphasize that you never know what the long-term benefit of a relationship will be. Few stories drive home the importance of building relationships more poignantly than this one. Trust, grounded in a relationship, encourages new deal opportunities and helps overcome seemingly intractable obstacles.

The Deal of a Lifetime: How Kirby Puckett Bonded with Carl Pohlad, the Minnesota Twins, and the Twin Cities

Passing up instant gratification isn't an easy choice to make, but it is one that's often worth it. Back in 1992, Kirby Puckett, the superstar of the Minnesota Twins, was about to become a free agent. He had built his career with the Twins and he wanted to stay with them. With us as his agent, Kirby had a history of negotiating WIN–win deals with the team. At this point, we knew that Kirby might have to make some sacrifices to stay since Minnesota is a small revenue market.

Large, medium, small, or minuscule market, we were miles apart when the negotiations began. To use the baseball cliché, we weren't in the same ballpark. We felt Kirby's value was in the range of $35 million over five years. The Twins first offer was $12 million over three years. Worse than the dollars per year—our $7 million versus their $4 million—was the discrepancy in contract length—our five years to three. We were $23 million and two years apart.

Still, Kirby and his family wanted to remain in the Twin Cities. Throughout the summer, I kept going back and forth with the team's general manager,

Andy MacPhail. Finally, in August, Andy MacPhail brought us a five-year offer of $28 million. This brought them up to $5.6 million per year. The dollars weren't as high as we had hoped, or as high as we believed Kirby's market value to be, but we knew enough about the Twins' finances to know the club was close to the limits of its resources.

I didn't tell Kirby to take it. I didn't tell him to turn it down. I said, "Kirby, how do you feel about the offer?" Kirby did what he always does with a major decision. He talked it over with his wife, Tonya. After a lot of soul-searching, they concluded they'd take the offer.

But before Kirby accepted, we put in a call to Donald Fehr, the then-leader of the Major League Players Association. Don had been criticized by some for wanting to squeeze every last dime from every team owner. It so happens, that criticism was undeserved. Don Fehr was determined that each ballplayer be in the best situation for that player. When we called and told Don the Twins offer, he asked only one question. "Kirby, are you happy with it?"

Kirby said, "Yes, I am."

Don said, "Then you should take it."

Then, Carl Pohlad overruled Andy MacPhail and retracted the offer. Kirby was greatly disappointed. I was discouraged. Andy was disheartened that the deal he had worked so hard to make had fallen apart. Negotiations were stalled. Throughout the fall, nothing occurred to encourage us.

Finally, reluctantly, we went into the free-agent market. Remember, win–win (and certainly WIN–win) isn't lose–win, where you give up everything just to make some kind of a deal. We explored other cities but kept the door open to the Twins' front office in case they should have a change of heart. I followed a personal axiom, "Be hard on issues, soft on people." We went to Boston and Philadelphia and learned from the Red Sox and the Phillies what we suspected. Kirby Puckett could get a lot more as a free agent, well into the mid-$30 million range for five years, maybe higher.

Financially, things were looking up. However, Kirby and Tonya still wanted to live in Minneapolis. I called Andy MacPhail in late November and told him, "You're going to lose Kirby." Standard negotiation was getting nowhere. To change the course of what now appeared to be almost inevitable would require a change of normal procedure. We suggested an informal meeting with Carl Pohlad, perhaps over a meal. The message came back that Carl and Eloise Pohlad would like to have Kirby and Tonya Puckett, me, my partner, Michael Maas, and Andy MacPhail to dinner at their home. We had no specific agenda and, frankly, we had no expectations.

It was a lovely evening, a great dinner of wine and good food, during which we discussed community involvement, family, priorities—everything but baseball. At the end of the night, Carl turned to Kirby and said, "What do I have to do to keep you here?" Kirby replied, "I just want to be treated fairly." Carl nodded and saw us out.

I went back to the Pucketts' house with them. We talked past midnight, well into the morning. Could we work something out? Could we find a way to make a deal in the Twin Cities? Could we do it in time? At this point, we were facing deadlines from the other interested teams. At 3:30 A.M., I called Andy MacPhail at home. We talked about what kind of a deal would work: Something in the range of $30 million, five years, game tickets worth several hundred thousand dollars, and other support for Kirby's charitable endeavors. Clearly, Andy would have to talk to Carl Pohlad about those kinds of numbers. Somewhere between 4:00 and 5:00 A.M., Andy called back, "Deal." Kirby got $30.5 million, tickets for the underprivileged kids he helped, and a pledge of further aid to Kirby's causes. The relationship between Kirby and Carl contributed to changing the owner's stance. Before Kirby formally accepted, I talked heart-to-heart with Kirby. "You know, in the next few weeks, someone is going to get $35 or maybe $40 million (and it happened). Think about that before you decide."

Kirby looked at me and said, "You're probably right. But no matter how much they get, nobody will be happier than me."

We told Andy MacPhail, "Deal."

We had negotiated. We'd gotten stalled. We explored alternatives but didn't burn bridges. We tried an unconventional approach. We didn't jump at a deal; instead we opted to build a relationship. The Pohlads and the Pucketts had rebonded. The Twins kept their superstar. Kirby's family stayed in Minneapolis. If that amounted to the total result of building a relationship, it would've been more than worth the effort.

But, as it turned, out, there was more to the story. At the beginning of the 1996 baseball season, as Kirby entered the fourth year of his contract, he noticed a problem with his vision. The problem quickly evolved into a serious condition. The sight in Kirby's right eye was fading and fading fast. By July, his career as a major league ballplayer was over. The superstar who couldn't be stopped by 100 mph fastballs was stopped by the insidious disease glaucoma.

You have to know Kirby Puckett to appreciate the way he handled this tragic situation. I remember the news conference at which his retirement was announced. Hardened baseball players, callous reporters, and veteran team officials were all in tears. Kirby sat behind the microphone, flashed his big, broad smile and said, "Don't worry about me. It may be cloudy in my right eye, but the sun is always shining in my left eye."

Although he maintained a confident, positive attitude, his life was now filled with agony and uncertainty. What would he do? How would they live? What did the future hold? Of course, the agony did not abate but the uncertainty did. Immediately, propositions came to Kirby for this next phase of his life. He was practically overwhelmed with offers, from individuals and businesses around the Twin Cities, as well as from far away. It seemed that everywhere and everyone with whom Kirby had "built relationships" reciprocated with opportunities. Among them was a proposal from Carl Pohlad. He wanted Kirby to work with the Twins. But beyond that, he asked Kirby if he would participate in other Pohlad business enterprises. That dinner in November of 1992 had not only sealed a baseball contract, it had strengthened a relationship between two people and two families that lasted through good times and challenging times. The bond transcended the deal. The relationship outlasted a baseball career. The Power of Nice paid off again.

REFRESHER

Chapter 11: Building Relationships

> WIN—win deals build relationships.

Negotiations that build relationships provide you with a return-on-effort by increasing the retention rate of current deals, as well as making more future deals, and, in turn, increasing revenues and profits.

> Bonding leads to relationships where none previously existed.

No "faux bonding": Pretending you have a shared interest when you don't will backfire.

Rules of Bonding

1. *Meet face-to-face*: Can't bond with a stranger.
2. *Go to their turf*: Learn more about someone in the comfort of their home/office.
3. *If negotiation breaks down, rebond*: Go back to what you have in common, not where you differ.

Practice Makes Bonding (Exercise)

- Find a stranger.
- Find links.
- Use the Quick Guide to Bonding.

How to Bond

Start with Interests—Then move on to Goals, Struggles, and Stressors, if appropriate.

Body Language—Don't forget that more information is communicated nonverbally than verbally.

It's a Balance—Bonding requires two-way communication and should be beneficial for both parties.

Never underestimate the value of relationships.

"You can't talk to him like that, Herman! He makes your salary every time he trots lethargically to right field."

CHAPTER **12**

Putting It All Together

Most effective negotiations use the three key principles behind the Power of Nice—the 3Ps. One negotiation may exemplify the value of the 3Ps with the emphasis on preparation, another on utilizing probing and, in particular, listening skills, another on the best way to propose, and another on how to deal with difficult negotiators, each with various combinations of these tools. But once in a while, a negotiation comes along that highlights the application of all of the principles of *The Power of Nice*. The following is a case history, which illustrates and utilizes all the power of *The Power of Nice*.

THE MAJOR LEAGUE BASEBALL OWNERS VERSUS THE MAJOR LEAGUE UMPIRES (AND THE MAJOR LEAGUE UMPIRES VERSUS THEMSELVES)

What's a negotiator's worst nightmare? Too high a price? Too low? Bad terms? No, it's when your negotiation strategy literally self-destructs. Not only does the deal blow up, but so does all of your negotiating leverage and perhaps even the viability of your negotiation team. What do you do? Give in? Give up? Or take an entirely different approach?

In the summer of 1999, the negotiations between the Major League Umpires Association (the "Association") and the Major League Baseball Owners backfired so badly that, in a matter of days, the Association lost virtually all of its bargaining power. *In fact, the Association was instantaneously so crippled, the umpires would first have to negotiate with themselves to regain a measure of unity and a fresh start just to get back to the table with the owners.*

It couldn't have begun worse, a textbook case of how not to negotiate, a win–lose strategy deteriorating into a lose–lose outcome (a loss for the umpires of their bargaining leverage and an eventual loss of umpire talent for baseball). But later, through an eleventh-hour adoption of the Power of Nice philosophy and its systematic approach, it became a case study in *how to negotiate*, putting the umpires back into a position to bargain effectively.

The triggering event occurred on July 14, 1999, with the Association Executive Director Richie Phillips' attempt to force early renegotiation of the umpires' collective bargaining agreement. Phillips followed the ill-fated strategy of 12,000 air traffic controllers in 1985—when they struck illegally, President Reagan swiftly dismissed them and immediately ordered the hiring of replacements.

When Phillips, a renowned hardball negotiator, advised members of the umpires' Association to tender their resignations to Major League Baseball, the umps met a similar fate to the one meted out by Reagan. Sandy Alderson, then Major League Baseball's executive vice president for operations, responded: "This is either a threat to be ignored or an offer to be accepted." Baseball took the latter option and began hiring replacements.

Many of the 50-plus umpires who resigned tried to rescind their resignations, but sadly 22 were left without jobs. Suddenly the Association, which Phillips had helped build, was practically powerless. Although he worked to obtain many benefits for umpires through the years, he may be most remembered for this faulty strategy.

My relationships with umpires went back a long way, both on and off the field. After spending 25 years in baseball and attending hundreds of games, I not only watched the "men in blue" call balls and strikes on my baseball clients, but I got to know and respect them as human beings. In late 1991, I became deeply involved with umpire Steve Palermo. Steve had been shot and paralyzed while coming to the aid of two waitresses who were being mugged in Dallas. Steve's heroism cost him the profession he loved. Without adequate compensation or benefits, Steve struggled financially as well as physically. On behalf of Steve and his wife, Debbie, I negotiated with then Acting Commissioner Bud Selig to hire Steve as a special assistant in the Commissioner's Office and provide him with needed benefits and compensation. With this professional stability, Steve was able to focus on his physical rehabilitation. Steve's professional role grew to his being a supervisor of umpires for Major League Baseball and his physical rehabilitation progressed to the point where he could walk without crutches.

Several years later, the personal side of umpires became even clearer during the infamous Roberto Alomar–John Hirschbeck "spitting incident." I knew John Hirschbeck, one of the most respected umpires in the game, having interviewed him on my television show on Baltimore's NBC affiliate. He talked about the loss of his son, John, to adrenoleukodystrophy (ALD), a rare genetic brain disease, and the challenge he and his wife, Denise, faced knowing that their other son, Michael, was also afflicted with the disease.

Sometime later, an unfortunate on-field incident brought John and me together again. After disputing a call, the perennial All-Star Roberto Alomar shocked the baseball world by spitting on John Hirschbeck. Having dealt with superstar athletes for many years, I fully expected the media feeding frenzy that followed. John asked for my advice. He made it clear, from the beginning, that he wanted to put the incident behind him and I encouraged him to do so. Rather than holding a lifetime grudge and treating each other with animosity, John and Roberto both ultimately practiced the Power of Nice, extending their hands to one another when they next met on the playing field and maintaining their mutual respect thereafter. These experiences emphasized to me, not only an umpire's dedication to the game, but the human dimension of these "men in blue" that few see when they are on the field.

My role of working with individual umpires like Steve and John actually evolved into a role of helping a larger group of umpires in the summer of 1998. Back then, when some umpires began to feel uncomfortable with their union leadership, Joe Brinkman, another highly regarded umpire, asked if I would lead an election challenge to Phillips. I declined to challenge Phillips for the post of Executive Director of the umpires' union. But I did offer to advise the group (Brinkman had been joined by John Hirschbeck, Tim Welke, and several other umpires) pro bono. I agreed with their feeling that they would be better served with nonconfrontational leadership and sent them copies of the first edition of this book, which had just been published.

In a meeting of the Association in February of 1999, Brinkman, Hirschbeck, and Welke were unable to garner enough votes to prevent the reappointment of Phillips as executive director. Brinkman and Hirschbeck were dejected. They felt that they had tried a new approach and failed. I comforted them with a bold prediction: Within six months,

Phillips would do something "so outrageous and so negative, you'll find renewed strength for real opposition." It took only five months.

When Phillips had suggested the "mass resignation" tactic in July of 1999, many of his troops obediently followed. As one umpire put it, "We drank the Kool-Aid." But only hours later, the same ump thought, "What have I just done?" The uneasiness spread; the umpires put their careers in jeopardy. In one case, an umpire said that he signed the resignation because of the intense peer pressure at the meeting.

When he arrived home, he replayed the strategy and outcome with his most important advisor, his wife. She summed up the thoughts of families, fans, and experts around the country when she exclaimed, "What in the world were you thinking!" Within 24 hours of the mass resignation meeting, umpires were calling me for help.

Practicing what we preach, I began my own preparation. I called distinguished labor lawyers who represented both union and management perspectives in several industries. Their unanimous response was, "What in the world were they thinking!" These advisors told me the umpires' only hope was to rescind their resignations as soon as possible. I conveyed this advice to those umpires who called me, encouraging each to hire his own counsel, to pass the word to other umpires to do likewise, and for all of them to weigh the option of rescinding their resignations.

Further, we started to share ideas with other umpires and legal experts in a series of conference telephone calls. Each call became a mini-seminar in *The Power of Nice* negotiation principles: The **3Ps—prepare, probe,** and **propose**—as well as lessons in dealing with difficult negotiators, listening, and bonding (all in contrast to Phillips's combative style).

On September 27, 1999, we conducted a call with a group of umpire representatives in my Baltimore law office and with more than 40 umpires on phones around the country. During that call, several labor lawyers agreed that the first step to rebuilding the umpires' strength would be to decertify the existing union. A new union was the only hope for dealing constructively with Major League Baseball and possibly helping the 22 unemployed umpires.

Thus began a new negotiation—a negotiation within a negotiation—by Hirschbeck, Brinkman, and their allies to obtain the support of enough umpires to achieve decertification of the union. If the previous strategy of the Major League Umpires Association was a case study in *how not to negotiate*, this new negotiation to decertify the union and start fresh would be textbook Power of Nice.

Initially, I led them through the use of the first of the 3Ps, *Preparation*. Learn everything about the current union: its rules, legal documents, and finances. Use the Preparation Checklist: Gather and analyze information about *precedents* for decertification, as well as the applicable labor law. Find *alternatives* to Phillips's leadership of the umpires' Association, as well as alternative approaches to waging a successful decertification campaign. Learn how the *interests* of the undecided umpires would impact the process. Become fully familiar with the timetable and deadlines governing the election process. Analyze the relative *strengths and* weaknesses of the existing umpires' union and of those of the group being led by Hirschbeck and Brinkman. And finally, set goals for the Hirschbeck–Brinkman group; establish team assignments for the leaders of the group while analyzing Phillips' team; map out a strategy for a successful election campaign; prepare *scripts* for meetings and conference calls.

Then, together, we practiced the second P, *Probing*—patiently asking every umpire for goals, objections, and worries, both rational and emotional. We instructed our leadership team in using the **W.H.A.T.** system to frame questions. Find out **W**hat is important to the constituents, **W**hat *else* is important, **W**hich element is most important, and **W**hy it is important. **H**ypothesize, by asking questions in the form of "what ifs" rather than direct or threatening questions. To gather additional information, **A**nswer their questions with your own questions. And, in your never-ending quest for more and more knowledge, encourage respondents to **T**ell *me more*. From time to time, I would point out to Hirschbeck (emerging as a leader) the principles they were practicing. "Keep probing; keep asking, and don't hesitate to ask them to tell more and more." "Learn what others want; understand their needs." "The best way to get what you want is to help others get what they want."

Another important call came on Sunday, October 3. Hirschbeck conducted the telephone meeting with me quietly offering advice. The subject was key; it involved asking the other umpires to fund the projected $100,000 expense of a decertification effort at a cost of $3,000 per umpire. If this **P**roposal, the third P, had been made earlier, it would have likely been rejected. However, because Hirschbeck, Brinkman, and their team had taken the time to *Prepare,* and because they spent countless telephone calls *Probing* the interests of the other umpires, when it came time to make this proposal, sharing the cost was not a bombshell, but, instead, a foregone conclusion.

Hirschbeck, following a script, which we had devil's advocated, asked for questions and concerns. A novice at the start of this process, John was becoming a seasoned negotiator, utilizing the lesson of *Listening* by encouraging his leadership team to "let others vent opposing views," "diffuse anger," practicing the lesson that "listening isn't just waiting to talk." Because the conference calls extended to three hours, some umpires became frustrated with the apparently slow movement. John counseled them to be patient with another Power of Nice principle, *"Negotiation is a process, not an event."* Ultimately, the Sunday call was a huge success. The umpires were becoming comfortable with decertification and creation of a new union.

Support was growing. Forty-nine of the 93 umpires joined with Hirschbeck, Brinkman, and the rest of our core group on the next call. The $100,000 decertification fund had been raised. On October 16, the petition to decertify the old union was submitted to the National Labor Relations Board (NLRB). The issue would be put to a vote. All umpires were invited to a meeting in Baltimore on November 2.

On the evening before the meeting, our team met until 10 P.M. The preparation session was interrupted with news that Phillips had filed a defamation suit against Hirschbeck and others. I advised the group that the suit was probably without merit, simply a part of Phillips's strategy of intimidation. When dealing with difficult people, *"Don't take it personally and don't get personal."* Rather than take the bait and get distracted by the lawsuit, I told the umpires, "When people are under pressure, they revert to habits. Richie's habit is to intimidate. Let's make sure our habit is *Preparation.*"

We then reviewed 21 questions, ran our lead umpires, Brinkman and Hirschbeck, through their drill, playing devil's advocate, preaching, and practicing, "prepare, prepare, prepare." At midnight, Hirschbeck and others were still up making notes.

At a Days Inn Hotel in Baltimore the next day, 52 umpires appeared in person. They walked past a banner reading: "Vote for Our Future—Vote Right," referring to the fact that the new union they were forming, the World Umpires Association (WUA), appeared on the right side of the ballot in the coming decertification election. The atmosphere was highly charged. One staunch opponent fired a steely glare at me and refused to shake my hand when I extended it to him. Looking me in the eye, he told me, "Go **** yourself." Despite the emotions in the air, we reminded ourselves to neutralize our emotions, to maintain self-control, and not to take any of it personally.

Hirschbeck conducted a democratic meeting. He went through 21 different questions; he listened; he probed; he patiently waded through disagreements; he let everyone have their say regardless of their point of view. To umpires who were accustomed to meetings where dissent was squelched, where the floor was owned by the few who could shout the loudest, Hirschbeck's open, approachable, and fair style was a welcome change. Even some of those who vehemently opposed the new union were the first to agree that this meeting had demonstrated the integrity of the people behind it. At the end of the meeting, the umpire who previously would not shake my extended hand, found me, reached his hand toward mine, and said, "Nice job."

The preparation paid off. Skeptics and several opponents were won over. The official vote finally came on November 30. In a crowded hearing room at the NLRB in New York, the umpires' ballots were counted. In an overwhelming victory, the tally was 57 to 35 and the World Umpires Association replaced the Major League Umpires Association as the certified bargaining agent for all major league umpires. The umpires would once again be in a position to negotiate effectively.

Phillips appealed, but the NLRB's decision stood. By this time, I had stepped aside from my volunteer advisory role. The World Umpires Association and its team of lawyers took on their first task, negotiating a new collective bargaining agreement that was completed on September 2, 2000. Phillips and the Major League Umpires Association filed a grievance on behalf of the 22 umpires who lost their jobs and would not relinquish its control to the new umpires' union. Despite the fact that in May 2001, an arbitrator reinstated 9 of the 22, the lives of these umpires and their families had been profoundly altered because of an ill-advised, and ultimately failed, strategy. With that sad exception, the World Umpires Association had achieved its objective—a sound collective bargaining agreement with Major League Baseball. The umpires had learned and practiced one more principle of the Power of Nice: *Building* (or, in this case, rebuilding) *relationships* for more deals and better deals in the future.

Speaking to the *New York Times* shortly after the election victory, John Hirschbeck summed it up: "We learned from Ron Shapiro and from his book, *The Power of Nice*. We were prepared in all respects, from every angle, in every phone call."

Thanks, John. We couldn't have said it better ourselves.

REFRESHER

Chapter 12: Putting It All Together

Think WIN–win rather than Win–Lose—The best way to get what you want is to help the other side get what they want.

Remember the Three Ps (Prepare, Probe, Propose)—A systematic approach empowers you.

- *Prepare*—Research, study, stockpile knowledge, learn everything you can about the situation and the others. Use the Preparation Checklist and its six Information Gathering steps—*Situation Summary, Precedents, Interests, Alternatives (including Highest Goal and Walkaway), Strengths and Weaknesses, and Team*—and its two Action Planning steps—*Strategy and Scripts*—to guide the process.
- *Probe*—Ask questions, look for common ground, determine needs, try to understand the other person's situation.
  - Practice **W.H.A.T.**—the probing technique
    - **W**—What is important? What else is important? Which element is most important? Why is it important?
    - **H**—Hypothesize, by asking questions in the form of "what ifs" rather than direct or threatening questions.
    - **A**—Answer their questions with your own questions.
    - **T**—Tell Me More. Keep probing; keep asking, and don't hesitate to ask them to tell more and more.
  - **Listen**—Listening is not waiting to talk. Gain information and let the other side vent. The others may unload their emotional baggage and, at the same time, may be telling you what it takes to make a deal.
- *Propose*—Try not to go first. Don't hurry, let discussions become offers. Know your alternatives.

Dealing with a difficult negotiator—Neutralize your emotions. Don't take it personally and don't get personal. When people are under pressure, they revert to habits. Make sure your habit is preparation.

Script—For crucial conversations, draft your proposal and find a *devil's advocate*—someone with whom you can practice your strategy and scripts.

Build relationships—Leads to more deals and better deals in the future.

> Negotiation is a process, not an event.

Epilogue

Nelson Mandela—When the Power of Nice Changed a Nation

On December 5, 2013, Nelson Mandela, the heroic leader of South Africa's Liberation Movement who helped end apartheid in his country, passed away. His loss triggered worldwide attention and countless testimonials. I, like so many others, greatly admired the way he lived his life. Mr. Mandela and his methods are a fitting coda to this book. Excerpted below is an op-ed piece I wrote for *The Baltimore Sun* just prior to his passing, focusing on his approach to negotiation and the lessons that other leaders could learn from it.

> I wondered . . . what lessons the leaders of our polarized political parties might learn from the example of Nelson Mandela. He did not succumb to pure partisanship as he led South Africa from the violence and repression of Apartheid to a multicultural functioning democracy. When Mr. Mandela was released from prison in 1990, South Africa's racial and political divisions were in many ways sharper than the economic divide that is tearing our Congress apart. Mr. Mandela negotiated his path to South Africa's presidency and his nation toward reconciliation by doing something which appears unthinkable to many leaders today: taking into account the interests and feelings of the other party while seeking to achieve his own objectives.

> President F. W. De Klerk, who had ordered President Mandela's release from prison, engaged in discussions with him for almost four years on the future of the South African government until the adoption of a new constitution in 1994. Mr. De Klerk and his National Party were fearful of the inevitable—relinquishing control of the government to Mr. Mandela and his African National Congress Party (ANC). Impressively, during these

talks Mr. Mandela did more than merely assert the will of the
black majority, which was largely represented by the ANC.
He also recognized the need to be mindful of the interests
of Mr. De Klerk and the white minority. Mr. Mandela saw
meaningful bridge-building as attainable "only if both parties
[were] willing to compromise." Thus, during these negotiations,
Mr. Mandela was mindful of the interests of Mr. De Klerk and
the white minority.

Mr. Mandela's approach allowed him to narrow the gap between
the black majority and the white minority. After the new
constitution was adopted, he supported the formation of the
Government of National Unity (GNU), a multiracial and multi-
party government. The GNU entitled parties with parliamentary
minorities to proportional representation in the cabinet....
Reflecting later on this approach, Mr. Mandela remarked: "You
mustn't compromise your principles, but you mustn't humiliate
the opposition. No one is more dangerous than one who is
humiliated."

The partial U.S. government shutdown and debt-ceiling
brinkmanship [of 2013] illustrate this point. Congress was at
an impasse. Neither Democrats nor Republicans were willing
to make any concessions, and an agreement was reached only
when disaster was imminent. The standoff caused significant
economic and political damage. Moreover, the agreement was
only a temporary solution. A similar crisis may occur . . . [in the
future]. Hopefully, U.S. politicians in the meantime might
examine Mr. Mandela's bold Win–win approach to bridging
divides.

The power of Mr. Mandela's approach became most apparent
as he guided the nation toward the creation of the Truth and
Reconciliation Commission in 1995. During this period, there
were polarized views regarding the treatment of those who par-
ticipated in human rights violations during the Apartheid era.
At one extreme was Mr. De Klerk and his National Party fol-
lowers. They sought complete forgiveness of those responsible
for Apartheid-spawned violence. In contrast, some black parties
demanded Nuremberg trial–like accountability for their former
oppressors—no amnesty....

Mr. Mandela chose a different path. He understood the need to account for what took place during Apartheid and would not accept Mr. De Klerk's call for general amnesty. Mr. Mandela's authorized biographer, Anthony Sampson, describes Mr. Mandela's support of a kind of "specific" amnesty, which was conditioned on perpetrators revealing the truth and proving that their actions were "politically motivated." Additionally, the commission's framework gave the victims of Apartheid violence and human rights violations a platform to describe the horrors they experienced, as well as an opportunity to receive reparations. . . . the Truth and Reconciliation Commission framework for dealing with the abuses of Apartheid, demonstrated Mr. Mandela's ability to walk the South African tightrope of black African majority rule while still accommodating white Afrikaner interests.

So from the halls of government to the administration of justice in dealing with approaches to human rights abuses, Nelson Mandela recognized the power of reconciliation as a building block in the foundation of a new South Africa. He did so without ignoring the most vital interests of black South Africans, but also without completely trampling the needs of whites. And while South Africa is not trouble free today, Mr. Mandela's approach to reconciling the different points of view of his countrymen is an example for others to weigh. Perhaps by studying it, U.S. politicians [and leaders everywhere] will stop practicing the stifling politics of polarization.

Nelson Mandela's life and actions are proof, at the highest global level, with the greatest issues at stake, that there is genuine power in considering the wants, needs, and motivations of the other side. There is true empowerment in recognizing that a win is not a win at all if the other side is shamed, destroyed, or pushed so far that they are only waiting for the chance to someday even the score. Humiliating the other side isn't winning. Finding workable solutions is real winning. Imagine how much we might all benefit—on a world stage, in national or local politics, or in daily dealings—by shifting from win–lose negotiation to Power of Nice negotiation.

Reinforcement Tools Link

SNI (Shapiro Negotiations Institute) is a premier global provider of sales, negotiation, and influence training and consulting based on the guiding principles of the Power of Nice. SNI focuses on maximizing our clients' ability to create mutually beneficial and profitable long-term relationships with peers, vendors, and customers both internal and external to the organization. Its success is built on helping professionals at all levels use a systematic approach to accomplish more, faster, and with a higher degree of effectiveness. By taking more than 40 years of lessons learned in real-life situations, the Institute's team digs into specific industry and client challenges, so its tools and techniques can be implemented immediately with precision.

For reinforcement of the Power of Nice systematic approach, and for information about SNI, go to: **bit.ly/PONtools**.

FOR MORE INFORMATION

Shapiro Negotiations Institute
3600 Clipper Mill Road
Suite 401
Baltimore, Maryland 21211
Phone: 800-665-4SNI(4764)
E-mail: sni@shapironegotiations.com
Website: www.shapironegotiations.com

Post-Negotiation Assessment Questionnaire

The best negotiators learn from their successes and mistakes, as well as those of the other side. Use this post-negotiation assessment to analyze your performance and identify ways to improve results in your next negotiation.

YES	NO	PREPARE
——	——	1. Was your pre-negotiation preparation thorough?
——	——	2. Did you establish an aspiration level and a walkaway position?
——	——	3. Did you obtain information about the other side?
——	——	4. Did you formulate a negotiation strategy and put it in writing?

YES	NO	PROBE
——	——	1. Did you ask questions to determine the other side's interests?
——	——	2. When you probed, did you utilize W.H.A.T.?

YES	NO	PROPOSE
——	——	1. Were you able to get the other side to make the first offer?
——	——	2. Did you aim high with reason?
——	——	3. Did you utilize Scripting: Draft, Devil's Advocate, Deliver?

YES   NO   CHALLENGING NEGOTIATIONS
              (If Applicable)

——   ——   1. Were you able to control your emotions?

——   ——   2. Did negotiations reach a deadlock?

——   ——   3. Did you consider "no deal" as an option?

YES   NO   RELATIONSHIP BUILDING

——   ——   1. Were you "hard on interests but soft on people"?

——   ——   2. Did you acknowledge the other side's concerns and interests?

——   ——   3. Did you engage in sufficient bonding during the negotiation?

YES   NO   THE DEAL

——   ——   1. Did you achieve most of what you wanted?

              2. How satisfied are you with the deal? (On a scale of 1 to 10)

              3. How satisfied do you think they are with the deal? (On a scale of 1 to 10)
              a. What did you do best as a negotiator?

              _____

              _____

              _____

              b. What information about the other side and the way they negotiate will be useful to you in the future?

              _____

              _____

              _____

              c. What should you do differently the next time?

              _____

              _____

              _____

For a more comprehensive discussion of post-negotiation assessment and their benefits see Chapter 14 in Charles Craver's *The Art of Negotiation in the Business World* (LexisNexis, 2012).

THE POWER OF NICE®
NEGOTIATOR'S TOOLBOX

THE PREPARATION CHECKLIST

PREPARE

Information Gathering
Situation Summary
Precedents
Interests
Alternatives
Strengths & weaknesses
Team

Action Steps
Strategy
Scripts

PROBE

What is important? What is most important? **Why?**

Hypothesize

Answer questions with questions

Tell me more   listen, **listen**, **listen**

PROPOSE

Try not to make the first offer.
Don't (immediately) accept the first offer
Set your aspirations high, within reason
Be creative – increase the pie
Script – *draft, devil's advocate, deliver*

- Negotiation is a **process**, not an event

- In order to get what you want, **help them** get what they want

- It's **WIN-win**, not wimp-wimp

- **Preparation** – the only aspect over which you have complete control

- Much is lost for want of **asking**

- Don't get **personal**, don't take it personally

www.shapironegotiations.com

Index

A

Action planning steps, 3, 93–94
Active listening, 129
Addicted negotiator, 53
Adversaries. *See* Enemies
Agreement, points of, 17, 200
Air traffic controllers, 238
Albright, Madeleine, 169, 219
Alderson, Sandy, 238
Allies, 182–184, 186
Alomar, Roberto, 239
Alternatives, 75, 90–91, 210–211, 241
Amiable negotiator, 53–54, 175
Analytic personality, 174
Angelos, Peter, 170
Anger, 171
Answers, 123–124, 241
Anxious negotiator, 53
Apartheid, 247–249
Apathetic negotiator, 53
Aramark, 184
Arbitration, 208
Aristocratic negotiator, 53
Arms summit, 201
Asking questions, 71–72, 123–124, 168, 179–180, 223, 241
Attanasio, Tony, 184

B

Bacon, Francis, 19
Bain & Company, 219–220
Baltimore Orioles, 58–59, 73–78, 169–170, 203–205, 220–221
Baltimore Police Department, 198–199
Baltimore Ravens, 48
Baltimore Symphony Orchestra, 117–120
Barriers, removing, 154–155
Barshefsky, Charlene, xi–xiii, 90
Baseball, 38–45, 58–59, 73–78, 183–184, 202–205, 220–221, 231–235. *See also* MLB (Major League Baseball)
Basketball, 91–92, 166–167, 221
Bedtime negotiation, 21–23
Begin, Menachem, 114–117
Bell, Alexander Graham, 87
Benefit, mutual, 50–51
Best offer. *See* First offer
Bias, 106
Bids, sealed, 207
Binding arbitration, 208

Bisciotti, Steve, 48
Blackstone, Mike, 91–92
Bonding, 221–222
  exercise, 229–231
  faux, 227–228
  practice, 228–231
  rules, 228
Bottom line, 91, 210
Bradley, Bill, 29
Brainstorming, 187–192, 201,
    205
Brinkman, Joe, 239–240, 242
Bronner, Jim, 184
Bulls (Chicago), 166–167
Burwell, Bryan, 33–34

C

Camp David Peace Accords,
    114–117
Carter, Jimmy, 114–117
Case study:
  deadlocks, 198–199
  proposal writing, 146–147
  situationally difficult
      encounters, 169–170
  Sur-Real Sales Challenge,
    97–103
  Wimp-Wimp negotiations,
    54–55
  WIN-win negotiation, 58–59
  World Series, 220–221
Casserly, Charlie, 175
Change, 195–199
Chicago Bulls, 166–167
Cialdini, Robert, 157
Cialdini's Law of Reciprocation,
    157–158

Circus, 37–38
Clinton, Bill, 40
Cochran, Jeff, 96–97, 156
Cochran's Law of Deflation, 156
Commerce of information, 19–20,
    21, 71, 77
Communication, 56–57, 185
Compensation, deferred, 205
Concerns, acknowledging,
    168–169
Concessions, 93, 156
Confidence, 8, 104, 151, 152,
    185–187
Confucius, 10
Conversations, exploratory, 153
Counterproposals, 153–158
Creativity, 18, 200–205
Credit card company, 24–25, 188
Criteria, external, 208
Curie, Madam Marie, 5
Customer retention, 219–220

D

Deadlines, 31
Deadlocks, 195–218
  tools used to break, 196–199
Deal fever, 209–215
Dealmaking, 12–13
Defeat, 29
Deferred compensation, 205
Deflation, 156
De Klerk, F.W., 247, 248
Delivery, 151, 152
Depersonalization, 206–208
Dessen, Sarah, 130
Devil's advocate, 50, 93, 151, 152,
    242

Distrust, 40
Drafting, 151, 152
Duncan, Tim, 221

E

Economic impact, 76
Economy of scale, 212–213
Ego, 17, 205–206
Emotions, 170–173, 210
    neutralizing, 164, 166–167
Empathy, 168
Enemies, 29–31
Engagement, 10
Entrenched positions, 31–32
Epictetus, 128, 139
Exasperation, 172
Expectations, 151, 157
Exploratory conversations, 153
External criteria, 208
Extroverts, 173
Eye contact, 134

F

Facebook, 106
Farmer/farmland, 162–165
Faux bonding, 227–228
Fehr, Don, 183, 184, 232
First offer, 146–147, 148,
        149–150
    encouraging the other side to
        make, 152–153
Flattery, false, 172–173
Football, 33–35, 48
Frankel, Ryan, 104
Franklin, Benjamin, 82, 110
Free agency, 75, 91–92, 220,
        232

G

Gain, ultimate, 20–21, 71, 77
Gatti, Joe, 23
Gilbert, Sean, 175
Gilhooley, Bob, 184
Gillick, Pat, 169–170
Ginobli, Manu, 221
Goals, 241
    expanding, 181–182, 186,
        187
    highest, 90–91, 92, 151, 152
    identifying, 49, 75
    losing sight of, 210
God, 175
Good will, 37
Google, 106
Gorbachev, Mikhail, 201
Growth, revenue, 220
Guilt, 172

H

Habits, 70
Harris, Kelly, 133–134
Hendricks, Randy, 184
Herwald, Kurt, 201
Highest goals, 90–91, 92, 151,
        152
Hirschbeck, John, 239–244
"Hit and run" negotiations,
        32–35, 222
Hock, Dee, 200
Hoffberger, Jerold "Chuck,"
        73–78
Horse trading, 154
Hunt's tomato sauce, 213–215
Hurston, Zora Neale, 113, 138
Hypothesis, 122–123, 241

I

"I Lose–You Win" negotiation, 18
Impact, economic, 76
Inexperience, 57
Information:
　checklist, 107
　commerce of, 19–20, 21, 71, 77
　gathering, 3, 89–91, 223
　sources of, 105–107
Instagram, 106
Instant gratification, 32, 211, 231
Insults, 171
Intangibles, 181
Interests, 90, 129, 154, 202, 241
　identifying, 49
　maximizing, 60
　satisfying, 50–51
Interrogation *vs.* interview, 127
Interruption quotient, 130
Interview *vs.* interrogation, 127
Intimidation, 242
"I Win–You Lose" negotiation, 9,
　　14–16, 18, 29–45
　dissatisfied parties in, 43–44

J

Jackson, Phil, 166–167
Jacobs, Eli, 58
James, William, 161
Jankowski, Mark, 67–70
Jefferson, Thomas, 166
Jernigan, Dean, 146–147
Justification, 156–157

K

Keeping Faith (Carter), 116
Kelleher, Herb, 201

Kennedy, John F., 5
Knowledge, 8
Knowledge network, 106
Korte, Diana, 91

L

Labor dispute, baseball, 183–184
Lenhart, Todd, 62, 181–182
Levine, Randy, 183, 184
Lincoln, Abraham, 81
LinkedIn, 106
Listening, 18, 31, 56–57, 72, 77,
　　114–117, 128–137, 197,
　　242
　checklist, 136–137
　learning how, 135–136
　test, 130–134
Location, 196, 204
Long run, 219–221
Lose-in-order-to-win negotiation,
　　54–55
Lose-lose negotiations, 237
Lucchino, Larry, 58, 203–204,
　　205

M

MacPhail, Andy, 232, 233
Major League Baseball Owners,
　　237–245
Major League Umpires
　　Association, 237–245,
　　243
Mandela, Nelson, 247–249
MBNA, 24–25, 188
Mechanisms, objective, 205–208
Mediation, 117–120, 197–199
Meet-and-bond style, 222–225

Mercer, Johnny, 195
Middle East peace talks, 114–117
Miller, Jon, 169
Mindreading, 126–127
Minnnesota Twins, 231–234
MLB (Major League Baseball),
        183–184, 237–245.
        See also Baseball strike
Modell, Art, 48
Munger, Charlie, 156
Munger's Law of Justification,
        156–157
Murray, Eddie Clarence, 202–205

N

Namath, Joe, 47
National Football League. *See*
        NFL (National Football
        League)
National Labor Relations Board
        (NLRB), 242
Navratilova, Martina, 30
NBA (National Basketball
        Association), 91–92
Negotiation(s), 5–27
  assessment questionnaire,
        253–254
  biggest roadblock to success,
        205
  and deadlocks, 195–218
  dealing with difficult
        negotiators, 166–170
  difficult, 9–10, 161–178
  against God, 175
  key subjects of, 129
  "no deal is the best deal,"
        209–215

preparation phase (*see*
        Preparation)
probing phase (*see* Probing)
proposal phase (*see* Proposal)
  real estate, 107–109
  and relationship building,
        51–52
  and results, 7
  risk, 109
  strengthening team, 182–184
  systematic approach, 3,
        67–79
  toolbox, 9, 18
  from weakness, 179–194
  what it can be, 23–25
  what it is, 19–21
  what it isn't, 11–14
Networking, 74, 106
Neubauer, Joe, 184
News Radio (TV show), 123–124
NFL (National Football League),
        33–35, 48
"No deal is the best deal"
        negotiation, 209–215
Numbers and Letters Game,
        83–87

O

Objections, overcoming, 188
Objective mechanisms, 205–208
Observation, 223
O'Connor, Sandra Day, 87
Opportunists, 35
Options, power of, 91
Orioles (Baltimore), 58–59,
        73–78, 169–170,
        203–205, 220–221

P

Pain, removing, 154–155
Palermo, Steve, 238
Parker, Dave, 203
Parker, Tony, 221
Participation, 10
Past, power of, 90
Peace talks, Middle East,
    114–117
PEP (participate, engage,
    personalize), 10
Perfecting Your Pitch (Shapiro),
    152
Personality traits, 173–176
Personalization, 10
Perspective, new, 197
Peters, Hank, 74–78, 203
Pharmaceutical sales, 62–63
Phillips, Richie, 238, 239–243
Pilot's Checklist, 96–97
Pinterest, 106
Pitch, 93
Pizza Hut, 213–215
Pohlad, Carl, 231–234
Police, 198–199
Position phase, 58, 120–122
Post-Negotiation Assessment
    Questionnaire, 253–254
Potential, 155
Power of Nice:
    expected objectives, 8–10
    philosophy, 6, 237–245
Power of options, 91
Power of the past, 90
Pragmatists, 174
Precedents, 74–75, 76, 90, 151,
    241

Preparation, 9, 50, 71, 73–74,
    81–111, 241
    and difficult negotiators, 167
    how to, 87–89
    insufficient planning, 56
    personal feelings about, 85
    readiness quiz, 82
    system for, 89
    why people don't do it,
        87–88
Preparation Checklist, 3, 89–97,
    241
    sample, 97–103
    template for, 94–96
Probing, 9, 71–72, 113–140,
    204, 241
    don'ts of, 126–128
    overcoming resistance to,
        125–126
    readiness quiz, 114
    W.H.A.T.? technique,
        120–126
Problem solving, 202
Proposal, 9, 72–73, 93, 141–160,
    241–242
    case study, 146–147
    three rules behind, 149–153
Psychology of Influence, The
    (Cialdini), 157
Publisher-Agent Game, 141–146,
    180
Puckett, Kirby, 231–234

Q

Questions, asking, 71–72,
    123–124, 168, 179–180,
    223, 241

R

Rajneesh, Bhagwan Shree, 133
Ravens (Baltimore), 48
Reagan, Ronald, 201
Real estate sales, 85–87,
    107–109
Reality checks, 211
Rebonding, 225–227
Reciprocation, 157–158
Redskins (Washington), 175
Reference sources, 105–106
Refocusing technique, 166–167
Reich, Tom, 183–184
Rejection, 151
Relationships:
  building, 30, 51–52, 78, 120,
    219–236, 243
  tools for building, 221–225
  value of, 222, 231–234
Restatement technique, 125
Return-on-effort, 219–220
Revenue growth, 220
Rewards, 155–156
Rhett, Errict, 33–34
Ringling Brothers and
    Barnum & Bailey
    Circus, 37–38
Ripken, Cal, 58–59, 147–149,
    169–170
Risk, 109, 155
Robinson, Brooks, 73–78
ROI (return on investment), 60,
    61–62
Role playing, 141–146
Rosenhaus, Drew, 33–35
Rouse, Jim, 114–115
Ryan, Nolan, 203, 204

S

Sadat, Anwar, 114–117
Sa'di, 141
Sales challenge, 97–103
San Antonio Spurs, 221
Sandberg, Sheryl, 67, 179
Sarda, Kunal, 104
Saving face, 169
"Says who?" technique, 126
School ties, 224–225
Scripting, 3, 76–77, 93, 151–152,
    241
Sealed bids, 207
Search engines, 105–106
Secrets, 202
Selig, Bud, 39, 238
Shapiro Negotiations Institute
    (SNI), 251
Shark Tank (tv show), 104–105
"Show-me-how" technique,
    125–126
Sidetracks, 127
Sinai, 115
Situationally difficult encounters,
    168–169, 169–170
Situation summary, 89–90
Skydiving, 67–70
"Slowing down" technique, 127,
    167–168
Social media, 106
Sotomayor, Sonia, 43
South Africa, 247–249
Southwest Airlines, 201
Spacey, Kevin, 161
Sports agency business, 32
Spurs (San Antonio), 221
Stevens Aviation, 201

STORAGE USA, 146–147
Strategy, 93
Strengths, 50–51, 92, 146, 180, 241
Strikes:
  MLB, 38–45, 237–245
  symphony orchestra, 117–120
  umpires, 237–245
Sullenberger, Sully, 97
Sunseri, Gus, 175
Super Bowl, 48
Sur-Real Sales Challenge, 97–103
Swanson, Dennis, 37
Swimming with Sharks (movie), 161
Symphony orchestra, 117–120

T

Tacking, 168–169
"Take it or leave it" negotiation, 31
Team, negotiation, 92–93, 182–184
"Tell me more" technique, 124–125, 241
$10 Game, 16–18, 47, 211–212
3 Ds process, 151–152
3 Ps, 9, 50, 67–79, 237–245
  as systematic approach to negotiations, 70–77
Time-outs, 167
Trade, 154
Truman, Harry S., 2, 88, 110
Trump, Donald, 31
Trust, 30, 40, 180, 231
Truth and Reconciliation Commission, 248–249

Twain, Mark, 219
Twins (Minnesota), 231–234
Twitter, 106

U

Ultimate gain, 20–21, 71, 77
Umpires, baseball, 237–245
Usery, William, 40, 41–42

V

Value, 60
Value/Pay Grid, 60–62, 62–63
Value swapping, 154
Van Buren, Abigail, 11
Victory, 29
Vincent, Fay, 39
Vulnerabilities, 92

W

Walkaway position, 3, 90–91, 92, 210
Washington Redskins, 175
Weaknesses, 50–51, 92, 146, 179–194, 241
  perceived *vs.* real, 179
Welke, Tim, 239
W.H.A.T.? technique, 120–126, 241
Williams, Edward Bennett (EBW), 58, 203–205
Wimp-wimp negotiations, 52–55
Win, maximizing, 3, 62
Winfield, Dave, 203
Winfrey, Oprah, 36–37
Win-lose negotiations, 35–43, 220, 237
Win-win negotiations, 47, 232

WIN-win negotiations, 3, 8–9,
        47–65, 113, 165, 198,
        220, 232
    achieving, 17–18, 49–51
    case study, 58–59
    obstacles, 18, 55–57
    reality of, 47–48
    temptations, 35–43
Withdrawal, 185
Wooden, John, 88, 110

World Series, 39, 220–221
World Umpires Association
        (WUA), 242, 243
World Wars, 15

Y

Yahoo!, 106
"Yellow pad checklist," 94
"You cut–I choose" technique,
        206